THE
ANCIENT
WORLD

PRENTICE HALL
Needham, Massachusetts
Upper Saddle River, New Jersey
Glenview, Illinois

Program Authors

Heidi Hayes Jacobs

Heidi Hayes Jacobs has served as an educational consultant to more than 500 schools across the nation. Dr. Jacobs is an adjunct professor in the Department of Curriculum on Teaching at Teachers College, Columbia University. She completed her undergraduate studies at the University of Utah in her hometown of Salt Lake City. She received an M.A. from the University of Massachusetts, Amherst, and completed her doctoral work at Columbia University's Teachers College in 1981.

The backbone of Dr. Jacobs' experience comes from her years as a teacher of high school, middle school, and elementary school students. As an educational consultant, she works with K–12 schools and districts on curriculum reform and strategic planning.

Brenda Randolph

Brenda Randolph is the former Director of the Outreach Resource Center at the African Studies Program at Howard University, Washington, D.C. She is the Founder and Director of Africa Access, a bibliographic service on Africa for schools. She received her B.A. in history with high honors from North Carolina Central University, Durham, and her M.A. in African studies with honors from Howard University. She completed further graduate studies at the University of Maryland, College Park, where she was awarded a Graduate Fellowship.

Brenda Randolph has published numerous articles in professional journals and bulletins. She currently serves as library media specialist in Montgomery County Public Schools, Maryland.

Michal L. LeVasseur

Michal LeVasseur is an educational consultant in the field of geography. She is an adjunct professor of geography at the University of Alabama, Birmingham, and serves with the Alabama Geographic Alliance. Her undergraduate and graduate work is in the fields of anthropology (B.A.), geography (M.A.), and science education (Ph.D.).

Dr. LeVasseur's specialization has moved increasingly into the area of geography education. In 1996, she served as Director of the National Geographic Society's Summer Geography Workshop. As an educational consultant, she has worked with the National Geographic Society as well as with schools to develop programs and curricula for geography.

Special Program Consultant

Yvonne S. Gentzler, Ph.D.
School of Education
University of Idaho, Moscow, Idaho

Content Consultant on The Ancient World

Maud Gleason
Department of Classics
Stanford University
Stanford, California

PRENTICE HALL
Needham, Massachusetts
Upper Saddle River, New Jersey
Glenview, Illinois

ISBN 0-13-050218-9

5 6 7 8 9 10 11 12 13   06 05 04 03 02

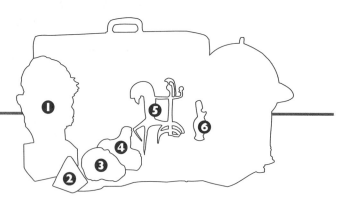

On the Cover

❶ Head of Poseidon, Greek god of the sea

❷ Capstone of an Egyptian pyramid

❸ Fragment of a Roman statue

❹ Model of Egyptian sphinx

❺ Reproduction of an iron sculpture of the goddess Athena in her chariot

❻ Reproduction of an ancient Greek vase

Content Consultants for the World Explorer Program

Africa
Barbara Brown
Africa Studies Center
Boston University
Boston, Massachusetts

Ancient World
Maud Gleason
Department of Classics
Stanford University
Stanford, California

East Asia
Leslie Swartz
Harvard University
    East Asian Outreach Program at
    the Children's Museum
    of Boston
Boston, Massachusetts

Latin America
Daniel Mugan
Center for Latin American Studies
University of Florida
Gainesville, Florida

Middle East
Elizabeth Barlow
Center for Middle Eastern and
    North African Studies
University of Michigan
Ann Arbor, Michigan

North Africa
Laurence Michalak
Center for Middle East Studies
University of California
Berkeley, California

Religion
Michael Sells
Department of Religion
Haverford College
Haverford, Pennsylvania

Russia, Eastern Europe,
Central Asia
Janet Vaillant
Center for Russian, Eastern
    European, and Central Asian
    Studies
Harvard University
Cambridge, Massachusetts

South Asia
Robert Young
South Asia Regional Studies
University of Pennsylvania
Philadelphia, Pennsylvania

Western Europe
Ruth Mitchell-Pitts
Center for West European Studies
University of North Carolina
Chapel Hill, North Carolina

Teacher Advisory Board

Jerome Balin
Lincoln Junior High School
Naperville, Illinois

Elizabeth Barrett
Tates Creek Middle School
Lexington, Kentucky

Linda Boaen
Baird School
Fresno, California

Nikki L. Born
Harllee Middle School
Bradenton, Florida

Barbara Coats Grabowski
Russell Middle School
Omaha, Nebraska

Stephanie Hawkins
Jefferson Middle School
Oklahoma City, Oklahoma

Fred Hitz
Wilson Middle School
Muncie, Indiana

William B. Johnson
La Mesa Junior High School
Canyon Country, California

Kristi Karis
West Ottawa Middle School
Holland, Michigan

Kristen Koch
Discovery Middle School
Orlando, Florida

Peggy McCarthy
Beulah School
Beulah, Colorado

Cindy McCurdy
Hefner Middle School
Oklahoma City, Oklahoma

Deborah J. Miller
Department of Social Studies
Detroit Public Schools
Detroit, Michigan

Lawrence Peglow
Greenway Middle School
Pittsburgh, Pennsylvania

Lyn Shiver
Northwestern Middle School
Alpharetta, Georgia

Mark Stahl
Longfellow Middle School
Norman, Oklahoma

TABLE OF CONTENTS

THE ANCIENT WORLD 1

OF SPECIAL INTEREST

A hands-on approach to learning and applying key social studies skills

Engaging, step-by-step activities for exploring important topics in ancient history

LITERATURE

High-interest selections from the mythology of ancient civilizations

CITIZEN HEROES

Profiles of people who made a difference in their country

Detailed drawings show how the use of technology makes a country unique

STUDENT ART

A view of a country through the eyes of a student artist

MAPS

CHARTS, GRAPHS, AND TABLES

READ ACTIVELY

How can I get the most out of my social studies book?
How does my reading relate to my world? Answering questions
like these means that you are an active reader, an involved reader. As an
active reader, you are in charge of the reading situation!

The following strategies tell how to think and read as an active
reader. You don't need to use all of these strategies all the time. Feel
free to choose the ones that work best in each reading situation. You
might use several at a time, or you might go back and forth among
them. They can be used in any order.

BEFORE YOU READ

Give yourself a purpose

The sections in this book begin with a list called "Questions to Explore." These questions focus on key ideas presented in the section. They give you a purpose for reading. You can create your own purpose by asking questions like these: How does the topic relate to your life? How might you use what you learn at school or at home?

Preview

To preview a reading selection, first read its title. Then look at the pictures and read the captions. Also read any headings in the selection. Then ask yourself: What is the reading selection about? What do the pictures and headings tell about the selection?

Reach into your background

What do you already know about the topic of the selection? How can you use what you know to help you understand what you are going to read?

WHILE YOU READ

Ask questions

Suppose you are reading about the continent of South America. Some questions you might ask are: Where is South America? What countries are found there? Why are some of the countries large and others small? Asking questions like these can help you gather evidence and gain knowledge.

Predict

As you read, make a prediction about what will happen and why. Or predict how one fact might affect another fact. Suppose you are reading about South America's climate. You might make a prediction about how the climate affects where people live. You can change your mind as you gain new information.

Connect

Connect your reading to your own life. Are the people discussed in the selection like you or someone you know? What would you do in similar situations? Connect your reading to something you have already read. Suppose you have already read about the ancient Greeks. Now you are reading about the ancient Romans. How are they alike? How are they different?

Visualize

What would places, people, and events look like in a movie or a picture? As you read about India, you could visualize the country's heavy rains. What do they look like? How do they sound? As you read about geography, you could visualize a volcanic eruption.

Respond

Talk about what you have read. What did you think? Share your ideas with your classmates.

Assess yourself

What did you find out? Were your predictions on target? Did you find answers to your questions?

Follow up

Show what you know. Use what you have learned to do a project. When you do projects, you continue to learn.

THE ANCIENT WORLD

The cities of ancient times bustled with traffic. People shopped at the market, worked, and lived in families, as people do today. Builders, teachers, rulers, and scientists invented objects and systems that we still know and use. The ancient peoples developed great civilizations. They traveled, traded, conquered, and settled. Who could have known how their beliefs and customs would affect the modern world?

Guiding Questions

The readings and activities in this book will help you discover answers to these Guiding Questions.

- ☞ What methods do people use today to try to understand cultures of the past?

- ☞ How did physical geography affect the growth of ancient civilizations?

- ☞ How did the beliefs and values of ancient civilizations affect the lives of their members?

- ☞ How did civilizations develop a government and an economic system?

- ☞ What accomplishments is each civilization known for?

Project Preview

You can also discover answers to the Guiding Questions by working on projects. Preview the following projects and choose one that you might like to do. For more details, see page 222.

Ancient World Travel Guide Write a travel guide to the world of ancient times, pointing out places of historical interest.

The Hall of Ancient Heritage Create a poster comparing ancient customs to similar customs in today's world.

Ancient Debate Stage a debate to argue which ancient civilization contributed the most to the modern world.

Life in the Ancient World Organize an Ancient World Fair, featuring foods, activities, artwork, and costumes of six ancient civilizations.

On a hilltop above the ancient Greek city-state of Athens stood the Acropolis, or high city, pictured above left. The photograph above shows the Great Wall of China as it appears today. Over the centuries, the wall was extended and rebuilt many times. The picture on the left shows a page from the ancient Egyptian Book of the Dead.

EXPLORER'S JOURNAL

A journal can be your personal book of discovery. As you explore ancient history, you can use your journal to keep track of the things you learn and do. You can also record your thoughts about your journey. For your first entry, suppose you could meet a boy or a girl from the past. What things might you ask about the way he or she lives? Write down questions and topics to explore.

ACTIVITY ATLAS

The Ancient World

Learning about the ancient world means being an explorer and a geographer. No explorer would start out without first checking some facts. Begin by exploring the maps of the ancient world on the following pages.

LOCATION

1. Explore the Ancient World's Location To begin your exploration, locate the ancient worlds on the political map. Which was the largest? Which was the smallest? On which continent was each one located?

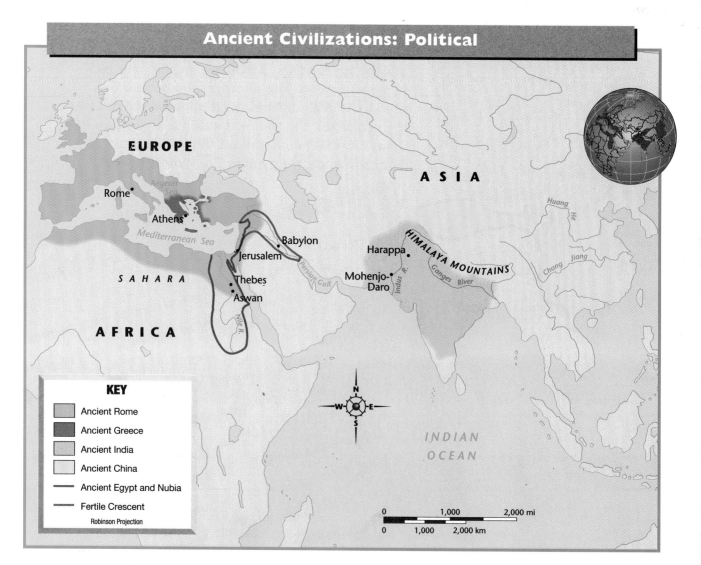

Ancient Civilizations: Political

EUROPE

Rome
Athens

Aegean

ASIA

Huang He

Mediterranean Sea

Babylon

Harappa

HIMALAYA MOUNTAINS

Jerusalem

Persian Gulf

Chang Jiang

SAHARA

Mohenjo-Daro

Indus R.

Ganges River

Thebes

Aswan

Nile R.

AFRICA

INDIAN OCEAN

KEY

- Ancient Rome
- Ancient Greece
- Ancient India
- Ancient China
- Ancient Egypt and Nubia
- Fertile Crescent

Robinson Projection

0   1,000   2,000 mi

0   1,000   2,000 km

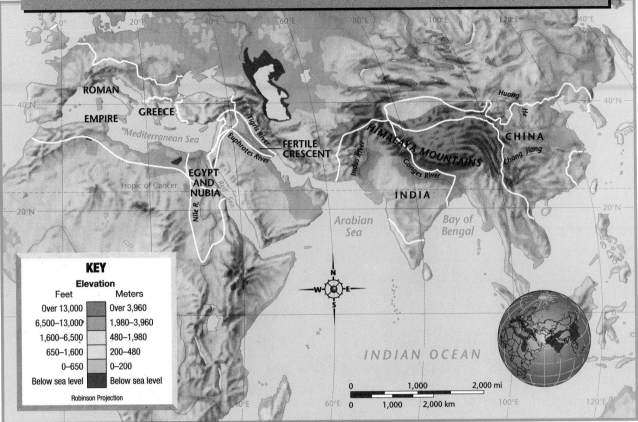

Ancient Civilizations: Physical

KEY

Elevation

Feet		Meters
Over 13,000		Over 3,960
6,500–13,000		1,980–3,960
1,600–6,500		480–1,980
650–1,600		200–480
0–650		0–200
Below sea level		Below sea level

Robinson Projection

0   1,000   2,000 mi
0   1,000   2,000 km

INTERACTION

2. **Consider How Geography Affects Settlement** Describe the geographic features of each of the six ancient areas of civilization. How are they different from one another? People often settle in an area because of its physical features. Which features do the six regions have in common?

REGIONS

3. **Find the Dates of Ancient Civilizations** Look at the table. Which civilization lasted for the longest time? Which ones existed at the same time? Name the civilization that began first. Which was the last to end?

Ancient Civilizations

Location	Time Span
Fertile Crescent	about 3500 B.C.–500 B.C.
Egypt and Nubia	about 3100 B.C.–A.D. 350
India	about 2500 B.C.–185 B.C.
China	about 2000 B.C.–A.D. 1911
Greece	about 2000 B.C.–146 B.C.
Rome	about 900 B.C.–A.D. 476

4. Find Geo Cleo Geo Cleo is excited about traveling to the sites of ancient civilizations. Read each of the postcards Geo Cleo sent home to her friends. Unfortunately, part of each message was washed away. Use the maps on the first two pages of this Activity Atlas to fill in the missing information.

The people who lived here in ancient times were cut off from the rest of the world for centuries by a mountain range. The world's highest mountains, the Himalaya Mountains, form a natural barrier to the north. I enjoyed traveling in this Asian country of _____.

This city, called _____, has some of the oldest ruins in the world. Located between two rivers, it was the home of a famous civilization of the Fertile Crescent.

I am on the banks of the world's longest river. It runs for 4,132 miles (6,648 km), about the distance between the American cities of Chicago and Honolulu. This river, called the _____, empties into the Mediterranean Sea. In the distance, I can see pyramids and this huge lionlike sculpture called the Sphinx.

GEO CLEO

I am standing on an ancient wall in northern China, not far from a muddy, yellow river. In ancient times, this river often flooded and wiped out whole villages. It lies to the north of another major Chinese river, the Chang Jiang. This river is named _____.

MOVEMENT

5. Trace Greek Settlements Powerful civilizations often expanded to include more land than they originally had. From time to time throughout their history, the city-states of ancient Greece found that they needed more land. The mountainous countryside made it difficult to farm, and the populations were growing quickly. Many of the city-states sent groups of citizens to look for new homes elsewhere. The Greeks established settlements all across the Mediterannean and Black seas, spreading the Greek civilization. Look at the area of Greek settlements on the map. Compare it to the area of the Greek mainland. Which is greater? Near what physical feature are all of the settlements located? How do you think the settlers traveled to their new homes?

LOCATION

6. Locate the Greek Settlements These new settlements became independent cities. Which new city was the farthest from the Greek mainland? Why do you think the new cities might have become so independent? Explain how you think Greek settlements might have affected Mediterranean cultures in general.

▼ The Ancient Greeks traveled across the sea to find new homes in boats like the one painted on this cup.

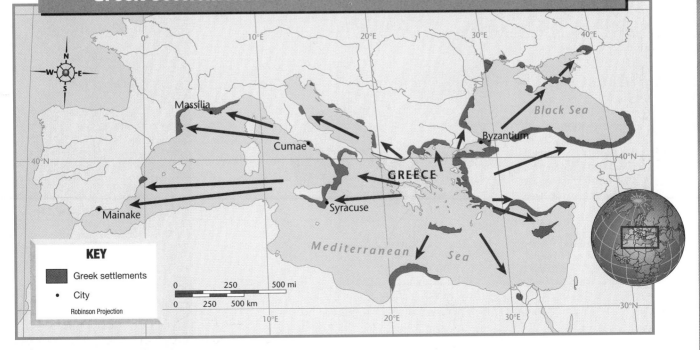

Greek Settlements From About 1100 B.C. to 500 B.C.

INTERACTION

7. Think About How Isolation Affects Civilizations You already know that some civilizations existed at the same time but in different places. Look at maps of two of these civilizations below and right.

The Fertile Crescent had few natural barriers to stop invaders. Over time, different peoples conquered and ruled this region. Look at the landforms on the map below. How do you think conquering peoples reached the area? How do you think the culture of this area was affected by these changes?

Look at the map of ancient India. What major landforms do you see? For many years, the people there were left alone. Why do you think this is so? How do you think this affected the culture of ancient Indian empires?

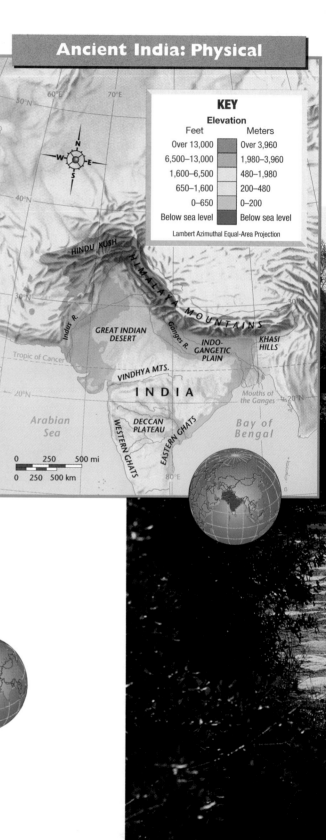

Ancient India: Physical

KEY
Elevation

Feet		Meters
Over 13,000		Over 3,960
6,500–13,000		1,980–3,960
1,600–6,500		480–1,980
650–1,600		200–480
0–650		0–200
Below sea level		Below sea level

Lambert Azimuthal Equal-Area Projection

HINDU KUSH
HIMALAYA MOUNTAINS
Indus R.
GREAT INDIAN DESERT
Ganges R.
INDO-GANGETIC PLAIN
KHASI HILLS
Tropic of Cancer
VINDHYA MTS.
INDIA
Mouths of the Ganges
Arabian Sea
DECCAN PLATEAU
WESTERN GHATS
EASTERN GHATS
Bay of Bengal

0   250   500 mi
0   250 500 km

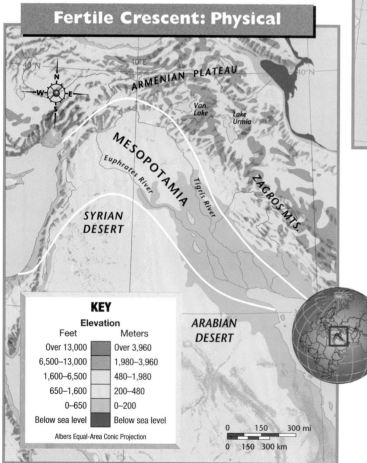

Fertile Crescent: Physical

ARMENIAN PLATEAU
Van Lake
Lake Urmia
MESOPOTAMIA
Euphrates River
Tigris River
ZAGROS MTS.
SYRIAN DESERT
ARABIAN DESERT

KEY
Elevation

Feet		Meters
Over 13,000		Over 3,960
6,500–13,000		1,980–3,960
1,600–6,500		480–1,980
650–1,600		200–480
0–650		0–200
Below sea level		Below sea level

Albers Equal-Area Conic Projection

0   150   300 mi
0   150 300 km

MOVEMENT

8. Consider How Roads Help a Civilization Grow Romans built the largest road system in the ancient world. Look at the roads shown on this map. On how many continents do the roads run? Estimate the greatest distance from one end of the road system to the other. Which city has the most roads leading to it? Why do you think that is? Explain why you think the Romans built so many roads over such a large area.

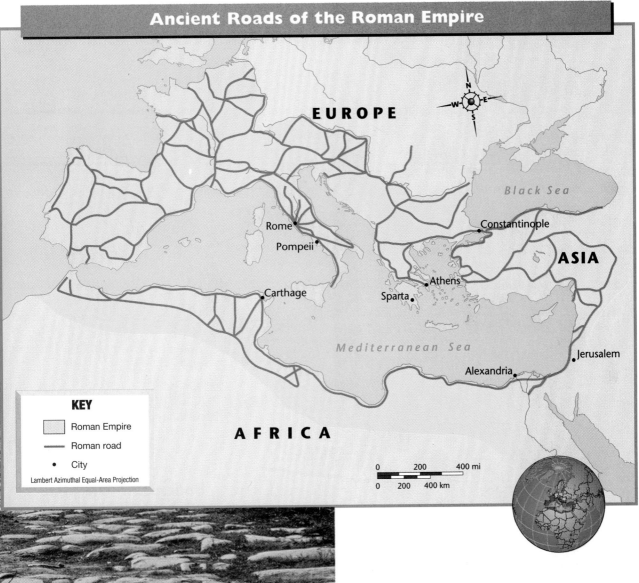

Ancient Roads of the Roman Empire

EUROPE

N
W E
S

Black Sea

Rome

Pompeii

Constantinople

ASIA

Athens

Carthage

Sparta

Mediterranean Sea

Jerusalem

Alexandria

KEY

Roman Empire

Roman road

• City

Lambert Azimuthal Equal-Area Projection

AFRICA

0   200   400 mi

0   200   400 km

◄ Roads of ancient Rome looked quite different from most of our modern roads. Why do you think the Romans built their roads differently than we do today?

CHAPTER 1

The Beginnings of Human Society

SECTION 1
Geography and History

SECTION 2
Prehistory

SECTION 3
The Beginnings of Civilization

PICTURE ACTIVITIES

This bull is one of hundreds of animals painted on the walls and ceilings of Lascaux (las COH) Cave in France. The people who painted these pictures lived about 15,000 years ago. To create their paintings, the artists traveled hundreds of yards into the dark cave. Often, they had to crawl through narrow, dangerous passages. To paint on the ceilings, they built rickety wooden platforms.

Understand the mind of the artist
Why do you suppose these people faced such dangers just to paint pictures on the walls? Why do you think they painted in caves rather than on rocks outside the caves?

Create a picture for the future
While the people who painted these cave pictures had no written language, they left pictures that tell us something about their lives. Draw a picture that will tell people a thousand years in the future about your life.

Geography and History

BEFORE YOU READ

Reach Into Your Background

Have you ever read a detective story or watched a mystery movie? Then you know what it's like to solve a mystery by using clues. The mystery you are about to read even begins with a dead body! Was he the victim of foul play? How can people figure out how he died? Read on . . .

Questions to Explore

1. What tools do we use to understand the past?

2. What is the connection between the geography of a place and its history?

Key Terms

history
prehistory
archaeologist
oral tradition

Key People

The Iceman of the Alps

His frozen body was found in a mountain pass in the Alps, on the Italian-Austrian border in Europe, so he is called the Iceman.

The Iceman was used to traveling the mountains. Usually, he was well able to survive alone. This day, however, he probably was caught by surprise by a fierce mountain storm. He stretched out near some rocks and covered himself with a cape made of woven grass. Soon, he fell asleep. As he slept, it grew colder. The Iceman froze to death without ever waking.

For thousands of years, the Iceman lay covered with snow and ice. In 1991, two hikers discovered him by chance. His body and possessions were taken to a laboratory, where scientists learned more about him. The Iceman lived before people kept written records. However, his clothing, tools, and his body were well preserved. They provided clues about the Iceman's life.

Scientists determined that the Iceman lived about 5,000 years ago, in about 3000 B.C. His clothes were made of finely stitched animal skins. That showed that the Iceman probably came from a community with people skilled in sewing.

▼ The Iceman was a skilled outdoorsman. Among his belongings were a wood frame pack, a bow, a flint dagger, and other gear suited to wilderness survival.

Experts analyzed many clues to learn about the Iceman. An artist studied the Iceman's skull to make this model of his head (below left). The Iceman's copper ax (below right) and unfinished arrows and a bow without a string suggest that he had been looking for materials needed to finish his weapons, when he met his death.

The most important clue about the Iceman's life was his copper ax. Copper was the first metal used by Europeans, beginning about 4000 B.C. There was no doubt that the Iceman lived after people had learned to use copper. Although the Iceman's people left no written record, scientists put together the clues he left to build a story of his life.

Understanding History

The scientists' curiosity about the Iceman's life was natural. We all are curious about our past. We want to know how our parents and grandparents and great-grandparents lived. We want to know where people in our community came from.

As human beings, we are curious about our origins. What was life like many thousands of years ago? About 5,000 years ago, people in Southwest Asia and in Africa developed systems of writing. With this, they began to keep written records of their experiences. That was the beginning of **history,** since history means the recorded events of people.

If you add the prefix *pre-* to the word *history,* you get the word *prehistory.* The prefix *pre-* means *before*. Therefore, **prehistory** means *before history.* Prehistory is the period of time in the past before writing was invented. How can we learn about the people who lived before written history?

The Iceman's Face Using measurements, X-rays, and computer views of the Iceman's head, a sculptor made a model of the skull. Then, with the help of other information, the sculptor added clay to the skull to show flesh. Finally, he used soft plastic and real hair to make a finished sculpture. It is an accurate model of the way the Iceman probably looked in life.

Prehistory: Digging Up the Past To learn about life in prehistoric times, scientists must rely on clues other than written records. Scientists known as **archaeologists** examine objects to learn about past people and cultures. They sift through the dirt of prehistoric camps to find bones, tools, and other objects. These objects may tell them something about the people who lived there. For example, the size of spear points made from a stone called flint shows what kinds of game the people hunted. To kill big game, such as bears, hunters had to use large, heavy spear points. Such points, however, would not work very well with birds and small animals.

History: A Record in Writing Historians do not have to rely on the objects discovered by archaeologists to learn about the past. They study the written record of human life and accomplishments to understand a society—its wars, its religion, and its rulers, among other things. Historians also look at what other groups living at the same time wrote about that society.

The Tools of Survival

Prehistoric peoples made tools and weapons from stone. These handaxes (1 and 3) and the sharp spear point (2) were fashioned from quartz some 50,000 years ago. **Critical Thinking** Which tool do you think would have been best for hunting? Why?

LINKS TO SCIENCE

Radiocarbon Dating All plants and animals have tiny amounts of a substance called radiocarbon in their bodies. After they die, the radiocarbon changes into another substance. Scientists know how long this change takes. They have tests that measure how much radiocarbon is left in ancient wood, grass, cloth, and flesh. Scientists can then calculate the age of the material.

Oral Traditions: A Record in the Spoken Word The written records studied by historians often began as **oral traditions,** which are stories passed down by word of mouth. Oral history can tell family history, such as stories of parents, grandparents, and great-grandparents. It can also tell stories about heroes or events in the past.

Oral traditions are still an important part of many societies today. Not all oral stories are historically accurate. Like myths and legends, they often mix facts with beliefs and exaggerations about heroes. Still, oral traditions tell about how a society lived and what the people considered important.

Linking Geography and History

Knowing when something happened is only the beginning for historians. Understanding why historic events took place is also important. Knowing the connection between geography and history is often the

Carrying On a Tradition

This man is a griot from the African country of Mali. Griots memorize important events from a village's past such as births, deaths, hunts, and wars. Griots may spend hours or even days retelling important events. Griots pass their knowledge on to young men who have been selected to become griots themselves. **Critical Thinking** How are oral traditions different from written history?

Rice Fields in the Hills

Wherever people farm, they must discover the most efficient way to grow crops and the best way to use available land. Rice grows best in fields covered with shallow water. On these hillsides along the Chang Jiang in China, rice farmers have built terraces into the hillsides. Terraces catch and hold rainwater and make it possible to grow crops on hilly land.

key to understanding why events happened. For example, to explain why the ancient Egyptians developed a successful civilization, you must look at the geography of Egypt.

Egyptian civilization was built on the banks of the great Nile River. Each year, the Nile flooded, depositing rich black soil on its banks. Because the soil was so rich, Egyptian farmers could grow enough crops to feed the large numbers of people in the cities. That meant everyone did not have to farm, so some people could do other things that helped develop the civilization. Without the Nile and its regular flooding, Egyptian civilization would not have become so successful. This is one way that geography affects history.

SECTION 1 REVIEW

1. **Define** (a) history, (b) prehistory, (c) archaeologist, (d) oral tradition.

2. **Identify** The Iceman of the Alps.

3. How do we learn what happened throughout history and prehistory?

4. Describe how geography can affect the history of a group of people.

Critical Thinking

5. **Understanding Cause and Effect** What effect has the geography of your community had on the way people live there?

Activity

6. **Writing to Learn** You may know stories that have been passed on by oral tradition. Ask a family member, teacher, or friend to share a story with you. The story should be about an important event in the person's life. Moving to a new country or home, the birth of a baby, or a move to a new school are all events that people share stories about. Write the words down. Try to write so the story sounds as if someone is speaking.

Prehistory

BEFORE YOU READ

Reach Into Your Background

For tens of thousands of years, our human ancestors lived and prospered using mainly stone tools. They used no metal of any kind. Look around the room in which you are reading this. What items are made of metal? How would your life be different if everything metal did not exist?

Questions to Explore

1. How did people live in the Old and New Stone Ages?

2. What is the effect of geography and climate on farming?

Key Terms

nomad
fertile
domesticate

Key Places

East Africa

▲ Prehistoric peoples had to make tools and other items out of materials they could find. This carving was made from a bone or tusk of a mammoth, or prehistoric elephant.

Long before humans used metal, about three-and-a-half million years ago, a huge explosion shook a part of what is now the country of Tanzania in East Africa. A volcano spit out clouds of fine ash that fell on the surrounding land. Then rain came. It turned the blanket of ash into thick mud. Before the mud dried, two individuals walked across the landscape. As they walked, they left their footprints in the mud.

In 1976, a group of scientists looking for evidence of early humans discovered the footprints, preserved in stone. They were amazed at their find. The footprints are almost identical to those made by modern humans walking in wet sand.

The Stone Age: From Hunting and Gathering to Farming

A million years after these footprints were made, human ancestors used tools. They used stones as hammers. With these hammers, they chipped sharp flakes from soft volcanic rock. They used the points they made to cut plants or meat.

This first use of stone to create tools began what we now call the Stone Age. The Stone Age gets its name from the fact that people made tools and weapons mainly from stone. These tools were very simple. Gradually, people began to make more complex tools from stone. Scientists think that the Stone Age continued for hundreds of thousands of years, until people learned to use metal for tools and weapons.

Some 18,000 years ago, people in central Russia depended on mammoths not only for food but also for shelter. People built huts like this one by fitting mammoth bones together. **Critical Thinking** Name some shelters other people have made from natural materials they gathered.

Archaeologists divide the Stone Age into three periods, the Old Stone Age, the Middle Stone Age, and the New Stone Age. During the Old Stone Age, people did not yet know how to farm. They lived by hunting animals and gathering roots, berries, leaves, and seeds. They used stone to make hunting weapons and tools to cut meat, scrape animal hides, cut skins to make clothing, and many other things. They also used other materials—bone and animal horns and tusks.

Gradually, Old Stone Age people learned to hunt in groups. Soon, they had developed the skill of cooperating in the hunt. Almost all of human prehistory took place during the Old Stone Age.

Fire!   Between about 500,000 years ago and about 1,400,000 years ago, there was another important development in human prehistory—the discovery of fire. No one knows for sure how it happened. Perhaps one day a small band of hunters saw a grass fire caused by lightning on the open plain. Terrified by the fire, they probably ran from it.

A great advance came when humans discovered how to make fire when they wanted it. They probably did this by rubbing two sticks together or by striking stones together to produce a spark. With the ability to make fire as they needed it, people could move to areas that had cold climates.

Predict Why would fire be useful to early people?

Predict After living as hunters and gatherers for many years, humans learned a skill that changed their lives. What do you think it was?

Settling New Areas   As people developed the use of tools, they left their original homes in Africa. This may have begun as early as 1 million years ago. Many Old Stone Age people became **nomads,** or people who had no single, settled home. They moved around to places where they were sure they would find food. These nomads stayed at a campsite for several days. When they had gathered all the food around, they moved on.

Humans eventually spread out over much of the Earth. There is evidence that people were living in Asia and Europe at least 500,000 years ago. Perhaps 30,000 years ago, humans crossed from Asia into North America. By 10,000 B.C., humans had reached Peru in South America. Though few in number, people lived in regions as different as the steamy rain forests in Asia, the cold lands near the Arctic Circle, and the very high altitudes of the Andes Mountains in South America.

The Beginning of Farming

For tens of thousands of years, humans continued to live as hunters and gatherers. Some societies entered the Middle Stone Age, characterized by the use of more refined tools. Then, about 11,000 years ago, people in Southwest Asia made an amazing discovery. They learned that if they planted the seeds of wild grasses, new crops of grass would come up. Thus

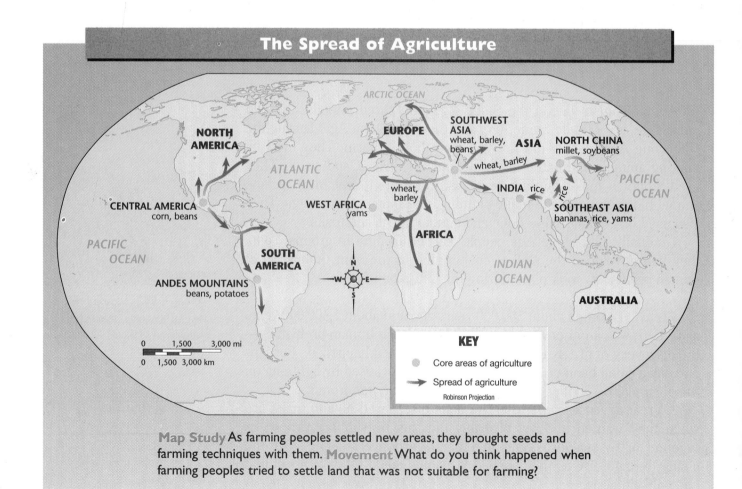

Map Study As farming peoples settled new areas, they brought seeds and farming techniques with them. **Movement** What do you think happened when farming peoples tried to settle land that was not suitable for farming?

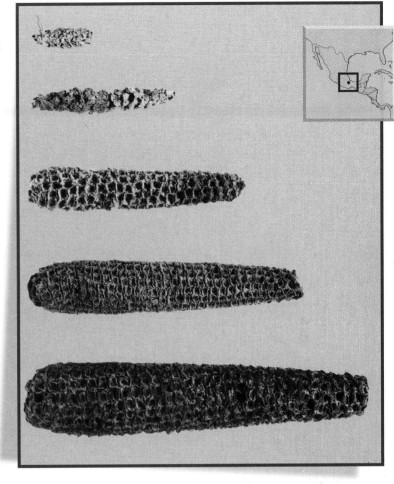

▶ Seven thousand years ago, an ear of corn did not make much of a meal (top). It took thousands of years of careful breeding for ears of corn to reach their present size.

began the New Stone Age in Southwest Asia. It was called the New Stone Age because people began to grow their own food. They were no longer nomads, although they still depended on stone tools. However, in many other parts of the world, the Old and Middle Stone Ages continued for many thousands of years. In some areas, Old Stone Age societies existed into the 1900s.

Since in most societies women were responsible for gathering plants and seeds, they may have first gotten the idea of planting seeds. Men usually were the hunters. Women began planting and harvesting their crops in the same place year after year.

Farming in Other Places

Some places were better for farming than others. Soil in some areas was very **fertile,** which means that the soil contained substances that plants need to grow. Plants also need light and warmth, so areas that had long springs and summers were good places to farm. Gentle rains were important sources of water for plants. In several places around the world, many miles apart, people discovered that the soil, the water, and the length of the summers were good for plants. These people took up the farming way of life. About 7,000 years ago, Chinese farmers began planting rice and other crops. A little later in Central America, people began to grow corn, beans, and squash.

While the kinds of plants grown by those first farmers are still important today, they looked very different. When people first began to plant seeds, they carefully chose the biggest, best-tasting plants. They selected those seeds to plant. Gradually, this careful selection of the biggest and best seeds and roots from each crop led to the kind of food that we eat today. For example, the earliest corn came from cobs only two or three inches long. Today, the corn-on-the-cob we eat may be four times that size.

Taming Animals
Humans learned another important skill during the New Stone Age. They learned to **domesticate,** or tame, animals. The first domesticated animals may have been dogs, because

Not Just Thousands of Years Ago Not all human groups took up farming. Even today, a few groups still live the way we believe Old Stone Age people did. Such groups include some living in the rain forests of the Amazon River Valley in South America, in the Kalahari Desert of Africa, and in parts of New Guinea, a Pacific Ocean island.

Beast of Burden

Camels are native to north Africa, southwest Asia, India, and the highlands of central Asia. They were domesticated long ago and have been used for their meat, milk, wool, and hides. Mostly, however, they have been used to carry loads. People in these regions still use camels to help them in their work.
Interaction How did humans benefit from domesticating animals?

they were valuable in hunting. By taming sheep, cows, and pigs, people developed a ready source of meat, milk, wool, and skins. Through careful breeding, the herders developed animals that were gentler than their wild ancestors and gave more milk or wool. By about 3000 B.C., cattle, camels, horses, and donkeys were trained to carry heavy loads.

SECTION 2 REVIEW

1. **Define** (a) nomad, (b) fertile, (c) domesticate.

2. **Identify** East Africa.

3. How did people of the Old Stone Age get their food?

4. How was life in the New Stone Age different from life in the Old Stone Age?

Critical Thinking

5. **Identifying Central Issues** Over the past two million years, human beings have made important discoveries and developed new ways of doing things. Name two of the most important developments and explain how they affect us today.

Activity

6. **Writing to Learn** Pretend you are a member of a hunting and gathering society. You get the idea to try growing plants for food. Write a journal entry describing what gave you the idea. Tell the differences your idea might make to your people.

The Beginnings of Civilization

BEFORE YOU READ

Reach Into Your Background

Look at the shoes you are wearing and the shirt or sweater you have on today.

Who made the fabric for your clothes? Who prepared the leather or canvas for your shoes? Who grew the grain for the cereal you ate for breakfast? All of these jobs were done by people who have special skills—weavers, shoemakers, farmers. Think what life would be like if families had to do all these things for themselves.

Questions to Explore

1. How did early cities develop?
2. What is civilization?

Key Terms

irrigation
surplus
artisan
civilization
social class

Under a fierce desert sun, long lines of people are digging a long trench, soon to become a deep canal. Other people lift heavy baskets of dirt dug from the canal onto their shoulders. They dump the dirt near the river where another crew of men is building a huge earthen dam.

These are some of the world's first construction workers. They are building an **irrigation** system, a network of canals to supply land with water from another place. One person directs the work at each site. Like the big construction projects of today, this job takes teamwork.

Soon, the dam will hold the spring flood waters of the river. A group of people are building wooden gates in the dam. Officials will open the gates in the dry summer. Water will flow through the canals, irrigating the growing crops.

▼ These people use traditional methods—an animal-powered pump—to irrigate their crops in the Nile Valley of Egypt.

Advantages of a Settled Life

Farming and raising animals was much harder work than hunting and gathering. However, it had far greater rewards. Producing food allowed people to have a steady supply of food year around. This meant they could stay in one place. People often had a food **surplus**—more than they needed. Surplus food could be stored for use at another time.

The Population Grows Having surplus food also affected the size of families. The hunting-gathering life did not allow parents to have many children. How could they feed them all? Now, food surpluses would feed many more people.

Larger families brought rapid population growth. Scientists estimate that about 10,000 years ago the population of the world was about 10 million people, which is about the number of people living in Los Angeles today. By 7,000 years ago, many people had settled into the farming life. The population had grown to about 66 million.

Early Villages and Towns People lived in New Stone Age farming settlements for many centuries before towns developed. Gradually, as the population increased, the settlements grew larger.

With food surpluses, people did not have to spend all their days producing food. Some people were able to switch from farming to other kinds of work. For example, some people became **artisans,** or workers who are especially skilled in making items such as baskets, leather goods, tools, pottery, or cloth.

The Growth of Cities

Not all early farming settlements grew into cities. Cities could develop where rich soil created large surpluses of food. People also needed a dependable source of drinking water and materials to build shelters.

Ask Questions Think of several questions you would like to have answered about the world's first cities.

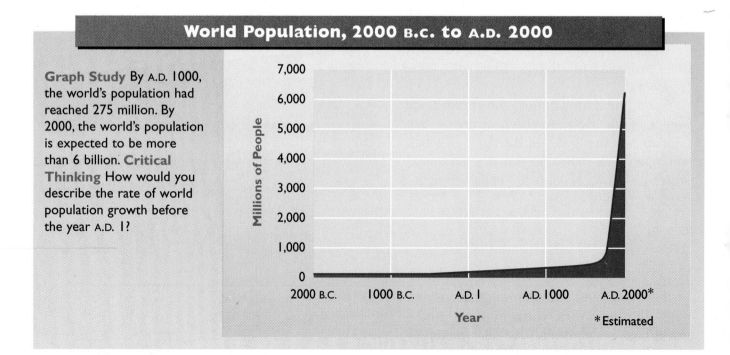

Graph Study By A.D. 1000, the world's population had reached 275 million. By 2000, the world's population is expected to be more than 6 billion. **Critical Thinking** How would you describe the rate of world population growth before the year A.D. 1?

World Population, 2000 B.C. to A.D. 2000

Millions of People

7,000
6,000
5,000
4,000
3,000
2,000
1,000
0

2000 B.C.   1000 B.C.   A.D. 1   A.D. 1000   A.D. 2000*

Year   *Estimated

These ruins of the village of Skara Brae are on one of the Orkney Islands, north of Scotland. Archaeologists think that farmers and herders settled here around 2000 B.C. People used stone to build shelters for themselves and their cattle, sheep, and pigs. Villagers spent their days tending their animals, collecting shellfish, hunting, making pottery, and repairing buildings. Experts think that a violent storm struck the area, causing the villagers to abandon Skara Brae. **Critical Thinking** Why do you think the villagers built their homes out of stone?

Some of the earliest cities grew up along big rivers, such as the Nile in Egypt, the Tigris and Euphrates (yoo FRAYT eez) rivers in Iraq, the Huang He (hwahng hay) in China, and the Indus River in Pakistan. Cities grew up there because the soil for farming is rich near riverbeds.

The Earliest Cities   The chart on the next page shows when the first cities developed in Asia, Africa, and the Americas.

Early cities were different from farming villages in some important ways. Cities were larger, of course. Cities also had large public buildings. There were buildings to store surplus grain, buildings for the worship of gods, and buildings where people could buy and sell goods. In villages, most people were farmers. In cities, workers had a wide variety of occupations. Most worked at a craft. As new skills developed, so did new occupations.

Governments Form   As the population of cities grew, so did the need for effective rules. Someone needed to be responsible for keeping order. Others had to settle disputes or manage such things as irrigation projects. People developed government to keep order in their society and to provide services.

The First Civilizations

Over time, some New Stone Age societies grew into civilizations. A **civilization** is a society that has cities, a central government run by official leaders, and workers who specialize in various jobs. This job

specialization leads to another feature of civilizations, social classes. Writing, art, and architecture also characterize a civilization.

By 6600 B.C., artisans in Europe and Asia had learned a key skill. They discovered that melting a certain rock at high temperatures would separate the metal copper from the rock. By 3000 B.C., artisans had learned to mix copper with another metal, tin, to make a mixture called bronze. Because bronze was much harder than copper, it had more uses—weapons, tools, helmets, and shields. This began the Bronze Age.

Trade Helps Civilizations Spread Traders took valuable items such as pottery, tools and weapons, baskets, cloth, and spices to faraway cities. They traded these items for food and goods that people at home wanted. By around 3500 B.C., some civilizations had developed a simple but amazing invention: the wheel and axle. With the wheel and axle, trade goods could be loaded into carts and pushed through the city to market. More goods could be transported farther and more easily.

Trade over water also developed. Merchant ships now carried goods across seas and rivers. With all this travel, people of many different cultures came into contact with one another. New tools and ideas from one society soon spread to others as people from different places traded information along with goods.

Cities and Civilization

Chart Study Cities arose at different times in different places. The city of Harappa (right) was one of the first cities built in what is now Pakistan. **Critical Thinking** About when was Harappa built?

Locations of the First Cities

Area	Date City Was Founded
Southwestern Asia	about 3500 B.C.
Egypt	about 3100 B.C.
Pakistan	about 2500 B.C.
China	about 1900 B.C.
Central America	about 200 B.C.

Ancient Jewelry

The artisan class arose because there was a demand for handicrafts. A European artisan made this bronze bracelet (left) in about 1000 B.C. The gold jewelry (right) was made in Southwest Asia as early as 2900 B.C.

Social Classes Develop Growing trade links brought new prosperity to the cities. This led to another major change in society—the development of social classes. Each person was part of a group, or class, made up of others with similar backgrounds, wealth, and ways of living. In the large cities, the king was by far the most powerful person. Next in importance were two classes of people. One was the priests of the city's religion. The other was the nobles, who were government officials and military officers. Below them were the artisans, small traders, and merchants. At the very bottom of the social ladder were common workers and farmers.

SECTION 3 REVIEW

1. **Define** (a) irrigation, (b) surplus, (c) artisan, (d) civilization, (e) social class.

2. Describe the important developments that led from the hunting-and-gathering way of life to villages and cities.

3. How were the large cities of early civilizations different from the early farming villages?

Critical Thinking

4. **Recognizing Cause and Effect** Name some reasons for the development of early civilizations.

Activity

5. **Writing to Learn** You are an early trader bringing tools and weapons made of bronze to people who have never seen this metal. Write a speech to persuade these people to trade for your bronze goods.

Using a Time Line

"Okay. If something happened in 1000 B.C., it happened 1,000 years ago. Right?" Derek looked at Maria.

"No." Maria smiled. " 'B.C.' stands for 'Before Christ.' That means it happened 1,000 years before Jesus was born. Christians believe he was born about 2,000 years ago. If something happened in 1000 B.C., it really happened about 3,000 years ago."

Derek was still puzzled. "Okay," he said slowly. "Then what does A.D. stand for? Does it mean After the Death of Christ?"

"No," said Maria. "It stands for *Anno Domini,* which is Latin for 'in the year of the Lord.' That is what the Christians called the time after Jesus was born. We still call it that—the years we count now are A.D."

Get Ready

A time line is an easy way to make sense of the dates and events of the past. A time line is a simple diagram that shows how dates and events relate to one another. It has a title, reads from left to right, has years that are evenly spaced, and labels major events.

The best way to understand how to use a time line is to make one yourself. Try making one of your own life! All you need is a pencil, a sheet of paper, and a ruler.

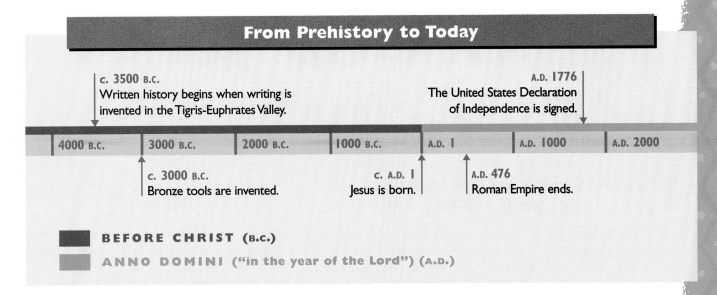

From Prehistory to Today

c. 3500 B.C.
Written history begins when writing is invented in the Tigris-Euphrates Valley.

A.D. 1776
The United States Declaration of Independence is signed.

| 4000 B.C. | 3000 B.C. | 2000 B.C. | 1000 B.C. | A.D. 1 | A.D. 1000 | A.D. 2000 |

c. 3000 B.C.
Bronze tools are invented.

C. A.D. 1
Jesus is born.

A.D. 476
Roman Empire ends.

BEFORE CHRIST (B.C.)

ANNO DOMINI ("in the year of the Lord") (A.D.)

Try It Out

A. Turn the sheet of paper sideways. Use the ruler to draw a straight line 7 inches long across the middle of the paper. Draw a big dot on the left end of the line.

B. Mark the years. Under the dot on the left, write the year you were born. Measure 1/2 inch along the line to the right, mark the spot with another dot, and write the next year under the dot. Continue until you reach the current year. Then write "Present" under the last dot. Your time line goes left to right, just as you read from left to right. Each space between two dots, or interval, represents twelve months.

C. Add the events. Above the first dot, write "Born in (write the name of the town where you were born)." Now write several other important events in your life above other dates on the time line. Connect each label to the right place on the time line with a vertical, or up-and-down, line. Remember, the space between the dots is the year; the dots themselves represent the first day of each year.

D. Give your time line an appropriate title. Now look at your time line, and ask yourself, "Does this make it easy for someone to learn about my life?" If you answer "yes," then you did a good job.

Apply the Skill

Complete the following steps by using the time line on these two pages.

1 Familiarize yourself with the time line. Look it over to get a sense of what the time line shows. What is the title? When does it begin and end? What types of events are shown? You used one-year intervals in your time line. What time intervals does this time line use?

2 Read the time line. Do you understand all of the labels and the dates on the time line? The Latin abbreviation *c.* stands for the word *circa*. *Circa* means "about." Why do you think some dates are marked "*c.*"? Why is 1776 not marked "*c.*"?

3 Learn from the time line. When did written history begin? Were bronze tools invented before or after writing? Can you tell if some events happened closer together than others? Which event happened closer to the birth of Jesus—the signing of the Declaration of Independence or the invention of writing?

4 Use the time line as a reference. A time line can help you remember dates and the order of important events. You may want to look back at the time line here as you read through this book.

Review and Activities

Reviewing Main Ideas

1. How do people today learn about people who lived tens of thousands of years ago?

2. Choose a landform or water body such as a river, mountain range, or lake and describe how it can affect the people who live around it.

3. Describe how Old Stone Age people in East Africa millions of years ago got food.

4. How did New Stone Age people get food?

5. Explain the connection between farming and the growth of early cities.

6. What caused social classes to develop?

Reviewing Key Terms

Use each key term below in a sentence that shows the meaning of the term.

1. prehistory
2. archaeologist
3. history
4. oral tradition
5. nomad
6. fertile
7. domesticate
8. irrigation
9. civilization
10. surplus
11. artisan
12. social class

Critical Thinking

1. **Drawing Conclusions** How does the geography of a place make it attractive or unattractive to settlers?

2. **Making Comparisons** Compare how New Stone Age farmers lived with how city people in early civilizations lived.

Graphic Organizer

Copy the web onto a sheet of paper. Then fill in the empty spaces with features of civilization to complete the web.

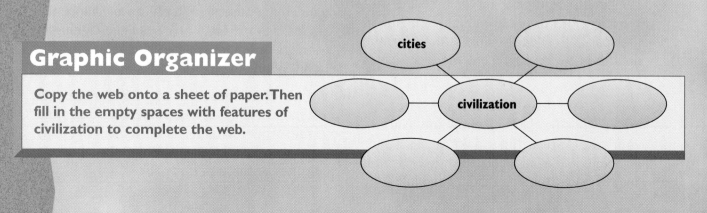

Map Activity

Agriculture

For each place listed below, write the letter from the map that shows its location.

1. Central America
2. Southwest Asia
3. North China
4. Southeast Asia
5. West Africa
6. India

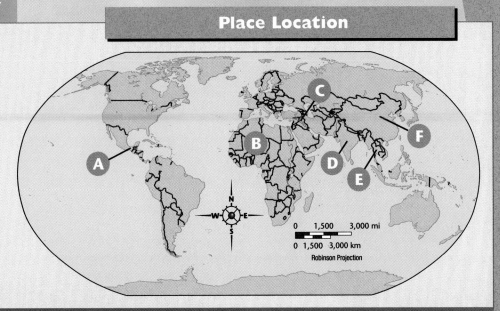

0   1,500   3,000 mi

0 1,500 3,000 km

Robinson Projection

Writing Activity

Writing Archaeology Notes

When archaeologists uncover prehistoric sites, they keep careful notes of each item they find. They use the items to help figure out things about the people who lived there. Choose a place you know well. Pick two or three items from the place and make detailed notes. From the items, tell what you can about the people who used them.

Internet Activity

Use a search engine to find **Flints and Stones: Real Life in Prehistory.** Click on the **Meet the Shaman** and **Meet the Archaeologist** links to learn about hunter-gatherers and the study of prehistory. Then return to the **Welcome** page and click on **Do the Food Quiz.** Take the quiz to see if you could survive today as a hunter-gatherer. Then write a description of a typical day for a hunter-gatherer.

Skills Review

Turn to the Skills Activity.

Review the steps for using a time line. Then complete the following: (a) Write a short definition of a time line. (b) How can you tell what the spaces between the years on a time line stand for?

How Am I Doing?

Answer these questions to help you check your progress.

1. Can I identify the methods that archaeologists and historians use to learn about the past?

2. Can I identify ways in which geography and history are connected?

3. Can I describe how Old Stone Age and New Stone Age people lived?

4. Do I understand how civilizations developed?

The Fertile Crescent

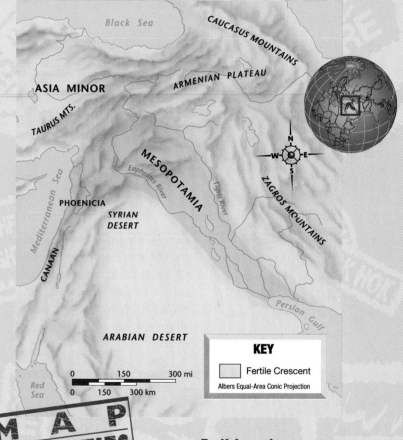

KEY

☐ Fertile Crescent

Albers Equal-Area Conic Projection

0   150   300 mi
0   150   300 km

MAP ACTIVITIES

The land that stretched in an arc from the Mediterranean Sea to the Persian Gulf had many attractions to the people of the ancient world. Get to know this land by completing the following activities.

Build a city

If you were to build three cities in the region shown on the map, where would you locate them? What makes these locations good places to build a city?

Protect yourself against invaders

Which areas might attract invaders? Why? How could people living in these areas protect their cities from invaders?

Land Between
Two Rivers

BEFORE YOU READ

Reach Into Your Background

What is the land like where you live? Is the area flat, hilly, or mountainous? Does it have any deserts, lakes, rivers, or cities nearby? What in the geography of the area do you think attracted people to first settle in your community?

Questions to Explore

1. How did the geography of Mesopotamia make this a likely area for the rise of civilization?
2. What was it like to live in a Sumerian city?

Key Terms
scribe
city-state
polytheism
myth

Key Places
Sumer
Mesopotamia
Fertile Crescent
Tigris River
Euphrates River

> **"M**y headmaster read my tablet and said: 'There is something missing,' and hit me with a cane . . . The fellow in charge of silence said: 'Why did you talk without permission?' and caned me.**"**

These words from the past come from a student at one of the world's first schools. He told what happened to him when his homework was sloppy or when he spoke without permission. Punishment was severe.

The first known schools were set up in the land of Sumer (SOO mur) over 4,000 years ago. Sumerian schools taught boys—and a few girls—the new invention of writing. Graduates of the schools became professional writers called **scribes.** Scribes were important people in Sumer because they were the only people in the land who could keep records for the kings and priests.

Learning to be a scribe was hard work. Boys normally began school at the age of 8 and didn't finish until they were 20.

The Geographic Setting of the Fertile Crescent

As you can see on the map on the next page, Sumer was located in a region called Mesopotamia (meh suh pah TAY mee uh). Like the place where you live, ancient

▼ The language on this clay tablet—Sumerian—is the oldest known written language.

Predict What might be some advantages and disadvantages to living between two rivers?

Mesopotamia had special attractions that drew people to settle there. Most important to the people, it had rich soil and life-giving rivers. These attractions drew people who became farmers and city builders. Sumer's central location within the ancient world drew many traders. Sumer became one of the most prosperous areas of the ancient world.

The Location of Mesopotamia Mesopotamia's name describes its location. The word *Mesopotamia* comes from Greek words that mean *between the rivers*. The map below shows that Mesopotamia lies between two rivers, the Tigris and the Euphrates.

Mesopotamia is part of a larger area that is called the Fertile Crescent. The Fertile Crescent is shown on the map at the beginning of this chapter. To see how this region got its name, place your finger at the eastern edge of the Mediterranean (med uh tuh RAY nee un) Sea on the map. Move eastward from the Mediterranean coast to Mesopotamia. Then move south to the Persian Gulf. Notice that the region you've traced is shaped like a crescent moon. The rivers of this crescent-shaped region made it one of the best places in Southwest Asia for growing crops.

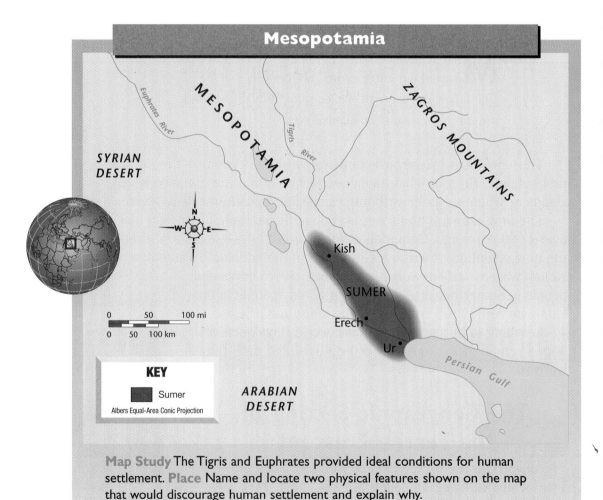

Map Study The Tigris and Euphrates provided ideal conditions for human settlement. **Place** Name and locate two physical features shown on the map that would discourage human settlement and explain why.

The Tigris and Euphrates meet in the southern part of modern Iraq. The land between the rivers continues to be good farmland. Iraqi farmers grow dates, barley, grapes, rice, and tomatoes in the Tigris-Euphrates valley.

Rivers of Life and Death The Tigris and Euphrates rivers were the source of life for the peoples of Mesopotamia. In the spring, melting snow picked up tons of topsoil as it rushed down from the mountains and flooded the land. The floods left this topsoil on the plain below. Farmers grew crops in this soil. The rivers also supplied fish; tall, strong reeds used to make boats; and clay for building.

The flood waters sometimes brought sorrows as well as gifts. The floods did not always happen at the same time each year. Racing down without warning, they sometimes swept away people, animals, and houses. Then, the survivors would slowly rebuild and pray that the next flood would not be so destructive.

The First Cities

As farming succeeded in Mesopotamia, communities began to have surpluses of food. In time, food surpluses encouraged the building of cities. By 3500 B.C., Mesopotamia had a number of growing cities in the region of Sumer. People coming to these cities were probably amazed. They saw high walls, built to keep out invaders. They stared at the large temples, the houses, the busy shops, and the splendid royal palace. They may have envied the large farms of the nobles outside the walls.

Independent Cities Form As the map on the previous page shows, cities grew up at different points along the Tigris and Euphrates rivers. These cities were separated by long distances, usually including

Around 2500 B.C., artists from the Sumerian city-state of Ur created this record of peacetime activities. The reverse side documents a battle. **Critical Thinking** How do the activities shown in the three rows provide clues about jobs and social classes in Ur?

a desert. This made it difficult for Sumerians in different cities to unite under one ruler. Each city acted as a state with its own special god or goddess, its own government, and, eventually, its own king. That is why they are called **city-states.**

A Brief Tour of a Sumerian City Some of the earliest cities arose in the region of Sumer. If you visited a Sumerian city, you'd spend much time in traffic jams. The streets were so narrow that carts could not get through them. People had to press themselves against the buildings to let donkeys squeeze by.

Sumerian houses faced away from the crowded streets, onto inner courtyards where families ate and children played. On hot nights, people slept outdoors on their homes' flat roofs. Oil lamps supplied light for Sumerian homes. Clay pipes, buried deep in the ground, carried liquid wastes away. Inventions like plumbing would not come to most other parts of the world for thousands of years.

The public squares buzzed with activity. Merchants displayed goods in outdoor stalls, shouting out to passersby to admire their goods. The streets filled with musicians, acrobats, beggars, and water sellers. Scribes wrote letters for those who could not read or write—for a price.

Sumerian Religion

A stranger coming to a Sumerian city would first notice a giant stone building at the center of the city. This was the ziggurat (ZIHG uh raht), the main temple to the gods of the city. Ziggurats were made of terraces,

Visualize What kinds of sights would you see and sounds would you hear on market day in a Sumerian city?

one on top of the other, linked by ramps and stairs. Some were more than seven stories high. At the top of the ziggurat was a temple. The Sumerians believed that gods descended to the Earth using the ziggurat as a ladder.

The people of Sumer worshipped not one, but many, gods and goddesses. This belief in many gods is called **polytheism.** To understand this word, break it up into its parts. *Poly,* a Greek word, means "many." *Theism* refers to gods.

Sumerian **myths,** or stories about gods that explain people's beliefs, warned that the gods would punish people who angered them. The myths also promised rewards to people who served the gods well. Sumerians made sure that their gods were properly cared for. Temple priests washed the statues of gods before and after each meal. Music sounded and incense burned as huge plates of food were laid before them. The god Anu was offered the following meal daily:

21 rams	7 ducks	3 cranes
60 birds	2 bulls	1 bullock
8 lambs	4 wild boars	3 duck eggs
3 ostrich eggs	29 bushels of	243 loaves of bread
2 vessels of milk	dates	

LINKS ACROSS TIME

Ur—Then and Now The Sumerian city-state of Ur was destroyed by war in 2006 B.C. In 1991, war came again to Ur. During the Persian Gulf War, the armies of the United States and Iraq fought not far from the ruins of this ancient city. Fortunately, what's left of Ur has survived the latest battles.

▼ This restored brick ziggurat once towered over the city of Ur.

The religious beliefs of the Sumerians give us an idea of what was really important to them. Notice the love of the city expressed in this Sumerian poem.

▼ In this statue grouping of Sumerian gods and worshipers from about 2500 B.C., height indicates importance. The tallest figure represents Abu, the god of vegetation. The smallest figures are worshipers.

> "Behold the bond of Heaven and Earth, the city.
> Behold the kindly wall, the city,
> its pure river,
> its dock where the boats stand.
> Behold . . . its well of good water.
> Behold . . . its pure canal."

Unfortunately for Sumer, the wealth of the city-states became their downfall. Sumerian city-states fought each other over land and, especially, the use of river water. Constant warfare weakened Sumer's rulers and exhausted its armies. Sumer was no longer a major power after 2000 B.C. It fell to a northern rival—Babylonia—in 1759 B.C.

SECTION 1 REVIEW

1. **Define** (a) scribe, (b) city-state, (c) polytheism, (d) myth.

2. **Identify** (a) Sumer, (b) Mesopotamia, (c) Fertile Crescent, (d) Tigris River, (e) Euphrates River.

3. What geographic features helped civilizations develop in Mesopotamia?

4. How did Mesopotamia become a center of trade?

Critical Thinking

5. **Distinguishing Fact From Opinion** Write one fact about Sumerian religion. Write one opinion.

Activity

6. **Writing to Learn** Pretend you are a student scribe in Sumer. Write a journal entry describing what you see on your walk to school.

Babylonia and Assyria

BEFORE YOU READ

Reach Into Your Background

Why do you think one country might decide to invade another country? List two or three reasons.

Questions to Explore

1. Why did civilizations rise and fall in Mesopotamia?
2. What characteristics describe the Babylonian and Assyrian empires?

Key Terms

empire
caravan
bazaar

Key People and Places

Babylonia
Assyria
New Babylonian empire
Nebuchadnezzar II

King Sargon II of Assyria (uh SEER ee uh) must have scowled when he heard the news. The nearby kingdoms of Urartu and Zikirtu had joined forces against him. How dare they challenge the most powerful monarch in the world? In the summer of 714 B.C., Sargon set out to "muzzle the mouths" of his enemies.

The rebels were no match for the powerful Sargon. His armies quickly overcame the forces of Urartu and killed all who resisted. The Assyrians howled with laughter when they saw the king of Urartu fleeing on an old horse. Sargon let him go. He knew that the survivors would serve as a grim warning to others who might later be tempted to oppose the mighty Assyrians.

The Two Empires of Mesopotamia

Sargon II was one of many kings who ruled Mesopotamia after the fall of Sumer. The history of Mesopotamia is filled with stories of conquest by one powerful warrior after another. This was a land worth taking. It brought great wealth to the army that could conquer it. But after winning it, each ruler became a target for another conqueror.

▼ This carving shows the powerful Assyrian warrior-king, Sargon II (left), and one of his officials.

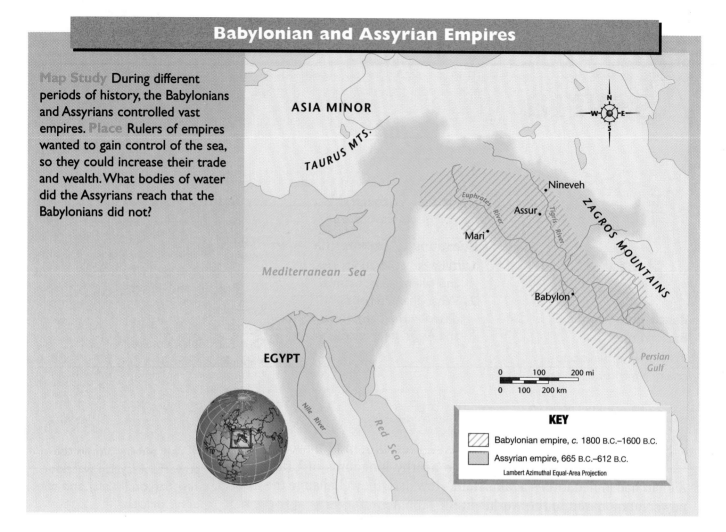

Map Study During different periods of history, the Babylonians and Assyrians controlled vast empires. **Place** Rulers of empires wanted to gain control of the sea, so they could increase their trade and wealth. What bodies of water did the Assyrians reach that the Babylonians did not?

KEY

◪ Babylonian empire, c. 1800 B.C.–1600 B.C.

▨ Assyrian empire, 665 B.C.–612 B.C.

Lambert Azimuthal Equal-Area Projection

READ ACTIVELY

Ask Questions What questions would you like to ask about the Babylonian empire?

The biggest and most important Mesopotamian civilizations were the empires of Babylonia (bab uh LOH nee uh) and Assyria. An **empire** is an area of many territories and people that are controlled by one government. The beautiful city of Babylon was the center of the Babylonian empire. This empire reached its height around 1750 B.C. The Assyrians, who got their name from the northern city of Assur, began expanding their lands in the 1300s B.C. By the 600s B.C., they controlled a huge empire. It stretched from the Persian Gulf across the Fertile Crescent and through Egypt.

The Babylonians and the Assyrians had two things in common. In their quest for riches, they were vicious warriors. And in the enjoyment of their riches, they built grand cities where culture and learning were highly valued.

The Babylonian Empire

A Babylonian king named Hammurabi (hahm uh RAH bee) created the Babylonian empire by uniting the cities of Sumer. Then, he conquered lands all the way to Asia Minor, the present-day country of Turkey, as you can see on the map above.

A Crossroads of Trade   Babylon's location made it a crossroads of trade. Caravans, or groups of travelers, coming and going from the cities of Sumer to the south and Akkad to the north, stopped in Babylon. In the city's bazaars, or markets, you could buy cotton cloth from India and spices from Egypt. Trade made Babylon rich. So did conquest.

Wealth Through Conquest   A conqueror—if successful—reaped great rewards. In about 1760 B.C., Hammurabi conquered the city of Mari. He seized Mari's war chariots, weapons, and tools, which were the best in the world. But all the wealth that Babylon gathered could not save it from conquest. By about 1600 B.C., the empire first conquered by Hammurabi had shrunk and was finally destroyed.

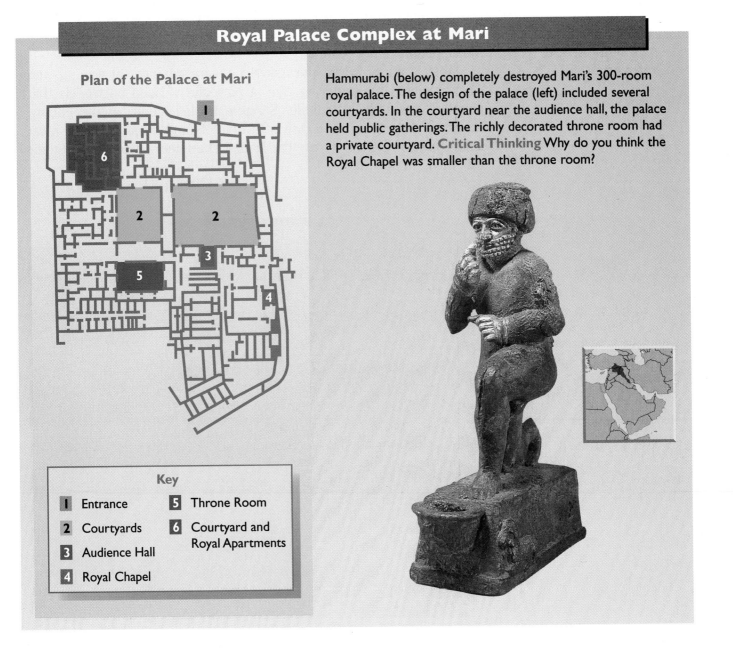

Royal Palace Complex at Mari

Plan of the Palace at Mari

Hammurabi (below) completely destroyed Mari's 300-room royal palace. The design of the palace (left) included several courtyards. In the courtyard near the audience hall, the palace held public gatherings. The richly decorated throne room had a private courtyard. Critical Thinking Why do you think the Royal Chapel was smaller than the throne room?

Key

1	Entrance	**5**	Throne Room
2	Courtyards	**6**	Courtyard and Royal Apartments
3	Audience Hall		
4	Royal Chapel		

The Empire of the Assyrians

North of Babylon was a small kingdom of a few walled cities known as Assyria. Its capital, Nineveh (NIHN uh vuh), was a sleepy village on the Tigris River. Assyria, as you can see on the map in this section, lay in an open land, which other peoples could easily invade.

Because they were constantly defending themselves, the Assyrians became skilled warriors. About 1365 B.C., they decided the best method of defense was to attack. By 650 B.C., Assyria had conquered a large empire. It stretched across the Fertile Crescent, from the Nile River to the Persian Gulf.

Assyria's Contributions The Assyrians were more than warriors. As Assyrian power grew, Nineveh became a city of great learning. Nineveh had a fabulous library that held thousands of clay tablets with writings from Sumer and Babylon. Because the Assyrians kept these records, we now know a great deal about life in early Mesopotamia.

Most of all, however, the Assyrians were geniuses at waging war. They invented the battering ram, a powerful weapon on wheels that pounded city walls to rubble. Slingers hurled stones at the enemy. Expert archers were protected with helmets and armor. But the most feared part of the army were the armed charioteers who slashed their way through the enemy.

LINKS TO LANGUAGE ARTS

The Epic of Gilgamesh Several clay tablets discovered in the great library of Nineveh contained a long narrative poem, or epic. This epic told of the Sumerian hero-king Gilgamesh. It described his adventures and his search for eternal life. It is the oldest epic ever discovered.

The Assyrian War Machine

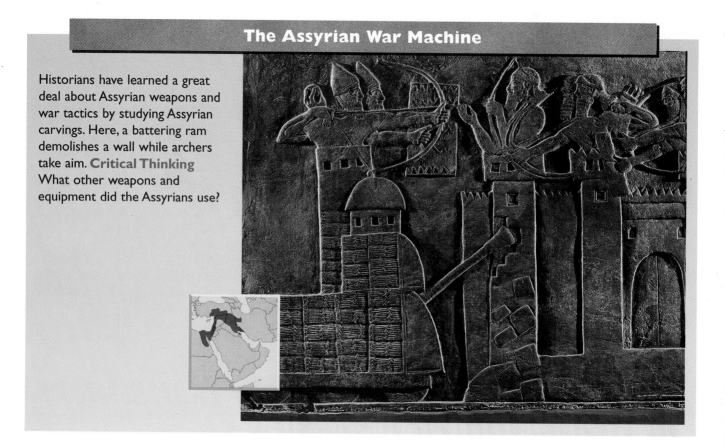

Historians have learned a great deal about Assyrian weapons and war tactics by studying Assyrian carvings. Here, a battering ram demolishes a wall while archers take aim. **Critical Thinking** What other weapons and equipment did the Assyrians use?

Assyria Overthrown The Assyrians had few friends in the lands that they ruled. Conquered peoples attempted a number of rebellions against Assyrian rule. Two groups, the Medes and Chaldeans (kal DEE uhns), joined together to smash the Assyrian empire in 612 B.C.

Babylonia Rises Again

Under the Chaldeans, Babylon rose again. It became the center of an even more splendid kingdom, known as the New Babylonian empire. Its greatest king was Nebuchadnezzar (nehb uh kuhd NEHZ uhr) II. Nebuchadnezzar rebuilt the city of Babylon, which the Assyrians had destroyed. He put up massive walls around the city for protection. He also built a gigantic palace, decorated with colored tiles. Carved on the tiles were plants, animals, birds, designs—and a boastful sentence by the king. "I am Nebuchadnezzar, King of Babylon," it said.

Nebuchadnezzar's royal palace was built on several terraces that rose to the height of some 350 feet (110 m). It had a dazzling landscape of trees and gardens. According to legend, he built the gardens for his wife, who came from the high plateau and hated the dry plains of Mesopotamia.

Under the Chaldeans, the New Babylonian empire became a center of learning and science. Chaldean astronomers charted the paths of the stars and measured the length of a year that was only a few minutes different from the length modern scientists have calculated. And Chaldean farmers raised "the flies which collect honey"—wild bees.

Like other Mesopotamian empires, the Chaldeans were open to attack by powerful neighbors. In 539 B.C., the New Babylonian empire fell. But the city of Babylon was spared.

▲ This clay tablet contains a map of the known world, which shows that the Babylonians were well aware of lands beyond their empire.

SECTION 2 REVIEW

1. **Define** (a) empire, (b) caravan, (c) bazaar.

2. **Identify** (a) Babylonia, (b) Assyria, (c) New Babylonian empire, (d) Nebuchadnezzar II.

3. Why did civilizations rise and fall in Mesopotamia?

4. How did Babylon become rich?

5. What accomplishments is Assyria known for?

Critical Thinking

6. **Cause and Effect** How did Babylon's location affect what happened to it?

Activity

7. **Writing to Learn** Write an epitaph, a statement carved on a tombstone, for Nebuchadnezzar.

SECTION 3

The Legacy of Mesopotamia

BEFORE YOU READ

Reach Into Your Background

What is your most prized accomplishment? Was it a sport or musical instrument you mastered? A friend you made? A job you did? Why does this accomplishment mean so much to you?

Questions to Explore

1. Why was Hammurabi's Code a major step forward for humankind?
2. How did writing develop in Mesopotamia?

Key Terms
code
cuneiform

Key People
Hammurabi

▼ King Hammurabi stands before Shamash, the god of justice. According to Babylonian legend, Shamash presented the code of laws to Hammurabi.

"If a man has destroyed the eye of a man of the class of gentlemen, they shall destroy his eye. If he has broken a gentleman's bone, they shall break his bone. If he has destroyed the eye of a commoner or broken a bone of a commoner, he shall pay one mina of silver. If he has destroyed the eye of a gentleman's slave, or broken a bone of a gentleman's slave, he shall pay half [the slave's] price. If a gentleman's slave strikes the cheek of a gentleman, they shall cut off [the slave's] ear."

—*from Hammurabi's Code*

Hammurabi's Code

What kind of justice system do you think we would have if our laws were not written down? What if a judge was free to make any law he or she wanted? What if the judge could give any punishment? Would people think that laws were fair? A written code, or organized list, of laws helps make sure laws are applied fairly to all.

We owe the idea that all laws should be written down and applied fairly to the Babylonians. It was King Hammurabi who set down rules for everyone in his empire to follow. These rules are known as

Hammurabi's Code. The code told the people of Babylon how to settle conflicts in all areas of life.

Hammurabi's Code contained 282 laws organized in different categories. These included trade, labor, property, and family. The code had laws for adopting children, practicing medicine, hiring wagons or boats, and controlling dangerous animals.

An Eye for an Eye Hammurabi's Code was based on the idea of "an eye for an eye." In other words, a man who blinded another person would have his own eye put out. However, the code did not apply equally to all people. As the laws at the beginning of this section show, the code gave different punishments for breaking the same rules. The harshness of the punishment depended on how important the victim was. The higher the class of the victim, the stiffer the penalty. Thus, an ox owner would pay half a mina of silver if the ox gored a noble. If the victim was a slave, the owner would pay only one third of a mina.

◀ This statue of a fierce lion dates from Hammurabi's time and probably served as a temple "guardian."

A person who accidentally broke a rule was just as guilty as a criminal. Results were what mattered. People such as doctors, who could not control the outcome of their work, had to be very careful, as the following law shows:

> **"If** a surgeon performed a major operation on a citizen with a bronze lancet [knife] and has caused the death of this citizen . . . his hand shall be cut off.**"**

Laws for Everyone   You probably know a lot of rules. There are rules for taking tests, playing ball, and just living in your home. People follow—or break—rules all the time. What, then, was the importance of Hammurabi's Code?

The laws are important to us because they were written down. With written laws, everyone could know the rules—and the punishments. These punishments may seem harsh to us. But they were the first attempt by a society to set up a code of laws that would apply to everyone.

The Art of Writing

Think how difficult it would be to carry on life if no one knew how to read and write. But writing did not just naturally develop. For most of human life, people did not have the art of writing.

Laws Set in Stone

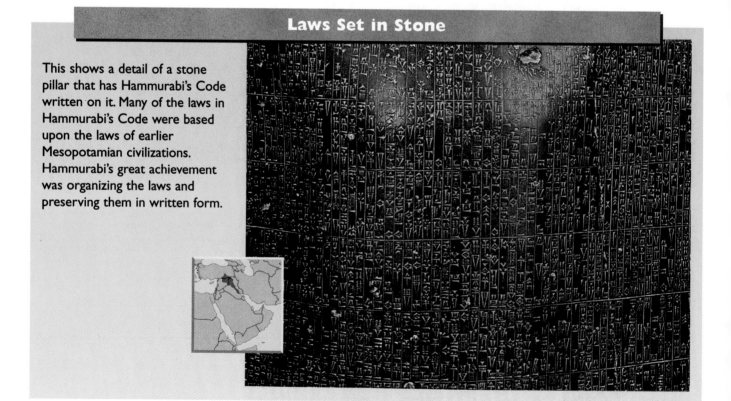

This shows a detail of a stone pillar that has Hammurabi's Code written on it. Many of the laws in Hammurabi's Code were based upon the laws of earlier Mesopotamian civilizations. Hammurabi's great achievement was organizing the laws and preserving them in written form.

▼ Scribes sometimes enclosed a message (left) in an envelope (right) made from wet clay. As the envelope dried, it formed a seal around the tablet.

Writing developed in Mesopotamia in about 3500 B.C. Long before Hammurabi issued his code, the people of Sumer developed a system of writing. Writing met the need of Sumerians to keep records. Record keepers were very important—and busy—people in Sumer. Since only a few people could write, it was one of the most valuable skills in the ancient world. Scribes held positions of great respect in Mesopotamia.

The scribes of Sumer recorded sales and trades, tax payments, gifts for the gods, and marriages and deaths. Some scribes had special tasks. Military scribes calculated the amount of food and supplies that an army would need. Government scribes figured out the number of diggers needed to build a canal. Written records then went out to local officials who had to provide these supplies or workers.

"Pages" of Hard Clay   What did the scribes of Mesopotamia write on? The Tigris and Euphrates rivers provided a perfect material —clay. Each spring, the rivers brought down clay from the mountains. Scribes shaped the soft, wet clay into smooth, flat surfaces called tablets. They marked their letters in it with sharp tools. When the clay dried, it left an almost permanent record.

The shape and size of a tablet depended on its purpose. Larger tablets were used for reference. They stayed in one place, like the heavy atlases and dictionaries in today's libraries. Smaller tablets, the size of

The Development of Writing

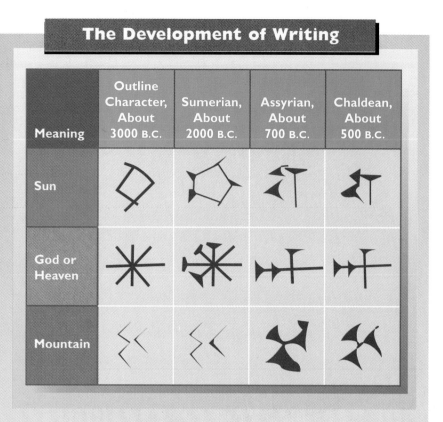

Meaning	Outline Character, About 3000 B.C.	Sumerian, About 2000 B.C.	Assyrian, About 700 B.C.	Chaldean, About 500 B.C.
Sun				
God or Heaven				
Mountain				

Table Study This table shows how writing based on pictures changed over time. These characters were used by civilizations in Southwest Asia for more than 3,000 years. The last clay tablets using them were written about 2,100 years ago. Then the languages of the tablets were forgotten. Scholars did not figure out how to read the tablets until the A.D. 1800s. **Critical Thinking** How does this form of writing differ from your own?

letters or postcards, were used for personal messages. Even today, these personal tablets can be fun to read. They show that Mesopotamians used writing during the ups and downs of everyday life:

"This is really a fine way of behaving! The gardeners keep breaking into the date storehouse and taking dates. You yourselves cover it up and do not report it to me! Bring these men to me—after they have paid for the dates."

From Pictures to Writing
Like most inventions, writing developed over time. At first, people drew pictures to represent what they wanted to say. Grain, oxen, water, stars—each important object had its own symbol.

As people learned to record ideas as well as facts, the symbols changed. Eventually, scribes combined symbols to make groups of wedges and lines known as **cuneiform** (kyoo NEE uh form). Cuneiform script could be used to represent different languages. This made it highly useful in a land of many peoples.

SECTION 3 REVIEW

1. **Define** (a) code, (b) cuneiform.
2. **Identify** Hammurabi.
3. **Why** was Hammurabi's Code important?
4. Why was the development of writing a big step in human history?

Critical Thinking
5. **Drawing Conclusions** What skills would help a student scribe succeed?

Activity
6. **Writing to Learn** Reread the letter that complains about the gardeners. Write a law that relates to the gardeners who stole the dates. What should their punishment be? What should happen to the people who didn't tell about the theft?

Mediterranean Civilizations

Reach Into Your Background

Just as people can chart the history of a civilization on a timeline, you can also chart your own personal history. What are some major events in the history of your family?

In what year did your family move to the home where you live now, for example? Make a time line that shows major events in your family history.

Questions to Explore

1. How did the Phoenicians help spread civilization throughout the Mediterranean area?
2. What were the major events in the history of the Israelites?

Key Terms

alphabet
monotheism
famine
exile

Key People and Places

Moses
Phoenicia
Canaan
Jerusalem
Israel
Judah

While the great empire of Hammurabi was rising and falling, the people of a poor city on the shores of the Mediterranean Sea were getting rich by gathering snails.

The snails that washed up on the shores of the city of Tyre (TY uhr) were not ordinary snails. These snails produced a rich purple dye. This dye was highly valued by wealthy people throughout the Mediterranean region. Ships from Tyre sold the dye at extremely high prices. The profits soon made Tyre a wealthy and active city.

▶ The Phoenicians left few details about the appearance of their ships. An Assyrian artist made this carving.

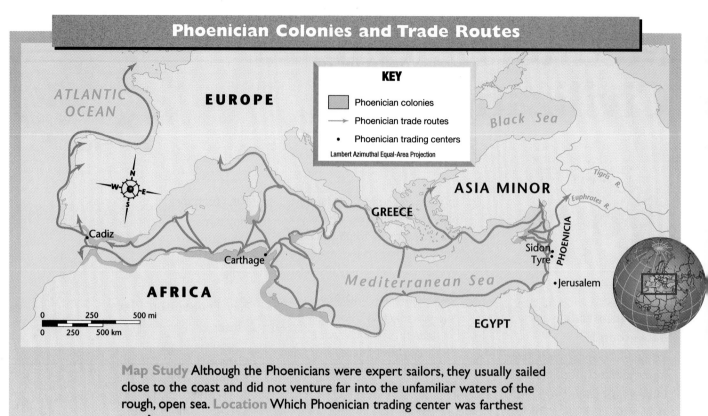

Phoenician Colonies and Trade Routes

KEY

Phoenician colonies
Phoenician trade routes
• Phoenician trading centers
Lambert Azimuthal Equal-Area Projection

Map Study Although the Phoenicians were expert sailors, they usually sailed close to the coast and did not venture far into the unfamiliar waters of the rough, open sea. **Location** Which Phoenician trading center was farthest west?

The Phoenicians: Sailors of the Mediterranean

Tyre was the major city in a region called Phoenicia (fuh NEE shuh), shown on the map. The Phoenicians' outlook was not eastward, toward Mesopotamia. Rather, the Phoenicians looked westward, toward the Mediterranean Sea and the cities that were growing up around it.

The Phoenicians had settled in a land that had few, but important, resources. Besides the snails, there were dense forests of cedar trees. Phoenicians sold these resources to neighboring peoples.

As trade grew, the Phoenicians looked to the sea to increase their profits. In time, they became the world's first trading empire. From about 1100 B.C. to 800 B.C., Phoenicia was a great sea power. Phoenician ships sailed all over the Mediterranean Sea. They even sailed out into the stormy Atlantic Ocean. They came back from these trips with stories of horrible monsters who lived in the ocean depths. Did the Phoenicians really believe these stories? Nobody knows for sure. But the stories did help keep other people from trying to compete for trade in the Atlantic.

Trade brought rich goods from lands around the Mediterranean Sea to the Phoenician cities of Tyre and Sidon (SY duhn). Bazaars swelled with foods brought from faraway places. These foods included figs, olives, honey, and spices. In the bazaars, merchants sold strange animals, such as giraffes and warthogs from Africa and bears from Europe.

Ask Questions What kinds of questions might you ask about the different and unusual lands that Phoenician sailors visited on their trading voyages?

Travelers throughout the Mediterranean area were awed by the grand ships and the overflowing markets of Tyre. This description of Tyre's bazaars appears in the Bible:

> "When your wares came from the seas,
>   you satisfied many peoples.
> With your great wealth and merchandise,
>   you enriched the kings of the earth."

Predict What would be some results of an easier, simpler system of writing?

The Phoenician Alphabet: One Sound, One Letter

Because they had so much trade, the Phoenicians needed to simplify writing. Cuneiform, with its hundreds of symbols, was just too complicated.

The Phoenicians found a way to write using just 22 symbols. This was the Phoenician alphabet, a set of symbols that represented the sounds of the language. It forms the basis of the alphabet that people in the United States and many other countries use today. Each of the 22 letters in the Phoenician alphabet stood for one consonant sound.

The simple Phoenician alphabet was far easier to learn than cuneiform. Before the alphabet, highly educated scribes controlled the power of writing. With the alphabet, many more people could learn.

The Phoenician Alphabet

The Phoenician Alphabet

A	𐤀	N	𐤍
B	𐤁	O	𐤏
C	𐤂	P	𐤐
D	𐤃	Q	𐤒
E	𐤄	R	𐤓
F	𐤅	S	𐤔
G	𐤂	T	+
H	𐤇	U	𐤅
I	𐤆	V	𐤅
J	𐤆	W	𐤅
K	𐤊	X	𐤎
L	𐤋	Y	𐤆
M	𐤌	Z	𐤈

Chart Study The chart (left) shows the Phoenician letters that correspond to our alphabet. The tablet (below) is an example of cursive Phoenician writing. **Critical Thinking** Use of the Phoenician alphabet spread throughout the Mediterranean. How do you think this occurred?

LINKS TO LANGUAGE ARTS

The Exodus The name given to the Israelites' escape from Egypt is the Exodus. It comes from an ancient Greek word meaning "going out." Scholars think the Exodus happened in the early 1200s B.C.

The Rise of the Israelites

South of Phoenicia, a small band of people settled along the shores of the Mediterranean. They were called Hebrews, and were later known as the Israelites. Although the Israelites never built a large empire, they made a deep impact on our civilization.

The Israelites traced their beginnings to Mesopotamia. For hundreds of years, they lived as shepherds and merchants who grazed their flocks outside Sumerian cities.

According to the Bible, a leader named Abraham led his people to a belief in one God. This practice is called **monotheism.** *Mono* is the Greek word for "one." *Theism,* as you know, refers to *gods.* The Bible explains that God promised Abraham that his people would have their own land if they would follow his word:

> **"G**et you out of your country, and from your kindred [relatives], and from your father's house, to the land that I will show you. And I will make of you a great nation.**"**

The Bible goes on to explain how, around 1900 B.C., Abraham led the Israelites from Mesopotamia to a new home in Canaan (KAY nuhn). Find Canaan on the map. Around 1800 B.C., a famine spread across Canaan. A **famine** is a time when there is so little food that many people starve. The famine caused the Israelites to flee south to Egypt.

In Egypt, the Israelites lived well for about 600 years. Many of them reached high positions in the government. Later, they were enslaved when an Egyptian king grew jealous of their wealth and suspicious of their power.

Return to Canaan The Bible tells how an Israelite hero named Moses led his enslaved people out of Egypt. For the next 40 years, the Israelites wandered through the desert of the Sinai (SY ny) Peninsula. Find the Sinai on the map to the left. The Bible says that while in the desert, God gave the Israelites the Ten Commandments, a code of laws. At last, the Israelites returned to Canaan. There, over time, the Israelites moved from herding to farming and built their own cities.

Conquest of Canaan As they moved further north into Canaan, the Israelites faced opposition. Slowly, through

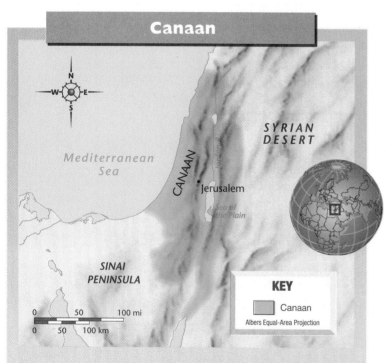

Canaan

KEY

Canaan

Albers Equal-Area Projection

0   50   100 mi
0   50   100 km

Mediterranean Sea

CANAAN

Jerusalem

SYRIAN DESERT

SINAI PENINSULA

Map Study Canaan's location between two deserts made trade over land difficult. Since Canaan bordered the Mediterranean Sea, the Israelites developed a sea trade. **Location** In what direction did the Israelites travel to return to Canaan from the Sinai Peninsula?

fierce wars, the Israelites conquered all of Canaan. Two kings led them to victory. Saul, considered the first king of the Israelites, defended them against many enemies. The next king, David, united the 12 Israelite tribes into a single nation. David established his capital at the city of Jerusalem.

After David died, his son, Solomon, inherited the kingdom. Under Solomon's rule, Israel grew prosperous through trade. The Israelites sold palm and olive oils, honey, fruits, vegetables, and grain to neighboring peoples. King Solomon also developed a sea trade with neighboring lands. On the very first voyage, an Israelite ship brought back more than 13 tons (11.8 metric tons) of gold.

▼ People have lived in Jerusalem since 1800 B.C. Today, centuries-old buildings stand not far from modern hospitals, apartments, and hotels.

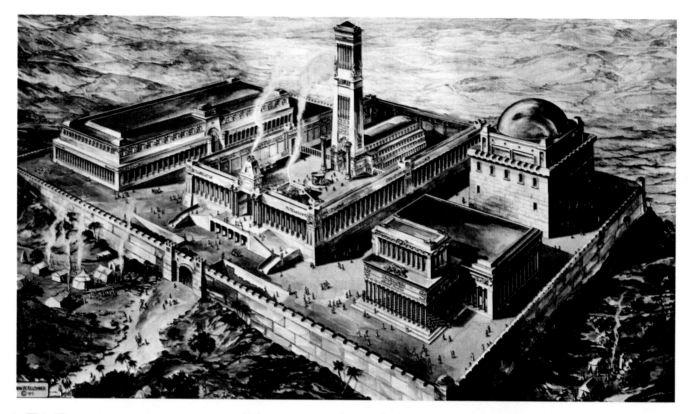

▶ This illustration captures the grandeur of what King Solomon's temple may have looked like. Solomon built the temple in about 1000 B.C.

Solomon transformed the city of Jerusalem into a magnificent capital. His most prized monument was a beautiful temple in the center of Jerusalem. It became the central place of worship for the Israelites.

Solomon's building projects were very expensive, however. The country faced hard times, and after his death, it split into two kingdoms. The northern kingdom was called Israel. The southern kingdom took the name Judah. The divided kingdom was ripe for invasion, and its dangerous neighbor, Assyria, was gaining power.

In 722 B.C., the Assyrians seized the kingdom of Israel. They punished the Israelites by exiling thousands to distant parts of their empire. To **exile** people means to force them to live in another country. About 135 years later, the kingdom of Judah fell to the Chaldeans. The Judeans were exiled as well.

SECTION 4 REVIEW

1. **Define** (a) alphabet, (b) monotheism, (c) famine, (d) exile.

2. **Identify** (a) Moses, (b) Phoenicia, (c) Canaan, (d) Jerusalem, (e) Israel, (f) Judah.

3. What impact did the Phoenicians have on the Mediterranean world?

4. Explain the importance of Phoenician writing.

5. Briefly trace the history of the Israelites from the leadership of Abraham to King Solomon.

Critical Thinking

6. **Identifying Central Issues** What important events in the history of the Israelites were shaped by movement and by war?

Activity

7. **Writing to Learn** Look at the poem about Tyre. Write one humorous verse about Tyre's markets.

Judaism

BEFORE YOU READ

Reach Into Your Background

Have you ever spent time away from home? If so, what did you do to stay in contact with family and friends?

Questions to Explore

1. How were Israelite religious beliefs unique in the ancient world?
2. What values did the Israelites have?

Key Terms

covenant
prophet
diaspora

Key People

Abraham
Deborah

The Bible records a promise made by God to the Israelite leader Abraham:

> "I will give you many descendants, and some of them will be kings. You will have so many descendants that they will become nations. . . . I will keep my promise to you and your descendants in future generations as an everlasting covenant. I will be your God and the God of your descendants."

This was the promise of a special relationship with God. It helped shape the history of the people of Israel from ancient times to the present.

The Israelites were among many peoples who lived in the Fertile Crescent. They came into contact with many other people and ideas. Over time, the Israelites developed their own ideas. These ideas reflected a blend of many traditions.

The early Israelites came to believe that God was taking part in their history. They recorded events and laws in their most sacred text, the Torah. The Torah is made up of five books. They are called Genesis, Exodus, Leviticus, Numbers, and Deuteronomy. The promise that you just read is from the Book of Genesis. Later, Christians adopted these books as the first five books of the Old Testament.

▲ All Jewish synagogues have a copy of the Torah, like the one above. The Torah's sacred text is handwritten on a parchment scroll.

2500 B.C.	2000 B.C.	1500 B.C.	1000 B.C.	500 B.C.

Sumer
3500 B.C.–1800 B.C.
- *c.* 3500 B.C. Sumerians develop writing.
- *c.* 2100–2000 B.C. Ziggurat of Ur built.

Babylonia
1800 B.C.–1600 B.C.
- *c.* 1792–1750 B.C. Hammurabi rules and produces code.
- *c.* 1760 B.C. Hammurabi conquers Mari.

Israel
2000 B.C.–587 B.C.
- *c.* 1800 B.C. Famine drives Israelites to Egypt.
- *c.* 1250 B.C. Moses leads Israelites back to Canaan.
- *c.* 1000–962 B.C. King David rules.
- 722 B.C. Israel falls to Assyria.
- 587 B.C. Judah falls to Chaldeans.

Assyria
1365 B.C.–612 B.C.
- 714 B.C. Sargon II conquers Urartu.
- *c.* 665–612 B.C. Assyrian empire

New Babylonia (Chaldeans)
612 B.C.–539 B.C.
- 605–562 B.C. Nebuchadnezzar rules.
- 587 B.C. Nebuchadnezzar captures Jerusalem.

A Covenant With God

To the Israelites, history and religion were closely joined. Each event showed God's plan for the Israelite people. In time, Israelite beliefs changed into the religion we know today as Judaism. You already know that Judaism was monotheistic from its beginning. It also differed in other ways from the beliefs of nearby peoples.

Most ancient people thought of their gods as being connected to certain places or people. The Israelites, however, believed that God was present everywhere. They believed that God knew everything and had complete power.

As you read, Israelites believed that God had made a covenant, or binding agreement, with Abraham. For this reason, Israelites considered themselves to be God's "chosen people." Moses renewed this covenant. He told the Israelites that God would lead them to Canaan, "the promised land." In return for God doing this, the Israelites had to obey Him faithfully.

Ask Questions What would you like to know about the Israelites' covenant with God?

The Ten Commandments At the heart of Judaism are the Ten Commandments. These are laws that Israelites believed God gave them through Moses. Some set out religious duties toward God. Others are rules for moral behavior. From Jewish scripture, here are five.

66 I the Lord am your God who brought you out of the land of Egypt. . . . You shall have no other gods beside Me. . . .
Honor your father and your mother, as the Lord your God has commanded. . . .
You shall not murder.
You shall not steal. 99

In addition to the Ten Commandments, the Torah set out many other laws. Some had to do with everyday matters, such as how food should be prepared. Others had to do with crimes. Like Hammurabi's Code, many of the Israelites' laws demanded an eye for an eye. At the same time, preachers called on leaders to carry out the laws with justice and mercy.

Some laws protected women. The Ten Commandments, for example, make respect for mothers a basic law. But, as in many other religions, women were of lower status than men. A man who was head of a family owned his wife and children. A father could sell his daughters into marriage. Only a husband could seek a divorce.

Early in Israelite history, a few women leaders, such as the judge Deborah, won honor and respect. Later on, women were not allowed to take part in many religious ceremonies.

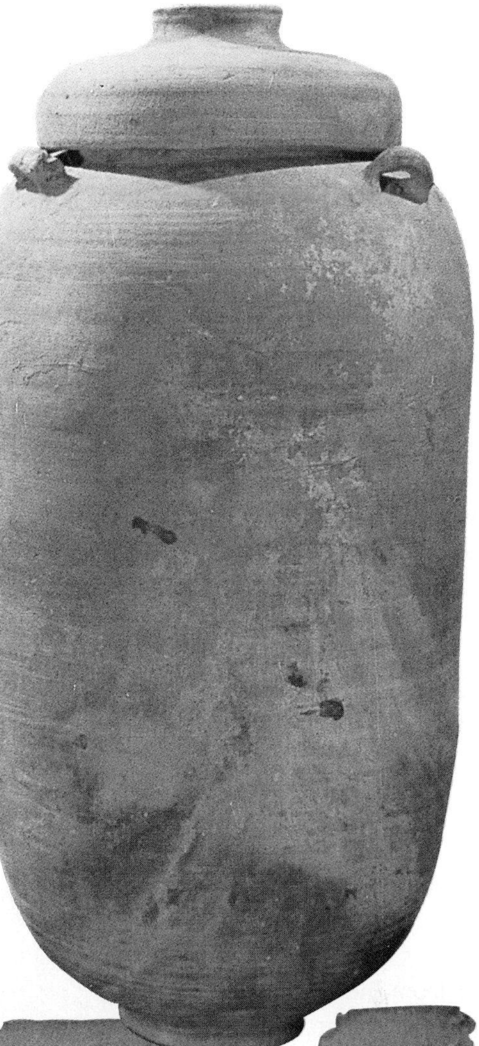

▼▶ Several ancient scrolls, concealed in jars like the one on the right, were found near the Dead Sea in 1947. Named the Dead Sea Scrolls, these manuscripts helped historians reconstruct the early history of the Israelites.

Justice and Morality   Often in the history of the Israelites, prophets, or religious leaders, appeared. They told the Israelites what God wanted them to do. The prophets warned the people not to disobey God's law. Disobedience would bring disaster.

Prophets preached a strong code of moral behavior. They urged the Israelites to lead moral lives. They also called on the rich and powerful to protect the poor and weak. All people, the prophets said, were equal before God. In many ancient societies, the ruler was seen as a god. To the Israelites, however, their leaders were human. Kings had to obey God's law just the way shepherds and merchants did.

Looking Ahead

In A.D. 135, the Romans added to the **diaspora** (dy AS puhr uh), or scattering of people, begun by the Assyrians and Chaldeans. After a rebellion, the Romans drove the Israelites out of their homeland. As a result, Israelites scattered to different parts of the world.

Wherever they settled, the Jews, as they had come to be called, preserved their heritage. They did so by living together in close communities. They took care to obey their religious laws and follow their traditions. These traditions set Jews apart. Yet, they also helped the Jews survive harsh treatment by others.

The Diaspora Because of the many dispersals of the Jewish people throughout history—known as the Diaspora—Jews settled in communities all over the world, including India, China, and Africa. The first Jewish settlers in the Americas arrived in Brazil in the 1500s.

▶ After defeating the Jews in battle in A.D. 70, Roman soldiers carried off precious and sacred objects from the temple in Jerusalem.

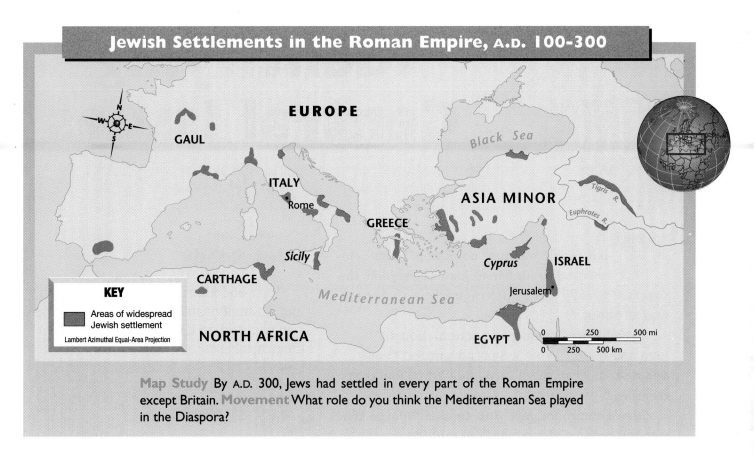

Jewish Settlements in the Roman Empire, A.D. 100-300

KEY

Areas of widespread Jewish settlement

Lambert Azimuthal Equal-Area Projection

EUROPE

GAUL

ITALY

Rome

GREECE

Sicily

CARTHAGE

Mediterranean Sea

NORTH AFRICA

Black Sea

ASIA MINOR

Tigris R.

Euphrates R.

Cyprus

ISRAEL

Jerusalem

EGYPT

0   250   500 mi

0   250   500 km

Map Study By A.D. 300, Jews had settled in every part of the Roman Empire except Britain. Movement What role do you think the Mediterranean Sea played in the Diaspora?

Judaism is one of the world's major religions because of its special religious ideas. It also had an important influence on two later religions, Christianity and Islam. Both of those faiths came from the same geographical area. Both were monotheistic. Jews, Christians, and followers of Islam all honor Abraham, Moses, and the prophets. They also share the same moral point of view that the Israelites first developed.

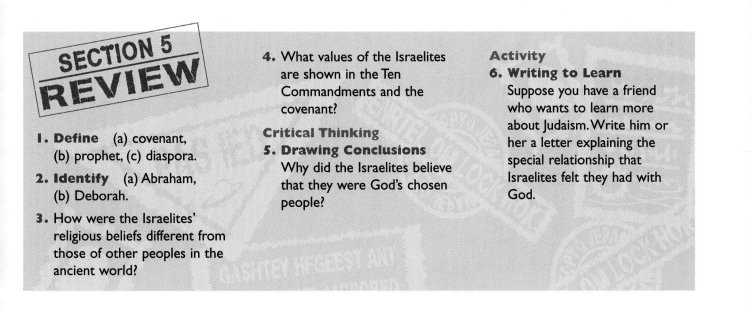

SECTION 5 REVIEW

1. **Define** (a) covenant, (b) prophet, (c) diaspora.

2. **Identify** (a) Abraham, (b) Deborah.

3. How were the Israelites' religious beliefs different from those of other peoples in the ancient world?

4. What values of the Israelites are shown in the Ten Commandments and the covenant?

Critical Thinking

5. **Drawing Conclusions** Why did the Israelites believe that they were God's chosen people?

Activity

6. **Writing to Learn** Suppose you have a friend who wants to learn more about Judaism. Write him or her a letter explaining the special relationship that Israelites felt they had with God.

Identifying Central Issues

"That movie was sure confusing," Bob commented to his friend Juan as they left the theater. "I really had trouble figuring out what it was all about."

"Well, it had some great action, though," Juan answered. "What a neat adventure! Those people really had to go through a lot to find that treasure."

Juan's comment gave Bob an idea. "Maybe that was the point of the movie," he said. "Maybe the whole idea was just to show the great adventures they had while they tried to find the lost treasure."

Get Ready

Juan and Bob got the idea. You can, too. To understand anything you read or see, you need to identify the main idea, or the central issue.

Try It Out

Try identifying central issues by reading the following paragraph. Think about its main idea. Then complete the steps that follow.

◀ A scene from *Raiders of the Lost Ark*. The adventure of finding lost treasure was a central issue of this movie.

In 1901, the Code of Hammurabi was discovered when a huge stele (STEE lee), or monument, was found. The stele was almost eight feet tall and more than seven feet around—a huge piece of deep black stone. At its top was a carved scene of a sun-god on a throne handing a scepter to the man in front of him. The scene represented Hammurabi receiving the code of laws from the sun-god. Below the scene, the laws were listed in more than 1,000 lines of writing in cuneiform characters. On the other side of the monument were 2,500 more lines. People soon translated the writing. They realized they had discovered a set of ancient laws.

A. Look for something that identifies the central issue. If you are trying to find the central issue in something you have read, you may find it in the title. Also, look for a sentence that identifies the central issue. Which sentence in the paragraph you just read does this?

B. Look for an idea that all the sentences (or scenes in a movie) have in common. Usually, most of the sentences provide details that support or explain the central issue. The idea they have in common is the central issue. What idea do the sentences in the paragraph have in common?

C. State the central issue in your own words. Write in your own words what you think the central issue is. You might want to write it in the form of a title. Write one or two versions, and then reread the passage to make sure that what you wrote accurately identifies the central issue. What might be a title for the paragraph?

Apply the Skill

The text in the box at right lists some laws from the Code of Hammurabi. Read them, and then follow the steps below.

1 **Follow the three steps for identifying a central issue.** Repeat the three steps you followed before. Does anything in the list of laws state the central issue? What do all the laws have in common? How would you state the central issue of the information in the box?

2 **Consider other peoples' statements of the central issue.** Compare your statement of the central issue with those of some of your classmates. Then, work with your classmates to compare your statements with what some scholars have identified as the central issue in the Code of Hammurabi. Do you agree with the the following statements? Explain your answers.

- The underlying principle of the Code of Hammurabi is that "the strong shall not injure the weak."
- The basic idea of the Code of Hammurabi is that "the punishment shall fit the crime."
- Every law in Hammurabi's Code follows this central idea: "the punishment for a crime shall be retaliation (revenge)."

Selections From the Code of Hammurabi

If a shepherd is careless and brings about an accident in the flock, the shepherd shall repay in cattle and sheep the loss he caused.

If a physician sets a broken bone, the patient shall give five shekels (Babylonian coins) of silver to the physician.

If a man cuts down a tree in another man's orchard without the consent of the owner of the orchard, he shall pay one-half mina (another Babylonian coin) of silver.

If a man opens his canal for irrigation and neglects it so that the water carries away soil from a nearby field, he shall give the owner of the field enough grain to replace what the field would have grown.

If a builder builds a house for someone and does not make its construction meet the requirements, and a wall falls in, that builder shall strengthen that wall at his own expense.

Review and Activities

Reviewing Main Ideas

1. Explain the importance of the Tigris and Euphrates rivers in the Fertile Crescent.
2. Describe Mesopotamia's location in the ancient world.
3. Explain how Mesopotamia's location shaped its development.
4. Give two examples of strong rulers in the Fertile Crescent.
5. How did rulers in the Fertile Crescent help shape the civilizations they ruled?
6. Explain how Assyria gained and used its power.
7. Name one improvement that Hammurabi's Code made in Babylonian society.
8. List two steps in the development of writing in Mesopotamia.
9. Explain two important cultural contributions of the Phoenicians.
10. List three major events in the history of the Israelites. Then, choose one of them, and describe its importance.
11. Identify one way in which the Israelites' religious beliefs were unique in the ancient world.

Reviewing Key Terms

Use each key term below in a sentence that shows the meaning of the term.

1. scribe
2. city-state
3. polytheism
4. myth
5. empire
6. caravan
7. bazaar
8. code
9. cuneiform
10. alphabet
11. monotheism
12. famine
13. exile
14. covenant
15. prophet
16. diaspora

Critical Thinking

1. **Comparing and Contrasting** Mesopotamian rulers used different methods of uniting their people behind the government. Contrast the ways of Sargon II with those of Hammurabi. How were they similar? How were they different?
2. **Expressing Problems Clearly** How did Assyria's location aid its development as a military power?

Graphic Organizer

Copy the chart onto a sheet of paper. Then fill in the empty boxes to complete the chart.

Civilization	Where They Lived	Their Challenges or Problems	Their Achievements
Sumerians			
Babylonians			
Assyrians			
Chaldeans			
Phoenicians			
Israelites			

Map Activity

Fertile Crescent
For each place listed below, write the letter from the map that shows its location.

1. Tigris River

2. Euphrates River

3. Mesopotamia

4. Fertile Crescent

5. Canaan

6. Mediterranean Sea

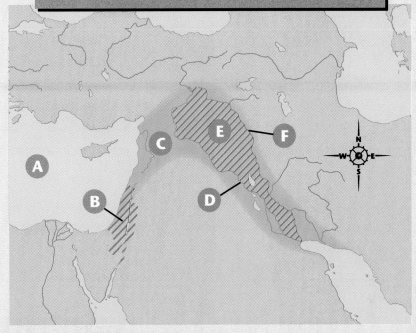

Writing Activity

Writing a Brochure
Choose a civilization that you read about in this chapter. Write a short, imaginary travel brochure telling an ancient visitor about the interesting features of the civilization.

Internet Activity
Use a search engine to search for the site **Cuneiform Connections.** Read the chart to learn some common cuneiform symbols. With a toothpick, scratch symbols from the chart onto self-hardening clay to create a list in cuneiform of items you would sell at a public market. Give your dried tablet to a friend to translate.

Skills Review

Turn to the Skills Activity.

Look again at the steps for identifying central issues. Then complete the following: (a) How would you define the term "central issue"? (b) Explain why understanding the central issue is important when you are reading social studies.

How Am I Doing?
Answer these questions to help you check your progress.

1. Do I understand how geography helped shape the civilizations of the Fertile Crescent?

2. Can I explain how civilizations in Mesopotamia and other areas of the Fertile Crescent affected human history?

3. Can I identify some historic events that shaped the culture and beliefs of the Israelites?

4. What information from this chapter can I use in my book project?

Ancient Egypt and Nubia

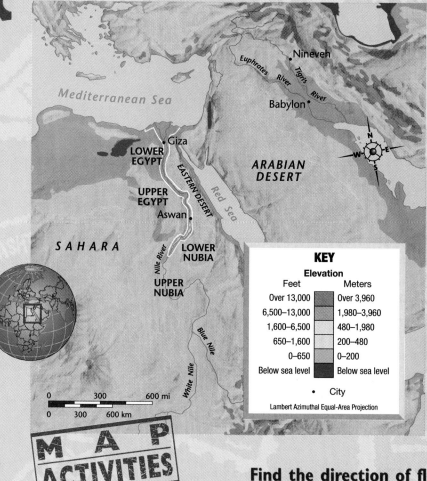

KEY

Elevation

Feet		Meters
Over 13,000		Over 3,960
6,500–13,000		1,980–3,960
1,600–6,500		480–1,980
650–1,600		200–480
0–650		0–200
Below sea level		Below sea level

• City

Lambert Azimuthal Equal-Area Projection

MAP ACTIVITIES

Water, as you know, always flows downhill. Whether the downhill direction is to the east, west, north, or south, water will flow that way. Study the map, and then carry out the following activities to understand the difference between up and down and north and south.

Find the direction of flow
Locate the Nile River and with your finger, trace its route. In what direction does the Nile flow? How do you know this?

Find Upper Egypt and Lower Egypt
Find the two areas labeled Upper Egypt and Lower Egypt. Is Lower Egypt north or south of Upper Egypt? Which area is up river from the other? In which region is the land higher? How do you know this?

The Geography of the Nile

BEFORE YOU READ

Reach Into Your Background

Perhaps you live near a river, lake, or ocean. If so, then you know that bodies of water affect your environment. You enjoy them for recreation. Perhaps your family depends on them for a living. Think of several ways nearby water can affect the way people live.

Questions to Explore

1. How does the geography of the Nile River change as it runs from its sources to the delta?
2. How did the Nile support human life in ancient times?

Key Terms
cataract
delta
silt

Key People and Places
Herodotus
Lower Nubia
Upper Nubia
Upper Egypt
Lower Egypt

"**E**gypt is the gift of the Nile," wrote the Greek historian Herodotus (huh RAHD uh tuhs). He explored Egypt in the 400s B.C. He saw the life-giving waters of its great river. He traveled upriver until he was stopped by churning rapids of white water. Unable to get past the rapids, he turned back. He never found the source of the river.

Herodotus wrote down his observations of Egypt and other lands. They still make interesting reading today. Despite his failure to locate the source of the Nile, Herodotus had learned a basic truth. There would be no Egypt without the Nile.

The Course of the Nile

The Nile is the world's longest river. It flows north from its sources in central Africa to the Mediterranean Sea for more than 4,000 miles (6,436 km). This is more than the distance across the United States.

The Nile has two main sources. The Blue Nile rises in the highlands of the present-day country of Ethiopia and races down to the desert in thundering torrents. The White Nile is calmer. It begins deep in central Africa and flows northward through swamps. The two

▼ Food was one of the gifts of the Nile. This Egyptian hunts waterbirds as he drifts along in a reed boat.

rivers meet at what is today the city of Khartoum (kahr TOOM) in the present-day country of Sudan. There, the Nile begins its journey through desert lands to the Mediterranean Sea.

The Nile Through Ancient Nubia   From Khartoum northward, the Nile makes two huge bends, forming an *S* shape. The northern tip of the *S* is at the city of Aswan in Egypt. Along this 1,000-mile (1,600 km) stretch of the Nile was a land called Nubia.

The Nubian section of the Nile contained six rock-filled rapids called **cataracts.** Between the First and Second Cataracts was Lower Nubia. In this region, the desert and granite mountains lined the riverbanks, leaving very little farmable land. Because it rarely rained in Lower Nubia, people had to live close to the Nile for their water supply.

Farther south, between the Second and Sixth Cataracts, lies the area that was known as Upper Nubia. In this region, rain does fall, so people could farm in the summer and fall. But the farmland was in a very narrow strip, no more than 2 miles (3 km) wide on each side of the river.

The Nile Through Ancient Egypt   The ancient Egyptian section of the Nile ran for about 700 miles (1,100 km) from the First Cataract at Aswan to the Mediterranean Sea. On its way, it passed through a narrow region called Upper Egypt. This fertile strip had an average width of around 6 miles (10 km) on each side of the river. In the north, the Nile spread out to form a fertile, marshy area called Lower Egypt. Dry deserts stretched on each side of the river's green banks.

READ ACTIVELY

Ask Questions What questions would you like answered about the importance of the Nile River to the ancient Egyptians and Nubians?

▼ Gold was an important Nubian resource. In this wall painting, Nubian princes bring gifts of gold to an Egyptian ruler.

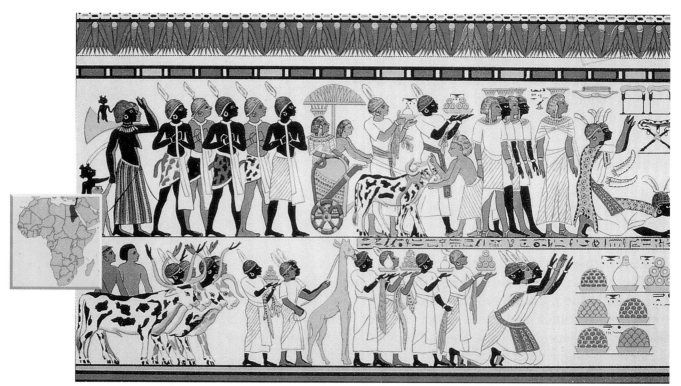

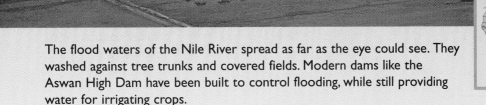

The flood waters of the Nile River spread as far as the eye could see. They washed against tree trunks and covered fields. Modern dams like the Aswan High Dam have been built to control flooding, while still providing water for irrigating crops.

At the end of the Nile in the north, the river split into several streams that flowed to the Mediterranean Sea. These streams formed an area shaped like a triangle and called the **delta.** The delta contained very fertile farmland.

The Gifts of the Nile   Every spring, far away in the highlands of Africa, waters came rushing down from the highlands. As they flowed, they brought rich, fertile soil called **silt.** Each spring the Nile spilled over its banks. It flooded the dry land and deposited a layer of thick silt that was ideal for farming. In gratitude, the Egyptians praised Hapi (HAH pea), the god of the Nile:

> **"H**ail to you, O Nile, who flows from the Earth and comes to keep Egypt alive.**"**

Black Land and Red Land   The ancient Egyptians called their land *Kemet* (KEH meht), "the black land," because of the dark soil left by the Nile's floods. The timing of the floods and the height of the flood waters might vary from year to year. But unlike the Mesopotamians, the Egyptians usually did not have to worry about flash floods. Dry years were rare, but they could cause famine.

LINKS ACROSS TIME

Saving Temples Lake Nasser is a lake created by the building of a dam on the Nile in the 1960s. The creation of Lake Nasser threatened to flood ancient temples that the Egyptians had carved in the cliffs above the Nubian Nile. Egypt, with the help of about 50 nations, saved the temples. Workers cut the temples into blocks. They moved the blocks to higher ground and rebuilt the temples.

Beyond the fertile river banks lay the "red land," the vast desert. It spread out on either side of the river. Most of the Sahara lay to the west, and the part of the Sahara called the Eastern Desert lay to the east. These lands were not friendly to human life. They were useless for farming. Only those who knew the deserts well dared travel over this blistering-hot land.

Yet the hostile deserts were a blessing to the Egyptians and Nubians. The hot sands shielded Egypt and Nubia from foreign attacks. This was a protection Mesopotamia did not have. The land between the Tigris and Euphrates rivers was wide-open to the raids of outsiders. The people of Mesopotamia were constantly facing invasions. Over a period of 2,000 years, the people of ancient Egypt and Nubia faced few invasions. Yet they were not isolated. The Nile Valley provided a path for trade with Central Africa. The Mediterranean Sea and the Red Sea provided access to Southwest Asia.

▼ The thriving crops and vegetation of the fertile Nile Valley contrast with the barren cliffs in the distance.

Although a modern tractor waits at the end of the field, this Egyptian farmer uses oxen and a traditional wooden plow to turn the soil in his field.

Civilizations Along the Nile

Communities appeared in the Nile delta of Lower Egypt by around 4000 B.C. The people of the delta built villages around the fertile river beds. Their homes were built of straw or of bricks made from a mix of mud and straw. To the south, in Upper Egypt, people built scattered farming villages along the banks of the Nile.

The first Nubian communities emerged around 3800 B.C. Because farming was difficult, Nubians also fished in the Nile and hunted ducks and other birds along its banks.

The Growth of Trade

The Nile was a highway for trade. Ships could float downriver because the Nile flowed north. But they could also sail upriver because the winds blew toward the south. Another trade link ran east across the desert and the Red Sea to Mesopotamia. Caravans loaded with gold, silver, copper, and fine pottery traveled the overland trade routes. Valuable goods such as cedar from the eastern coast of the Mediterranean Sea and gold from Nubia were sold in the bazaars of Egypt's towns.

READ ACTIVELY

Visualize Picture in your mind the way the Nile River valley looked before and after the yearly floods.

The ancient Egyptians built several kinds of boats for use on the Nile. Boats such as this one have been found in the tombs of Egyptian kings. Royal tombs contained objects that were thought to be needed by the dead—boats would help in making the voyage to the afterlife.

Because of the cataracts, people could not travel through Nubia by river. Instead, the Nubians developed trade routes over land. One of these routes was through the Nile Valley. The Nubians became famous traders of the ancient world as they carried goods from central Africa and Nubia into Egypt and southwestern Asia and back.

One Nubian caravan into Egypt had 300 donkeys. They carried ebony wood, ivory from elephant tusks, ostrich feathers and eggs, and panther skins. Another popular item was a "throw-stick," an African version of a boomerang.

SECTION 1 REVIEW

1. **Define** (a) cataract, (b) delta, (c) silt.

2. **Identify** (a) Herodotus, (b) Lower Nubia, (c) Upper Nubia, (d) Upper Egypt, (e) Lower Egypt.

3. How did the Nile River affect the lives of the early Egyptians and Nubians?

4. How did trade develop in various places along the Nile?

Critical Thinking

5. **Recognizing Cause and Effect** If the Nile River did not flood regularly, how might life along the Nile have been different?

Activity

6. **Writing to Learn** You are traveling along the Nile from its source to the Nile delta. Write a journal entry about the changes in the river you notice as you travel.

Egypt's Powerful Kings and Queens

BEFORE YOU READ

Reach Into Your Background

What would it be like to have total power over the lives of people? Very few leaders today have such sweeping powers. But at one time, kings and queens had the power of life and death over their people. How would it feel to be responsible for the well-being of thousands of subjects who looked upon you as a god?

Questions to Explore

1. How did Egyptian rulers unify their country?

2. What were some of the accomplishments of Egypt's greatest pharaohs?

Key Terms
pharaoh   regent
dynasty

Key People
Hatshepsut
Menes
Thutmose III

The statue you see here looks like the face of a powerful king of ancient Egypt. And indeed it is. But there's something wrong with this face. You see, there's a woman behind that beard.

The woman is Hatshepsut (haht SHEHP soot), who ruled Egypt during the New Kingdom. Hatshepsut was a bold leader who led her army into battle when enemies threatened Egypt's borders. But she is most known for creating a time of great peace and economic success. She encouraged trade with faraway places, sending a famous expedition to the land of Punt (puhnt) on the east coast of Africa. Egyptian traders returned with shiploads of ivory, gold, and spices.

Hatshepsut was not the only woman to rule Egypt. But the respected title of **pharaoh** (FAIR oh), or king, traditionally referred to a man. For this reason, Hatshepsut appears here with the clothing and symbols of a pharaoh—beard and all.

◄ Hatshepsut declared herself pharaoh of Egypt in 1503 B.C. She ruled with shrewdness and skill until her death.

Egypt's God-Kings

Hatshepsut was one of many famous Egyptian pharaohs to rule Egypt. Some, like her, were wise. Others were careless or cruel. Egypt's fortunes rested on the strength of its pharaohs.

From Dynasty to Dynasty   The history of ancient Egypt is the history of each of its dynasties. A dynasty is a series of rulers from the same family. Egypt had 31 dynasties until it was conquered by the Greek ruler Alexander the Great in 332 B.C. Historians group Egypt's dynasties into three main time periods, called kingdoms. The earliest time period is called the Old Kingdom. Next came the Middle Kingdom. The latest time period is called the New Kingdom. The time line on the next page shows the dates of each kingdom. Remember, these kingdoms are not places. They are time periods.

The gaps between the kingdoms were times of troubles—wars, invasions, weak rulers. These in-between periods were rare, however. For most of ancient Egyptian history, there was stable rule.

According to legend, Egypt's first dynasty began when a king named Menes (MEE neez) united Upper and Lower Egypt. Menes built a city named Memphis near the present-day city of Cairo (KY roh). From there, he ruled over the Two Lands, which is what the ancient Egyptians

Overcoming Obstacles A man named Nekhebu worked his way up from the bottom of society to become an architect during the Old Kingdom. At first, he carried other builders' tools for them. Eventually, his hard work paid off. The pharaoh made him Royal Architect. Nekhebu believed in always doing satisfactory work, and in never "going to bed angry against anybody."

▼ This plaque from about 3000 B.C. glorifies events of Menes' reign. At the left of the plaque, Menes looks victoriously on his dead enemies.

	c. 2700 B.C.–2200 B.C. Old Kingdom		2040 B.C.–1786 B.C. Middle Kingdom		1570 B.C.–1085 B.C. New Kingdom	
3000 B.C.	2700 B.C.	2400 B.C.	2100 B.C.	1800 B.C.	1500 B.C.	1200 B.C.

OLD KINGDOM

c. 2600 B.C. Builders begin Great Pyramid.

c. 2550 B.C. Statue of Sphinx built at Giza.

MIDDLE KINGDOM

c. 1991 B.C.–1800 B.C. Egypt expands into Lower Nubia.

c. 1991 B.C.–1800 B.C. Literature and art flourish.

c. 1878 B.C.–1840 B.C. Senusret III strengthens government.

NEW KINGDOM

c. 1503 B.C.–1482 B.C. Queen Hatshepsut rules.

c. 1333 B.C.–1323 B.C. King Tut rules.

c. 1290 B.C.–1224 B.C. Ramses II expands Egyptian territory.

▲ **Time Line Study** This time line shows the dates for each kingdom and lists important events and accomplishments of the kingdoms.

called Upper and Lower Egypt. Carvings from Menes's time show the pharaoh wearing two crowns—the white crown of Upper Egypt and the red crown of Lower Egypt. The uniting of Egypt began one of the most stable civilizations in history. It lasted for more than 2,500 years.

All-Powerful Pharaohs The pharaohs had absolute power over their people. Whatever the pharaoh decided became law. He decided when the fields would be planted. He received crops from the workers on his estates.

The pharaoh was also a religious leader. It was the pharaoh, Egyptians believed, who provided his people with the Nile's yearly floods and the harvests that followed. As one official wrote:

> "He is the god Re whose beams enable us to see. He gives more light to the Two Lands than the sun's disc. He makes the Earth more green than the Nile in flood. He has filled the Two Lands with strength and life."

Connect Compare the role of the Egyptian pharaoh with the role of the President of the United States.

Two Thousand Years of Power

Egypt grew and prospered during its first six dynasties, which included the Old Kingdom. It was blessed with able rulers and a well-run system of government. The pharaohs kept the peace and trade with Nubia, with only occasional conflicts. They sent merchants to the eastern coast of the Mediterranean to find timber. This timber was used in the building of houses, boats, and furniture. Egyptian merchants may have even traveled north across the Mediterranean in search of trade items.

About 2250 B.C., near the end of the Old Kingdom, governors in the provinces began to challenge the power of the pharaohs' government. Egypt's unity crumbled, and the dynasties grew weak.

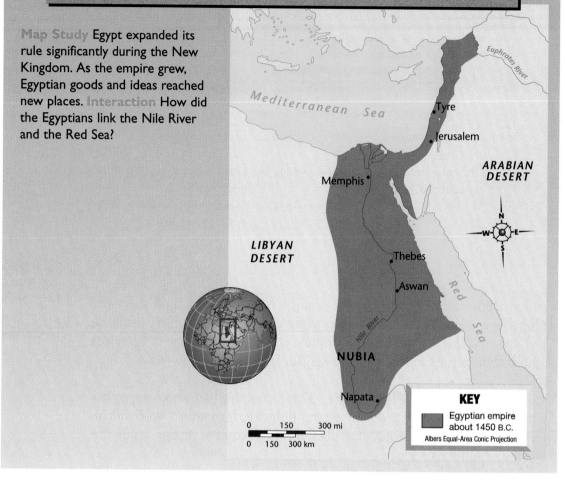

The Egyptian Empire About 1450 B.C.

Map Study Egypt expanded its rule significantly during the New Kingdom. As the empire grew, Egyptian goods and ideas reached new places. Interaction How did the Egyptians link the Nile River and the Red Sea?

KEY
Egyptian empire about 1450 B.C.
Albers Equal-Area Conic Projection

The early dynasties of the Middle Kingdom restored order and reunited the country. With calmer times, the pharaohs spent the nation's wealth on works such as irrigation projects instead of on wars. They also built a canal between the Nile and the Red Sea. Egypt grew even richer. However, less able rulers followed. In time, they lost control of the country to foreign invaders.

Egyptian princes became strong enough to drive out the foreign invaders around 1550 B.C. This event marks the start of the New Kingdom.

The first pharaohs of the New Kingdom were not content just to drive foreigners out of their country. They wanted to build an empire. The pharaohs created huge armies of foot soldiers, mounted warriors, and war chariots. Bronze swords and body armor made the Egyptians nearly unbeatable.

A Powerful Queen, a Great Pharaoh

Around 1500 B.C., a child named Thutmose III (thoot MOH suh) became pharaoh. Because of his youth, his stepmother was appointed **regent.** A regent is someone who rules for a child until the child is old enough to rule. His stepmother was Hatshepsut, whom you read about at the beginning of this section. Not content to be regent, Hatshepsut had herself proclaimed pharaoh. She ruled Egypt for about 22 years.

Hatshepsut's reign was good for Egypt. She apparently enjoyed her power, too. When Thutmose grew up, she refused to yield the throne to him. He took over when she died and had all her statues destroyed. We don't know if Thutmose had a hand in Hatshepsut's death.

Thutmose III was one of the greatest pharaohs of the New Kingdom. He led his army in wars against Syria and Phoenicia, in Southwest Asia. Egyptian troops advanced as far east as the Euphrates River and south into Nubia. Yet Thutmose was more than a conqueror. He was an educated man who loved to study plants. Unlike most rulers of his time, he treated defeated peoples with mercy.

▼ Queen Hatshepsut's temple at the foot of a dramatic limestone cliff in Dayr al-Bahri, Egypt, is one of the masterpieces of New Kingdom architecture.

Cleopatra: A Woman of Ambition

Cleopatra ruled Egypt from 51 B.C. to 30 B.C. The Egyptian carving (right) shows Cleopatra and Isis, a popular Egyptian goddess. Cleopatra, however, was not content to be queen of just Egypt. She wanted to rule the Roman Empire—and she almost succeeded. Cleopatra gained so much influence in Rome that her likeness appeared on roman coins (below).

The New Kingdom began to decline around 1075 B.C. Civil war left Egypt weak and poorly defended. The mighty kingdom fell to the famous conqueror Alexander the Great in 332 B.C. About 300 years later, Egypt was conquered by another powerful civilization of the ancient world: the Romans. Egypt became part of the Roman Empire. It would not govern itself again for almost 2,000 years.

SECTION 2 REVIEW

1. **Define** (a) pharaoh, (b) dynasty, (c) regent.

2. **Identify** (a) Hatshepsut, (b) Menes, (c) Thutmose III.

3. How did Egypt's rulers govern their empire?

4. Describe some of the accomplishments of each of the three Egyptian kingdoms.

Critical Thinking

5. **Expressing Problems Clearly** Explain why Egypt's rulers had more authority than most rulers have today.

Activity

6. **Writing to Learn** Write a paragraph explaining this statement: "Ancient Egypt was strongest when its rulers were strong."

Egyptian Religion

Reach Into Your Background

Have you ever tried to organize your friends or family to take a trip or to do something around the house?

If so, you've probably realized that getting people to do something together sounds easier than it actually is. People have their own opinions. It takes special skills to get the best work out of people. What do you think those skills are?

Questions to Explore

1. What role did religion play in ancient Egypt?

2. How did the Egyptians manage to build the pyramids without knowledge of the wheel?

Key Terms
afterlife
mummy
pyramid

Key Places
Giza

"You will live again. You will live forever. Behold, you will be young forever."

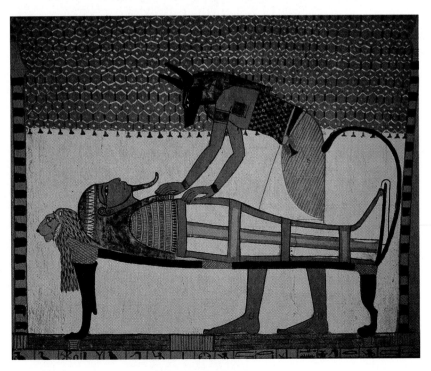

▼ The Egyptian god of the dead, Anubis, tends a dead pharaoh. According to myth, Anubis invented mummification.

The priest chanted the words as the royal family wept over the body of their most important member, the pharaoh. One hundred days had passed since he had died. During this time, the royal officials had worked on his body. After wrapping the body in many strips of fine linen, they placed the king in a gold-covered coffin. It was decorated to resemble the man in all of his royal glory.

The Egyptians believed in an after-life, a life after death. With each step of the funeral, there were prayers to help the pharaoh's soul on the way to the afterlife. Then the nobles and royal family followed the body as it was carried to the royal tomb. Workers closed the tomb and the mourners went home. The pharaoh's journey to the afterlife had begun.

▶Amon-Re's name meant "the hidden one." Some Egyptians believed that Amon-Re watched over and judged all human affairs from an unknown, hidden place.

Religion in Egyptian Life

For the people of ancient Egypt, religion was an important part of daily life. It was the way people explained the workings of nature. Why was there an unexpected long period without rain? What caused sickness and death? The Egyptians believed that only magical spirits could control these events. So they tried to please these spirits, their gods.

Each part of Egypt had its own gods and goddesses who had their own temples. The gods of Upper Egypt were different from those of Lower Egypt. Over the centuries, however, ancient Egyptians came to believe in several groups of gods. These included gods who were often shown as humans with animal heads. Among them was Osiris (oh SY rihs), the god of the living and the dead.

The chief god of the ancient Egyptians was Amon-Re. He protected the rich and the poor. The Egyptians believed that Amon-Re was born each morning in the east and died each evening in the west. That is why the west was believed to be the home of the dead. Egyptians preferred not to be on the west bank of the Nile after nightfall because they believed the spirits of the dead lived there.

According to Egyptian belief, Osiris, the god of the afterlife, had a family. Isis (EYE sihs), one of the most powerful of all Egyptian goddesses, was his wife. The god of the sky, Horus (HOH ruhs), was his son. Egyptians worshipped Isis as the great mother who protected the health of her children. In Egyptian art, Isis and Osiris are often shown together.

Scientists unwrapped the mummy of Ramses II and found that, although some 3,000 years had passed since his death, his facial structure and hair remained well preserved (left). The gold portrait mask (right) was one of many treasures found in King Tutankhamen's tomb.

Life Ever After

The ancient Egyptians believed the spirits of the dead made their way to the afterlife in heavenly boats. Once there, if they lived right in this life, they joined with Osiris and lived a life of ease and pleasure. They spent their days meeting and eating and drinking with their friends and family who had died. The souls of the dead could not survive without food, clothing, and other items from this life, however. The Egyptians took care of this by burying the dead with the possessions they had enjoyed in life. A pharaoh's tomb could contain everything from sandals to furniture to even his favorite horse.

Egyptians believed that if bodies were preserved, or made into mummies, the spirit would exist in the afterlife. The bodies of important people, usually royalty, were mummified. The process took two or three months. Workers carefully removed the organs. The body was then filled with a natural salt and stored for at least 42 days. During that time, it completely dried out.

Once dry, the body was cleaned and bathed in spices. Then it was wrapped with long linen bandages. Arms and legs were bandaged tightly to the body. A well-wrapped mummy had up to 20 layers of bandages.

While workers were preparing the mummy, artisans were busy carving the coffin. Actually, there were more than one of these wooden coffins. A pharaoh had three or four coffins. The coffins fit one inside the other like a nest of boxes. The innermost coffin was usually shaped like a human body, with the dead person's face painted on the cover.

LINKS ACROSS THE WORLD

A King With One God
Akhenaton (ah kuh NAH tuhn), who became pharaoh in 1353 B.C., gave up the old gods. He had their names chipped off temples. Like the Israelites, Akhenaton worshipped only one god. His god was Aton, the life-giving disk of the sun. The Egyptian people did not accept this monotheism. After the king's death, they went back to worshipping many gods.

Peering Into a Pyramid

The outside of a pyramid is extremely impressive, but the interior also reveals the high level of the Egyptians' building and design skills.

Critical Thinking Find the false burial chamber. Why do you think burglars would have wanted to rob a pharaoh's tomb?

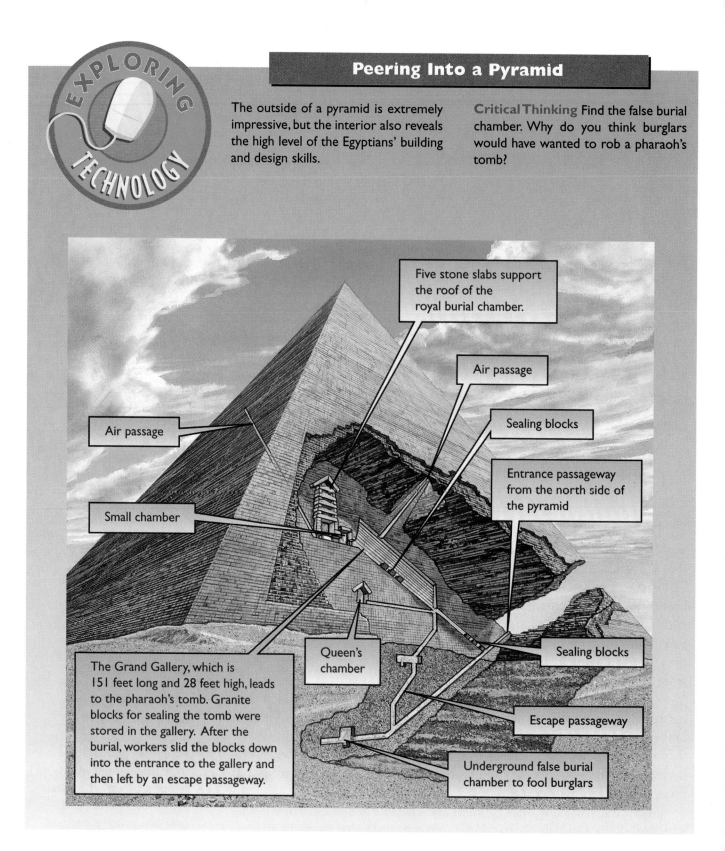

Five stone slabs support the roof of the royal burial chamber.

Air passage

Air passage

Sealing blocks

Entrance passageway from the north side of the pyramid

Small chamber

The Grand Gallery, which is 151 feet long and 28 feet high, leads to the pharaoh's tomb. Granite blocks for sealing the tomb were stored in the gallery. After the burial, workers slid the blocks down into the entrance to the gallery and then left by an escape passageway.

Queen's chamber

Sealing blocks

Escape passageway

Underground false burial chamber to fool burglars

Tombs for the Pharaohs

The planning for a pharaoh's tomb began as soon as he was crowned. The earliest royal tombs were made of mud brick. However, as time went on, tomb building became an art. The pharaohs of the

Fourth Dynasty built the largest and most famous tombs of all. These were the **pyramids,** huge buildings with four sloping outside walls shaped like triangles.

Most of the pyramids were built during the Old Kingdom. The largest is the Great Pyramid. It is one of several enormous monuments at a site called Giza. Find Giza on the map at the beginning of this chapter.

Building the pyramids required a great deal of organization. The Great Pyramid, for example, is made up of more than 2 million stones. The average weight of each stone is 5,000 pounds (2,270 kg). Each stone had to be hauled up the side and put into its right place.

It could take 20 or more years to build a pyramid. The project began with the selection of a site on the west bank of the Nile. Remember that the west bank was the land of the dead. Once the site was chosen, workers cleared the ground. Engineers set the pyramid square so that the sides faced the main points of the compass—north, south, east, and west.

Workers then cut the building blocks. Stone for the inner parts of the pyramids came from nearby quarries. But fine stone for the outside came from farther away. Some came all the way from Nubia. It had to be loaded onto barges and carried along the Nile or canals near the Nile to the building site.

Visualize What do you think the building site of a half-finished pyramid looked like? How many workers do you think were needed to push the huge blocks of stone up ramps?

▼ The Great Pyramid (center) is one of 10 located in Giza, Egypt. It stands about 450 feet (140 m) tall.

This large boat was discovered in the Great Pyramid. It was made of wood from cedar trees. Pharaohs were buried with boats so they could make the voyage to the afterlife.

At this time, the ancient Egyptians did not use the wheel. To get the blocks of stone into place, workers had to use sleds, wooden rollers, and levers. They dragged and pushed the huge blocks up ramps of packed rubble to the level they were working on.

Workers toiled all year either in the quarries or at the pyramid site. They had to be fed at least twice a day. Archaeologists have found the remains of their villages. They know that the builders of the pyramids ate huge quantities of wheat bread. Archaeologists actually found the remains of a bakery among grave sites of the workers.

Building pyramids was dangerous work. Each year, men lost their lives, crushed by falling blocks. But the workers believed in the importance of their work. To build a pyramid was an act of faith. It was a way of ensuring the pharaoh's place in the afterlife.

SECTION 3 REVIEW

1. **Define** (a) afterlife, (b) mummy, (c) pyramid.

2. **Identify** Giza.

3. How did the religion of the ancient Egyptians explain what happened to a person after death?

4. How was a pharaoh's tomb furnished?

Critical Thinking

5. **Expressing Problems Clearly** Describe how the ancient Egyptians organized the building of the pyramids.

Activity

6. **Writing to Learn** The pharaoh invites you to go with him to inspect his pyramid as it is being built. Write a journal entry describing what you see on your visit. What does the project tell about Egyptian religious beliefs? What does it tell about their skills in engineering?

The Culture of the Ancient Egyptians

BEFORE YOU READ

Reach Into Your Background

Imagine writing a school report or a letter to a friend using pictures instead of letters. A picture of an eye could stand for the letter *i*. A wavy line (a wave on the *sea*) could stand for the letter *c*. When you put them together you form the word *icy*. This is similar to the idea behind Egyptian picture writing.

Questions to Explore

1. How did the Egyptians live their daily lives?

2. What scientific contributions did the Egyptians make?

Key Terms

hieroglyph
papyrus
astronomer

Key People

Jean François Champollion

His name was Uni, and he was an Egyptian noble of the Old Kingdom. His life story—a success story—is recorded in his tomb.

Uni began his career in a simple way—running a storehouse. Later, he moved up the ladder to groundskeeper of the royal pyramid. In this job, he oversaw the quarrying and delivery of stone for the pyramid. Uni must have worked hard, because later he was made a general. Then, he became Governor of Upper Egypt, in charge of goods and taxes for half the kingdom. By the time of his death, we learn that Uni was royal tutor at the palace and an honored companion of the pharaoh.

Everyday Life of the Ancient Egyptians

Most of what we know of the everyday life of the Egyptians is based on paintings that cover the walls of tombs and temples. These paintings show royalty and ordinary people involved in all aspects of life. Written records also tell us much about their lives. Like Uni, they were busy and hard-working people. They also had a sense of fun and a love of beauty.

▼ Meri, a noble of the fourth dynasty, had his tomb carved with writings and with scenes of his life. Over the centuries, the paint has worn off the carvings.

Linteau et montant de porte provenant du tombeau du fonctionnaire MERI.
Sakkâra   IV: dynastie

Social Classes Egyptian society itself resembled a pyramid. At the very top stood the pharaoh. Beneath him was a small upper class. This group included priests, members of the pharaoh's court, and nobles who held the largest estates. The next level was the middle class, made up of merchants and skilled workers. At the base of the pyramid was by far the largest class, the peasants. Mostly, the peasants did farm labor. But they also did other kinds of labor, such as building roads and temples. A person could even rise to a higher class. Generally, the way to rise was through service to the pharaoh, as Uni knew.

Prisoners captured in wars were made slaves. Slaves formed a separate class, which was never very large. Egyptian society was flexible, however. Even slaves had rights. They could own personal items and inherit land from their masters. They could also be set free.

Lives of the Peasants Although peasants could own land, most worked the land of wealthier people. During the season of the flood, the peasants worked on roads, temples, and other buildings. As soon as the waters left the land, the fields had to be planted. This had to be done quickly while the soil was still moist. One farmer plowed the black earth with a team of oxen while another followed behind, scattering the seeds.

▼ These wooden figures depict workers in a bakery. The carved scene was found in a tomb. **Critical Thinking** Why do you think such scenes are useful to archaeologists?

Egyptian women worked hard in the fields with their husbands, as the tomb painting shows. But they also enjoyed using makeup and perfumes. The carving of the swimmer and the duck is actually a small case for makeup.

The harvest was the busiest season for Egypt's peasants. All men, women, and older children went into the fields to gather the crops of wheat or barley. Work went on from sunrise to sunset. Once the crops were gathered, the villagers feasted. Everyone made sure to offer food and drink to the gods in thanks for their help.

Egyptian Women: An Active Role   Egyptian women were looked upon as living models of Isis, the wife of Osiris. They had most of the rights that men had. They could own property, run businesses, and enter into legal contracts. For the most part, women traveled about freely. Egyptian paintings often show them supervising farm work or hunting. And women had many occupations—from priestess to dancer.

Noble women held a special position in Egyptian society. Sometimes they were in charge of temples and religious rites. They could also use their position to influence the pharaoh. Some women acted as regents until the pharaoh was old enough to rule on his own.

Achievements of the Egyptians

From the records of the ancient Egyptians, we know that they possessed an amazing amount of knowledge. They made important advances in such fields as writing, astronomy, and medicine. Among the people of the ancient world, Egypt was known as a land of great learning.

READ ACTIVELY

Connect What American holiday do we celebrate as a day of giving thanks? How is that holiday similar or different from the Egyptians' harvest feast?

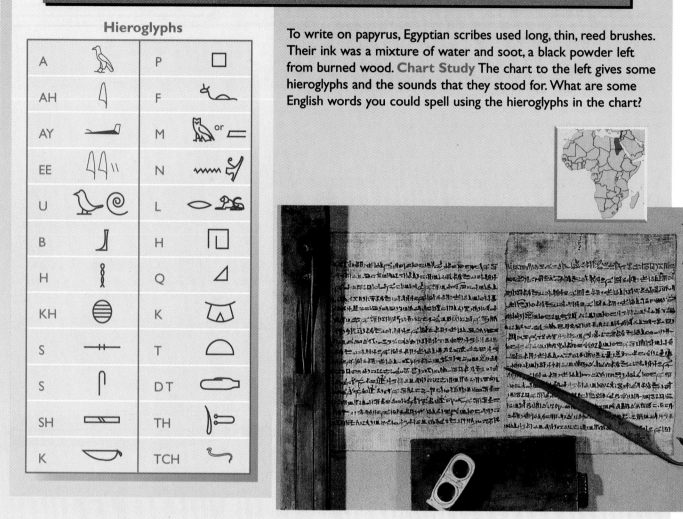

Hieroglyphs

A		P	
AH		F	
AY		M	or
EE		N	
U		L	
B		H	
H		Q	
KH		K	
S		T	
S		DT	
SH		TH	
K		TCH	

To write on papyrus, Egyptian scribes used long, thin, reed brushes. Their ink was a mixture of water and soot, a black powder left from burned wood. **Chart Study** The chart to the left gives some hieroglyphs and the sounds that they stood for. What are some English words you could spell using the hieroglyphs in the chart?

Ask Questions What would you like to know about the achievements of the Egyptians?

A New System of Writing In ancient Egypt, as in Mesopotamia, ideas were written down in picture-like symbols called hieroglyphs (HY ur oh glifs). In this script, some pictures stand for ideas or things. For example, two legs means *go.* Other pictures stand for sounds. For example, a drawing of an owl stands for *m,* as in *mother.*

The Egyptians began to use hieroglyphs because they needed a better way to keep track of the kingdom's growing wealth. As the Egyptian empire grew, it became necessary to create more pictures for more complicated ideas.

At first, the Egyptians wrote on clay and stone, as the Sumerians did. But they needed more convenient writing surfaces. They found it in papyrus (puh PY ruhs), an early form of paper made from a reed-like plant found in the marshy areas of the Nile delta. They first cut the stalks of the plant into narrow slivers. Then they soaked the slivers and pounded them flat. Left out in the air to dry, the pieces of papyrus became stiff. Joined side by side, the pieces formed a long roll.

Unlocking a Mystery   The meaning of ancient Egypt's hiero-glyphic writing was lost after the A.D. 400s. Scholars could not read the mysterious pictures. It wasn't until about 200 years ago, in 1799, that an important find took place. A soldier digging a fort near the Nile found a large black stone with three different types of writing on it. The upper part showed hieroglyphs, the middle part showed a different form of hieroglyphs, and the lower part showed Greek letters. This stone is called the Rosetta Stone because it was found near Rosetta, a city in the Nile delta near the Mediterranean Sea.

Many scholars tried to use the Greek letters on the Rosetta Stone to figure out the meaning of the hieroglyphs. But it was not an easy task. Then, in the 1820s, a young French scholar named Jean François Champollion (zhahn frahn SWAH shahm poh LYOHN) finally figured it out. When Champollion published his results, a new window onto the world of the ancient Egyptians opened.

Keeping Track of Time   Because they were an agricultural people, the Egyptians needed to be able to predict when the Nile would flood. This was the work of Egyptian **astronomers,** scientists who study the stars and other objects in the sky. They noticed that the Nile appeared to rise rapidly about the same time that they could see Sirius (SIHR ee us), the Dog Star, in the sky shortly before sunrise. They worked out the average time between the appearances of the star. They found that it came to 365 days. This became the length of their year.

Measurement Some units of measurement used by the Egyptians were based on the human body. The cubit was the distance from an elbow to the tip of the fingers. Of course, this length varied from person to person, so the Egyptians made a standard cubit out of black granite. The Egyptians used their accurate measuring system to build the Great Pyramid.

▼▶ The Rosetta Stone honored King Ptolemy V. The hieroglyphs circled by the ring below spell his name. This name and others were the key to finding the meaning of hieroglyphs.

Tomb robbers did not steal the treasures buried with King Tutankhamen, who died in 1323 B.C. Among the many beautiful objects found in his tomb were a wood and ivory game board and a pair of leather sandals. Critical Thinking Why do you think these objects were buried with the king?

Medicine Probably because of their work on mummies, the ancient Egyptians knew a great deal about the body. By studying the body, they learned to perform surgery. They could set broken bones and treat injuries of the spine.

The Egyptians also practiced herbalism, the art of creating medicines from plants. They used these natural remedies to help ease everyday illnesses such as stomachaches and headaches. Mothers prepared their own home remedies to reduce a child's fever. The Egyptians wrote much of their medical knowledge down on papyrus. The ancient Greeks and Romans used these records centuries later.

SECTION 4 REVIEW

1. **Define** (a) hieroglyph, (b) papyrus, (c) astronomer.

2. **Identify** Jean François Champollion.

3. How were the lives of Egypt's peasants ruled by the seasons?

4. What contributions did the Egyptians make in medicine and astronomy?

Critical Thinking

5. **Drawing Conclusions** What do you think were the two most important developments of ancient Egyptian culture? Explain your reasoning.

Activity

6. **Writing to Learn** You are a scribe at the court of the pharaoh. In a paragraph, describe how you use your skill in his service. Then, use the chart of hieroglyphs in this section to create a word you might have used as a scribe.

The Resource-Rich Cultures of Nubia

Prince Taharka of Nubia loved a good contest. He once held a 5-hour, 30-mile race across the desert. The athletes, Taharka's soldiers, ran at night to avoid the blazing heat. In the end, he gave prizes to the winners and losers alike.

In 690 B.C., Taharka himself received the ultimate prize: He was to be crowned king of both Nubia and Egypt. Taharka's father, Piye (PEE yeh), had conquered the mighty Egyptians. Now, Taharka was about to inherit this double kingdom. He would become the greatest ruler of his dynasty.

As the kingdom prepared for Taharka's crowning ceremony, what did the powerful warrior do? Like any good son, he invited his mom. And she came, traveling 1,200 miles from Nubia north to Memphis for the big celebration. The king wrote proudly, "She was thrilled to see me upon the throne of Egypt!"

Egypt's Friend and Rival

Taharka's homeland of Nubia was the birthplace of fascinating civilizations. An advanced culture

▼ The pharaoh Taharka of Nubia is shown offering two cups to a god. He is named in the Bible as a warlike and powerful ruler.

LINKS
ACROSS THE WORLD

Nubia and Egypt A recent discovery of a Nubian incense burner has some scientists thinking about the early relationship between Egypt and Nubia. Some scientists think the object was made around 3100 B.C. or even earlier. Carved on its side are a seated king and other figures that later became symbols of Egyptian pharaohs. Scientists are debating whether Nubia or Egypt had the first kings.

first appeared in Nubia about 8,000 years ago. This makes it one of the world's oldest cultures. During the long period of Nubian civilization, many kingdoms arose. They would grow and gain power for a time. Then they would become weak and die out. Tracing these events is like taking a slow-motion roller coaster ride through Nubian history.

For most of their long history, Nubia and Egypt both did well as peaceful, friendly neighbors. The Egyptians called Nubia *Ta Sety* (TAH seh tee), "the land of the bow." This probably referred to the Nubians' skill as archers. The Nubian archers were so good that Egypt hired many of them for its armies.

Early in its history, Egypt benefited greatly from goods brought into Egypt by caravans from Lower Nubia. But later, powerful kingdoms arose in Upper Nubia. These kingdoms began to rival Egypt for power and control of land. Three of the more powerful Nubian kingdoms grew up in the cities of Kerma (KUR muh), Napata (NAH pah tah), and Meroë (MER oh ee). Find these three cities on the map below.

The Kingdom of Kerma The Kerma kingdom rose in power at a time when Egypt was weakening. From the city of Kerma at the Third Cataract of the Nile, the kingdom expanded into parts of southern Egypt by 1600 B.C.

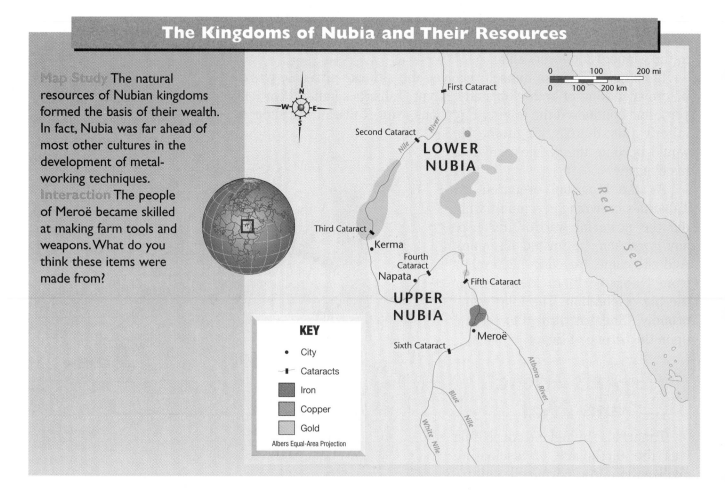

The Kingdoms of Nubia and Their Resources

Map Study The natural resources of Nubian kingdoms formed the basis of their wealth. In fact, Nubia was far ahead of most other cultures in the development of metal-working techniques. **Interaction** The people of Meroë became skilled at making farm tools and weapons. What do you think these items were made from?

First Cataract

Second Cataract

Nile River

LOWER NUBIA

Red Sea

Third Cataract

Kerma

Fourth Cataract

Napata

Fifth Cataract

UPPER NUBIA

Meroë

Sixth Cataract

Atbara River

Blue Nile

White Nile

0   100   200 mi
0   100   200 km

KEY
- City
- Cataracts
- Iron
- Copper
- Gold

Albers Equal-Area Projection

People of the Sudan still sleep on beds like this one. It is a reproduction based on remains found in a royal tomb. The jar shows the skill of Kerma potters. The long, thin piece is a spout for pouring.

Kerma gained not only power but wealth. It was noted for its **artisans,** or skilled workers. They made delicate pottery. Items made by Kerma artisans have been found in the tombs of pharaohs. This means the items were highly prized.

Kerma was a wealthy kingdom. One clue is the way the people buried their kings, in tombs under huge mounds of earth as large as football fields. They placed the kings on gold-covered beds and surrounded them with jewelry, gold, and ivory.

Around the late to mid-1400s B.C., Egypt began to regain its strength. Pharaoh Thutmose III sent his armies into Nubia. After a war that lasted about 50 years, the Egyptians took control of Nubia as far south as the Fourth Cataract. Egypt ruled Nubia for the next 700 years.

During this period, the Nubians adopted many Egyptian ways. They even began to worship Egyptian gods along with their own. Throughout these times of conflict and peace, people and goods continued to pass between Nubia and Egypt. The two cultures became mixed.

The Kingdom of Napata   In the late 700s B.C., Egypt was once again weak and divided. The Nubian kingdom of Napata expanded its power into Egypt. Napata was centered near the Fourth Cataract of the Nile.

The Napatan kings gradually took control of more of Egypt. They moved their capital city first to Thebes and then to Memphis. By the time of Taharka, whose coronation you read about earlier, the Napatans controlled all Egypt. The pharaohs of Egypt's Twenty-fifth Dynasty were Nubians.

The Napatan kings admired Egyptian culture. They brought back old Egyptian ways and preserved them. They even began building pyramids in which to bury their kings. The ruins of these small Nubian pyramids can still be seen today.

The rule of the Napatan kings did not last very long. About 660 B.C., they were forced back into Nubia. The Nubians never again controlled Egyptian land.

The Kingdom of Meroë   Moving south of Egypt's reach, the Nubians founded a royal court in the ancient city of Meroë. This city was located on the Nile between the Fifth and Sixth Cataracts. It became the center of an empire that included much of Nubia. It also stretched south into central Africa.

Predict What were some benefits Meroë gained from making and using iron tools and weapons?

Colorful Gold

Artisans of Meroë created some of the finest gold jewelry in the ancient world. This bracelet is decorated with colored enamel, another specialty of Meroë. Enamel is a glasslike material that is baked onto metal.

▶ Women like Queen Malakaye, who lived in the early 500s B.C., were important in Nubian culture. Over the centuries, several women held ruling power in Nubia.

The rocky desert east of Meroë held large deposits of iron ore. As a result, the Nubians began making iron weapons and tools. The people of Meroë became the first Africans to specialize in iron-working. Iron plows allowed them to produce good supplies of food. Iron weapons allowed them to control trade routes that ran all the way to the Red Sea. There they traded goods from central Africa for goods from India, the Arabian Peninsula, and Rome. Meroë grew rich on this trade.

Today, Meroë remains largely a mystery. The culture created its own system of hieroglyphic writing. But even today's powerful computers cannot figure out what it means, so scholars must get clues about these people from what they left behind. The kingdom of Meroë began to weaken in the A.D. 200s. However, features of Nubian culture have lasted for 3,500 years. To this day, Nubian styles of pottery, furniture, jewelry, beautiful braided hairstyles, and clothing survive among people of the modern-day country of Sudan.

SECTION 5 REVIEW

1. **Define** artisan.
2. **Identify** (a) Taharka, (b) Kerma, (c) Napata, (d) Meroë.
3. How would you describe the relations between Egypt and Nubia?

4. How did iron help make the kingdom of Meroë rich?

Critical Thinking

5. **Identifying Central Issues** Explain how the Nubians and the Egyptians borrowed from each other's culture. In what ways did each civilization benefit from the other?

Activity

6. **Writing to Learn** List the names of the three major Nubian kingdoms. Then briefly describe each one.

SKILLS ACTIVITY

Reading Route Maps

As the sky began to darken, the cool breeze shifted slightly. The leader of the caravan turned around and saw the storm at the horizon behind them. Then he looked ahead, straining to see some glimpse of Assur. The caravan had been traveling for many days with goods from Giza. Although his men were tired, he signaled for them to move faster. He wanted to reach the city before the storm reached them.

The pharaoh had chosen him to lead this trip because of his experience as a traveler. For years, he had brought goods from Lower Egypt to Syria and Sumer. This particular road, however, was new to him. He hoped they would reach Assur soon.

Get Ready

The caravan leader might have found a route map useful. This is a map that shows the routes, or paths, people follow. Reading a route map is simply a matter of reading a map and then reading the routes that are marked on it. As you do with all maps, you begin by reading the title, the key, the scale, the compass rose, and the labels on the map. Then, you study the map to figure out what it shows. Finally, you read the routes on the map by following the lines that show them.

Try It Out

Perhaps the best way to figure out how to use route maps is to make one of your own. You'll need a blank sheet of paper, colored pencils, and a ruler.

A. **Draw a simple map of the area that includes your school and your home.** Use the ruler as needed to make straight lines. Add a scale and a compass rose.

B. **Mark the location of your school and your home with symbols.** Explain the symbols in a map key.

C. **Draw routes.** Using a colored pencil, draw a line to show the route you take from home to school. Now use a different color to draw a line to show the route you take from your home to a friend's home. In the map key, explain the meaning of the different colored lines.

D. **Add symbols to your map.** For example, you might draw a symbol on the route from home to school to indicate you are carrying your lunch. Identify the symbols you use on the map key.

Apply the Skill

Use the Egyptian trade routes map to complete the steps that follow.

1 Familiarize yourself with the map. The first step in reading any map is to familiarize yourself with it generally. What is the title of the map? What region of the world does it show? What does the map key indicate?

2 Understand what routes are shown. You can learn this by studying the map key. How are Egyptian trade routes shown?

▶ As you might guess, trade routes followed the Nile River as well.

▼ This Egyptian tomb painting shows traders loading grain into a ship.

3 Use the map. According to this map, did Egyptian traders travel more by sea or by land? What city would a trader pass on the way from Giza to Assur? About how far is Assur from Giza?

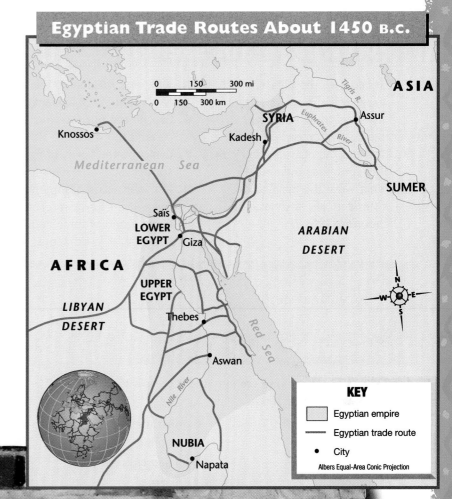

Egyptian Trade Routes About 1450 B.C.

KEY
- Egyptian empire
- Egyptian trade route
- • City

Albers Equal-Area Conic Projection

Review and Activities

Reviewing Main Ideas

1. Explain how the Nile affected everyday life in ancient Egypt.
2. How was trade important to Nubian civilization?
3. How did the pharaohs unify all of Egypt under their rule?
4. What were the main accomplishments of Hatshepsut and Thutmose III?
5. Why was religion so important to the people of ancient Egypt?
6. Explain the purpose of the pyramids.
7. Describe the levels of Egyptian society.
8. List four accomplishments of the ancient Egyptians. Then choose one of them and describe its importance.
9. Describe the relationship between Egypt and Nubia throughout their long history.
10. Name the three major Nubian kingdoms, and describe the location of each. Then choose one kingdom and describe it.

Reviewing Key Terms

Use each key term in a sentence that shows the meaning of the term.

1. cataract
2. delta
3. silt
4. pharaoh
5. dynasty
6. regent
7. afterlife
8. mummy
9. pyramid
10. hieroglyph
11. papyrus
12. astronomer
13. artisan

Critical Thinking

1. **Drawing Conclusions** Explain how Egyptian ideas about the afterlife have increased our knowledge of ancient Egypt.
2. **Making Comparisons** Compare the length of Egypt's civilization with that of the Assyrians and the Babylonians. How do you account for the differences?

Graphic Organizer

Copy the chart onto a sheet of paper and title it "Levels of Egyptian Society." Then fill in the empty spaces to complete the chart. Beside each space, describe briefly the group you wrote there.

Map Activity

Egypt and Nubia
For each place listed below, write the letter from the map that shows its location.

1. Nile River

2. Mediterranean Sea

3. Red Sea

4. Upper Nubia

5. Lower Nubia

6. Sahara

7. the Nile delta

8. Upper Egypt

9. Lower Egypt

Writing Activity

Writing a Poem
Sitting near the Nile waiting for it to flood, you think about the river and its importance to life. Write a poem expressing your thoughts and feelings.

Internet Activity

Use a search engine to find the site called **Egypt's Culture Net.** Click on **Museums.** Then click on **Museums in Egypt.** Select the **Egyptian Museum.** Explore the museum by selecting different links. Create a "What to See" list you would use if you visited the museum in person.

Skills Review

Turn to the Skills Activity.
Review the steps for understanding a route map. Then complete the following: (a) In your own words, explain what a route map is. (b) How is a route map different from other kinds of maps?

How Am I Doing?

Answer these questions to help you check your progress.

1. Can I describe the main geographic features of Egypt and Nubia?

2. Do I understand how Egyptian society was organized?

3. Can I identify the main historical periods of ancient Egypt?

4. Can I identify the important kingdoms of Nubia?

5. Can I describe the main features of Egyptian and Nubian culture?

6. What information in the chapter can I use in my book project?

CHAPTER 4

Ancient India

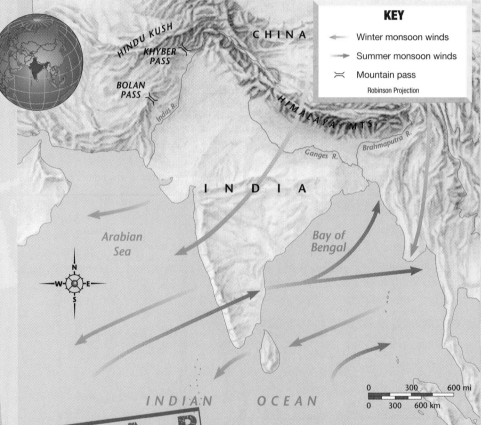

KEY

← Winter monsoon winds

→ Summer monsoon winds

⋈ Mountain pass

Robinson Projection

MAP ACTIVITIES

Important features of India are the mountains, the oceans, and the winds that blow across the region. They are shown on the map. To help you become acquainted with India's geography and climate, do the following activities.

Study the map
Describe the location of the mountains and oceans. What effect do you think these features had on the movement of people to and from India?

Follow the wind
Trace the wind arrows on the map with your finger. Which winds, winter or summer, do you think bring rain to India? Why? Which winds bring dry, cool air? Why?

The Indus and Ganges River Valleys

Reach Into Your Background

People all around the world are affected by their environment. In what ways does your environment influence the way you live your everyday life? In what ways do you affect your environment?

Questions to Explore

1. How did geography influence the history of India?
2. How did people live in one of the early cities in the Indus River Valley?

Key Terms

subcontinent   migrate
monsoon   caste
citadel

Key Places

Himalaya Mountains
Indus River Valley
Mohenjo-Daro
Ganges River Valley

For thousands of years, India was cut off from the rest of the ancient world by a great wall. Rising along India's northern border, the wall was more than 1,500 miles (2,400 km) long and nearly 5 miles (8 km) high. The wall was not made of stone or bricks. It was a wall of snow-capped peaks and icy glaciers. This great barrier is the Himalaya Mountains, the highest mountain range in the world.

▼ At 29,035 feet (8,850 m), Mount Everest is not only the highest peak in the Himalaya Mountains, but the highest in the world.

India's Geographic Setting

Stretching south from the Himalaya Mountains, the kite-shaped land of India bulges out from Asia into the Indian Ocean. Geographers refer to India as a **subcontinent,** or a large landmass that juts out from a continent.

For centuries, geography limited contact between the Indian subcontinent and the rest of the world. The Himalaya Mountains and the Hindu Kush separate India from Asia. Find

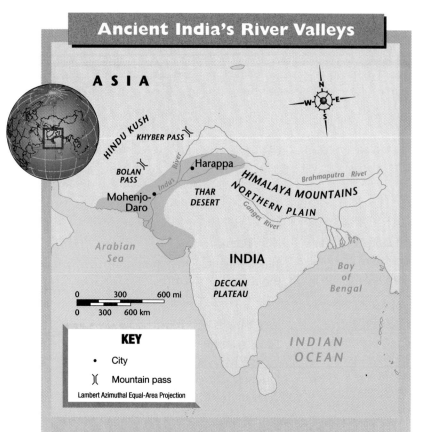

A S I A

HINDU KUSH

KHYBER PASS

BOLAN PASS

• Harappa

Indus River

Mohenjo-Daro •

THAR DESERT

HIMALAYA MOUNTAINS

NORTHERN PLAIN

Brahmaputra River

Ganges River

Arabian Sea

INDIA

DECCAN PLATEAU

Bay of Bengal

INDIAN OCEAN

0   300   600 mi
0   300   600 km

KEY

• City

)(Mountain pass

Lambert Azimuthal Equal-Area Projection

Map Study Passes through India's mountain ranges allowed people to move into and settle in two of India's fertile river valleys, the Indus and the Ganges. **Location** Invaders also used the mountain passes to get to the Indus River settlements. From what direction would such invaders have come?

LINKS TO SCIENCE

The Creation of the Himalaya Mountains
Millions of years ago, all of today's continents were part of a single continent called Pangaea (pan JEE uh). Then Pangaea slowly broke apart. Eventually, India broke loose from Africa and began moving northeast. About 55 million years ago, India began crashing into Asia. The force of the collision pushed up the earth to form the Himalaya Mountains.

them on the map at the beginning of the chapter. The Bay of Bengal, the Indian Ocean, and the Arabian Sea limit contact with lands to the east and west. These mountains and waters have been a major influence on the history and culture of the land.

A Climate of Monsoons
India's climate is dominated by the **monsoons,** strong winds that blow across the region at certain times of year. Look again at the map on the first page of this chapter. From October to May, the winter monsoon blows from the northeast, spreading dry air across the country. Then, in the middle of June, the wind blows in from the Indian Ocean. This summer monsoon picks up moisture from the ocean. It carries rains that drench the plains and river valleys daily.

The people depend on summer monsoons to provide life-giving rain. If the monsoon is late or weak, crops die, causing famine. If it brings too much rain, overflowing rivers may cause deadly floods.

Barriers and Pathways Although the mountains isolate India from other lands, they do have openings. Find the passages on the map above. For thousands of years, passes through the Hindu Kush mountain range have served as highways for invading people. The earliest people of northern India probably entered the valley of the Indus River through these pathways.

Great rivers rise in the mountains. Fed by melting snows and rain, the Indus and Ganges (GAN jeez) rivers cut through the mountains. They flow across the plains of northern India and make farming possible in the river valleys.

Life in the Indus River Valley

From the rich soil of the Indus River Valley, early farmers harvested a surplus of wheat and other grains. With a surplus of food, the population grew. Some villages became cities. From around 2500 B.C. to 1500 B.C., well-planned cities flourished in the valley. One of these, Mohenjo-Daro (moh HEHN joh DAH roh), lay along the banks of the Indus River.

The World's Earliest City Planners   Mohenjo-Daro was a large city that needed careful planning. Because the Indus River often flooded, the city's rulers built Mohenjo-Daro on a high mound of earth. To make travel easier in the city, streets were laid out in squares. People built their homes and shops along these squares. At the center of the city was the **citadel,** or fortress. It was a group of public buildings enclosed by a high brick wall. One building held a huge bath with dressing rooms for bathers. Nearby stood a storehouse for the city's grain supply.

Mohenjo-Daro must have been much cleaner than most other cities of the time. Clay pipes ran under the brick streets. They carried waste from homes and public buildings away from the city. Outside the city, canals ran along the Indus River, which often flooded. The canals controlled the flooding and directed water where it was most needed.

READ ACTIVELY

Predict What do you think life would have been like in an Indus Valley city?

▼ The baked-brick ruins of Mohenjo-Daro and its citadel are in the present-day country of Pakistan.

▶ Copper workers from Mohenjo-Daro forged this almost human-shaped weapon (below). Merchants may have used the seals (right) to identify their goods—much as businesses today use logos.

Connect How was Mohenjo-Daro similar to the Sumerian cities you read about?

Living in Mohenjo-Daro The city buzzed with activity. Merchants and artisans sold their wares from shops that lined the streets. Wagons loaded with grain rolled through the city. Traders came from as far away as Mesopotamia to buy and sell precious goods. The citizens of Mohenjo-Daro lived in homes that opened onto courtyards. Children played with toys and pets. Adults enjoyed games and music. Artisans fashioned jewelry and bright cotton clothing for the people to wear.

The language of the people is still a mystery. Their writings appear on square seals. But experts have not yet been able to figure out the writing. The form of government and the religion of Mohenjo-Daro are also unknown. No royal tombs or great temples have been found. But we do know they had a number of gods.

A Mysterious Decline About 2000 B.C., Indus River Valley farmers began to abandon their land. The climate may have changed, turning the fertile soil into desert. Or great earthquakes may have caused floods that destroyed the canals. Without enough food, people began to leave the cities of the Indus River Valley. Between 2000 B.C. and 1500 B.C., invaders from the north entered the valley. The people who remained at Mohenjo-Daro were too weak to resist them.

Conquest by the Aryans

The invaders called themselves Aryans (AIR ee uhnz), which in their language meant "noble" or "highborn." They **migrated,** or moved, from their homelands in central Asia. For several centuries, waves of these nomadic herders swept into India.

As the Aryans crossed the plains of northern India, the people of the Indus River Valley huddled behind the crumbling walls of their cities. They were no match for Aryan warriors armed with bows and arrows and axes. Especially terrifying were their chariots drawn by charging horses. Gradually, the Aryans conquered the people of the Indus River Valley. Many became slaves of the invaders.

The Forests of the Ganges River

Forests were once common along the banks of the Ganges River. Today, most forests are gone, but the river helps feed the people of India. People eat fish from the river and grow crops on the fertile land of the Ganges Valley. **Critical Thinking** How might this stretch of the river change if people settled nearby?

Aryans Occupy Northern India   After they had conquered the Indus River Valley people, the Aryans gradually moved into the Ganges River Valley to the east. By about 800 B.C., they had learned to make tools and weapons out of iron. With iron axes, the Aryans cleared areas of the thick rain forests of the northeast. Here they built farms, villages, and even cities.

Aryan Life   Most of what we know of early Aryan life comes from religious books called Vedas, which means "knowledge." At first, the Vedas were handed down from memory by Aryan priests. They were not written down for hundreds of years.

The Vedas tell us that the earliest Aryans were herders and warriors who lived in villages and tended flocks of cattle and sheep. Always on the move, these people did not build cities or spacious homes at first. For a long time, they had no written language. Priests, called Brahmins, performed religious services and composed hymns and prayers.

The Aryans organized their society around three classes. Priests guarded religious traditions, warriors fought, and ordinary people worked. Gradually, the Aryans drew the conquered people into their class system and made them a fourth class. This class included farmworkers, laborers, and servants.

By 500 B.C., there was a strict division of classes. Europeans later called it the caste system. Each caste, or class, had special work and duties to perform. Under the caste system, people always had to stay in the caste of their parents.

Over time, the caste system became more complicated. The main castes divided into hundreds of different groups, in which each person had the same occupation, or type of work. Shopkeepers, farmers, traders, barbers, and weavers each belonged to their own group. Since people could not leave their caste, they did the same work as their parents and other members of the group. A weaver's son would be a weaver. A barber's daughter would marry a barber.

SECTION 1 REVIEW

1. **Define**   (a) subcontinent, (b) monsoon, (c) citadel, (d) migrate, (e) caste.

2. **Identify**   (a) Himalaya Mountains, (b) Indus River Valley, (c) Mohenjo-Daro, (d) Ganges River Valley.

3. How did geography affect the way people lived in ancient India?

4. How did the leaders of Mohenjo-Daro plan their city?

Critical Thinking

5. **Drawing Conclusions**   The people of the Indus River Valley planned their cities with great care. What might this tell you about their form of government and their values?

Activity

6. **Writing to Learn**   List some words you think describe the city and the people of Mohenjo-Daro. Use these words to write a paragraph about life in the city.

The Beginnings of Hinduism

BEFORE YOU READ

Reach Into Your Background
Your beliefs and traditions are part of your life. They come from your family, your community, and your own ideas. Think about some of your beliefs and traditions. Consider where each came from.

Questions to Explore
1. How did the basic beliefs of the Hindu religion develop?
2. Explain the Hindu idea of reincarnation.

Key Terms
reincarnation
dharma
ahimsa

Key People
Brahma
Vishnu
Shiva

▼ Shiva is one of the Hindus' most important gods. Hindus believe that Shiva periodically destroys and re-creates the world.

"O Lord of the storm gods, may your grace come down to us. . . . Do not hide the sun from our sight. O Rudra, protect our horseman from injury and may we have worthy children through your grace. . . . Your glory is unbounded, your strength unmatched among all living creatures. O Rudra, wielder (handler) of the thunder-bolt. Guide us safely to the far shore of existence where there is no sorrow."

This prayer was part of one of the early Aryan Vedas. It praised gods of nature and asked for protection against ill fortune. What, do you think, is the meaning of the plea "Do not hide the sun from our sight"?

The Roots of Hindu Belief

The Aryans passed such hymns honoring their gods from generation to generation. As Aryan culture mixed with that of the people they conquered, new ideas and beliefs became part of the Vedas. From this blending came one of the world's oldest living religions, Hinduism.

STUDENT ART

Dhruv Khanna
age 12
India

Traditionally, artists' portrayals of the god Krishna show him as having blue skin. Other Hindu gods also have certain physical traits that help people identify them. For instance, paintings and sculptures of the god Shiva show him with four arms. **Critical Thinking** Krishna figures in many Hindu legends. He appears as a mischievous child, a cowherd, a chariot driver, and a hunter. In what role has the student artist shown Krishna?

READ ACTIVELY

Predict What are the Hindus' gods and goddesses like?

A Blend of Religions As Hinduism developed over 3,500 years, it absorbed many beliefs from other religions. This made Hinduism very complex. Many Hindus believe that since people are different, they need many different ways of approaching god. Thus, many different Hindu practices exist side by side.

Hinduism is more than one of the world's major religions. It is the national religion of modern India and a way of life for more than 700 million people today. Its beliefs have influenced people of many other religions. Yet Hinduism is unlike other major world religions. There is no one single founder, but Hindus have many great religious thinkers. Hindus worship many gods and goddesses, but they believe in one single spirit.

Hindu Gods and Goddesses The gods and goddesses of Hinduism stand for different parts of the single spirit. An ancient Hindu saying expresses this idea: "God is one, but wise people know it by many names." The most important Hindu gods are Brahma, the Creator; Vishnu, the Preserver; and Shiva, the Destroyer. These gods can take many different forms, both human and animal. Each of these gods is part of a single, all-powerful force called *brahman*.

Hindu teachings say that Brahma was born from a golden egg. He created the Earth and everything on it. However, he is not as widely worshipped as Vishnu and Shiva.

Hindus believe that Vishnu is a kindly god who is concerned with the welfare of human beings. Vishnu visits Earth from time to time in different forms. He does this to protect humans from disaster or to guide them.

Unlike Vishnu, Shiva is not concerned with human matters. He is very powerful. Shiva sometimes destroys the universe, but he also creates it again. Shiva developed from the god Rudra, the "wielder of the thunderbolt" in the prayer at the beginning of this section.

Hindu gods have their own families. Many Hindus, for example, worship Shiva's wife Shakti, who plays a role in human life. Like her husband, she is both a destroyer and a creator. She is both kind and cruel.

Basic Beliefs of Hinduism

All Hindus share certain central beliefs that are contained in religious writings or sacred texts.

The Upanishads One of the Hindu religious texts is the Upanishads (oo PAN uh shadz). *Upanishad* means "sitting near a teacher." Much of the Upanishads is in the form of questions by pupils and responses by teachers. For example: "Who," asks a pupil, "created the world?" The teacher replies, "Brahman is the creator, the universal soul."

When asked to describe brahman, the teacher explains that it is too complicated for humans to understand. Brahman has no physical form.

Common Roots The Hindu sacred books were written in a language called Sanskrit. It is one of the oldest known languages. Sanskrit is related to many other languages in the world, such as ancient Greek and Latin. Modern languages including Spanish, German, and English also have common roots with ancient Sanskrit.

▼ Special journeys to sacred places, such as this temple in southern India, are an important feature of Hindu life.

Reincarnation   One of the ideas in the Upanishads is **reincarnation,** or rebirth of the soul. The Hindus believe that a person may die, but the soul is reborn in the body of another living thing. Hindus believe that every living thing has a soul. This idea has been an important part of other Asian beliefs as well as Hinduism.

What body will the soul enter when it is reincarnated? According to Hindu belief, it is the actions of a person in this life that affect his or her fate in the next. Good behavior is always rewarded. Bad behavior is always punished. Faithful followers of Hinduism will be reborn into a higher position. Those whose acts have been bad may be born into a lower caste. They may even return as an animal. If a person leads a perfect life, he or she may be freed from this cycle of death and rebirth. The soul is then one with brahman.

A Hindu's Duties   To become united with the one spirit and escape the cycle of death and rebirth, a person must obey his or her dharma (DAHR muh). **Dharma** are the religious and moral duties of each person. These duties depend on factors such as a person's class, occupation, and age. By obeying his or her dharma, a person comes closer to brahman.

▼ In this scene from the ancient Hindu poem *Mahabharata,* the god Krishna drives the hero's chariot to victory. A major theme of the *Mahabharata* explores the proper conduct for different classes of people, including kings, warriors, and common folk.

The *puja*, or ceremonial worship of a god as a royal guest, is part of all Hindus' daily lives. Pujas may include ritual bathing and feeding and the offering of flowers, incense, perfume, and other gifts. **Critical Thinking** The way Hindus perform puja varies throughout India. Why do you think this is so?

Another important idea of Hinduism is **ahimsa** (uh HIM sah), or nonviolence. To Hindus, all people and things are part of brahman. This means they must be treated with respect. For this reason, many Hindus do not eat meat and try to avoid hurting living things.

Many Paths to Truth

Hinduism teaches that there is more than one path to the truth. No matter how a person searches for truth, he or she is accepted as a Hindu.

Because of this view, Hinduism allows its followers to worship in different ways. One Hindu may present gifts to a personal god. His or her devotion to the god brings the soul closer to brahman. Another may practice special exercises and deep thinking to help free the soul from the cares of the world. Still others hope to be united with brahman by learning the sacred writings.

SECTION 2 REVIEW

1. **Define** (a) reincarnation, (b) dharma, (c) ahimsa.

2. **Identify** (a) Brahma, (b) Vishnu, (c) Shiva.

3. How did the early Aryan religion grow into Hinduism?

4. How are good and bad behavior related to reincarnation in Hinduism?

Critical Thinking

5. **Identifying Central Issues** What does "escaping the cycle of birth and death" mean to Hindus?

Activity

6. **Writing to Learn** Hindu teachers often taught their students in the form of questions and answers. Write a dialogue in which a student asks questions about Hindu beliefs, and the teacher responds.

The Beginnings of Buddhism

BEFORE YOU READ

Reach Into Your Background

Everyone experiences changes in life. You may move to another community or attend a new school. Your ideas can change as well. Think about events or ideas that have changed your life. How did you react to these changes? Did the changes seem hard to accept at first?

Questions to Explore

1. How did the Buddhist religion come about?
2. How did the teachings of Buddhism develop and spread?

Key Terms
meditate
nirvana
missionary

Key People
Siddhartha Gautama

► Countless different paintings and sculptures of the Buddha (Siddhartha Gautama) exist all over the world. This golden statue from India shows the young Buddha.

According to Buddhist tradition, a young Hindu prince once lived a life of luxury in his palace in northern India. Protected by the walls of the palace, he saw none of the unpleasant troubles that touch other peoples' lives. He was content with his life, for he had everything he wanted.

Then, around the age of 30, he took some rides that changed his life—and changed the history of Asia. On his rides, he saw things he never imagined. He met a bent and tired old man. The prince had never realized that people grow frail. For the first time, he saw a man who was very sick. Finally, he saw death when he saw a body being carried to a funeral.

This suffering troubled the young man greatly. He wanted to know why there was so much suffering and pain in the world. He decided to change his life to find the answer. He gave up his wealth, his family, and his life of ease in order to find the causes of human suffering. The young man was named Siddhartha Gautama (sihd DAHR tuh goh TUH muh). What he discovered after seven years of wandering led him to found a major world religion, Buddhism.

The Teachings of Buddhism

As Gautama traveled in the 500s B.C., he sought answers to the meaning of life. At first, Gautama studied with Hindu philosophers. But their ideas did not satisfy him. He could not accept the Hindu belief that only Brahmins could pass on knowledge.

Gautama decided to stop looking outwardly for the cause of suffering. Instead, he tried to find understanding within his own mind. He did this by meditating. Meditating is thinking deeply about sacred things. Buddhist tradition says that Gautama fasted and meditated under a fig tree. After 49 days, he found the answers he sought. Now he understood the roots of suffering.

For the next 45 years, Gautama traveled across India and shared his knowledge. Over the years, he attracted many followers. Because he could explain things that troubled people, his followers called him the Buddha (BOO duh)—"The Enlightened One." His teachings became known as Buddhism.

The Middle Way Buddhism differed from earlier religions in one important way. Other religions worshipped many gods or one God. Buddha taught that the answer to human suffering lay not in worshipping gods, but in right thinking and self-denial.

Ask Questions What questions would you like to ask about the religion of Buddhism?

The Three Jewels of Buddhism

The Buddha (the teacher), *dharma* (the teaching), and *sangha* (the community of believers) are known as the three jewels of Buddhism. **Critical Thinking** How does this painting show the three jewels of Buddhism?

The Practice of Buddhism

Chart Study The Middle Way is also called the Eightfold Path. The chart shows the eight parts of the path and what they mean. Buddhists in Tibet use prayer wheels that contain a written holy verse. Each turn of the wheel is equivalent to saying the prayer aloud. **Critical Thinking** How do you think the prayer wheel helps the man follow the Eightfold Path?

The Eightfold Path

	Step	Meaning
1.	Right Understanding	Having faith in the Buddhist view of the universe
2.	Right Intention	Making a commitment to practice Buddhism
3.	Right Speech	Avoiding lies and mean or abusive speech
4.	Right Action	Not taking life, not stealing, not hurting others
5.	Right Livelihood	Rejecting jobs and occupations that conflict with Buddhist ideals
6.	Right Effort	Avoiding bad attitudes and developing good ones
7.	Right Mindfulness	Being aware of the body, feelings, and thoughts
8.	Right Concentration	Thinking deeply to find answers to problems

Adapted from *Encyclopaedia Britannica.*

READ ACTIVELY

Predict Why do you think some people might have been attracted to the religion of Buddhism?

Buddha taught that human suffering is caused by selfish desires for power, wealth, and pleasure. The way a person becomes free from suffering is by giving up these selfish desires. The way to do this is to follow the Middle Way. The Middle Way avoids two extremes—too much pleasure and too much worry about life.

Reaching Nirvana To find this Middle Way, Buddha taught, people must act unselfishly toward others and treat people fairly. They must tell the truth at all times. People should also avoid violence and the killing of any living thing. If people followed Buddha's path, their sufferings would end. They would eventually find **nirvana,** or lasting peace. By reaching nirvana, people would be released from the endless wheel of reincarnation.

Followers of Buddhism Buddhism also taught that all people are equal. Anyone, Buddha declared, could follow the path to nirvana, regardless of his or her social class. This idea appealed to many people.

Like other religions, Buddhism has priests. Anyone can become a Buddhist priest, or monk. Buddha encouraged his followers to establish monasteries. There they would learn, meditate, and teach. He also urged monks to become **missionaries,** or people who spread their religious beliefs to others.

Buddhism in India

After gaining the understanding of human suffering that he looked for, Buddha spent the rest of his life teaching. Followers flocked to hear his sermons. Rulers and ordinary people gathered around him. After his death, his teachings spread all over India. For many years, Buddhism and Hinduism existed side by side in India.

The Golden Age of Buddhism in India came during the rule of Asoka (uh SOH kuh), one of India's greatest rulers. You will read about him in the next section. However, Buddha's teachings did not last in the land of his birth. Over time, Buddhism died out almost completely in India.

However, as Hinduism and Buddhism coexisted in India, a number of fundamental ideas came to be shared by both. Hindus and Buddhists accept the idea that it is wrong to harm other living creatures and that nonviolence is to be valued. Many Hindus came to honor Buddha as a reincarnation of the god Vishnu. But, because Buddhists do not embrace the sacred texts of Hinduism, Buddha is a rarely worshipped god.

▼ Sculptures often show Buddha in one of three poses—meditating, teaching, or lying down. These poses may be linked to the great events of Buddha's life, his enlightenment, his teaching, and his reaching Nirvana.

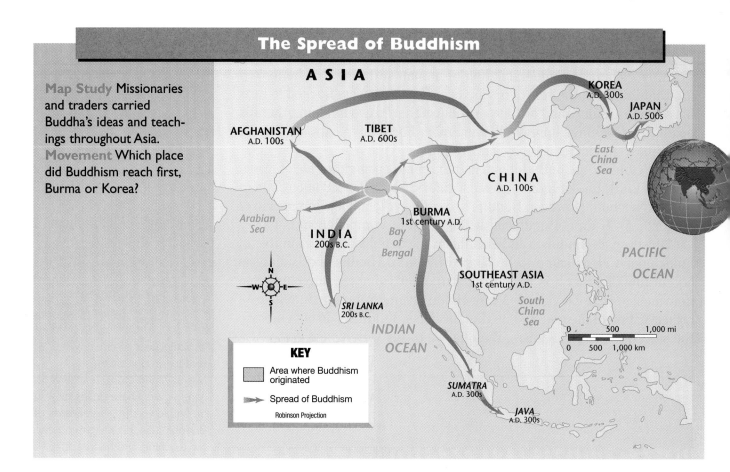

The Spread of Buddhism

Map Study Missionaries and traders carried Buddha's ideas and teachings throughout Asia. **Movement** Which place did Buddhism reach first, Burma or Korea?

ASIA

KOREA
A.D. 300s

JAPAN
A.D. 500s

AFGHANISTAN
A.D. 100s

TIBET
A.D. 600s

East
China
Sea

CHINA
A.D. 100s

Arabian
Sea

BURMA
1st century A.D.

INDIA
200s B.C.

Bay
of
Bengal

PACIFIC
OCEAN

SOUTHEAST ASIA
1st century A.D.

South
China
Sea

SRI LANKA
200s B.C.

INDIAN
OCEAN

KEY
Area where Buddhism originated
Spread of Buddhism
Robinson Projection

SUMATRA
A.D. 300s

JAVA
A.D. 300s

0   500   1,000 mi
0   500   1,000 km

Buddhism Spreads to Other Countries

Buddhism, however, was accepted by millions of people in other lands. Missionaries carried Buddha's message throughout Asia. It took root in China and grew there. Millions of Chinese became Buddhists. They mixed the ideas of Buddha with those of earlier teachers. Buddhist monasteries became centers of religious thought in China. From China, Buddhism spread to Korea and Japan. Today, Buddhism is part of the cultures of such countries as Japan, the Koreas, China, Tibet, and Vietnam.

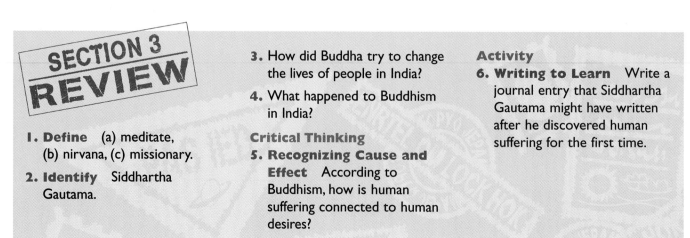

SECTION 3 REVIEW

1. **Define** (a) meditate, (b) nirvana, (c) missionary.

2. **Identify** Siddhartha Gautama.

3. How did Buddha try to change the lives of people in India?

4. What happened to Buddhism in India?

Critical Thinking

5. **Recognizing Cause and Effect** According to Buddhism, how is human suffering connected to human desires?

Activity

6. **Writing to Learn** Write a journal entry that Siddhartha Gautama might have written after he discovered human suffering for the first time.

The Golden Age of Maurya India

BEFORE YOU READ

Reach Into Your Background

Think about someone you admire and respect. What traits does that person have?

How does she or he act? How could you be more like that person?

Questions to Explore

1. Why is the Maurya empire considered a golden age in India?

2. Why is Asoka considered one of India's greatest leaders?

Key Terms
absolute power
convert

Key People
Chandragupta
Asoka

Around 330 B.C., a new ruler came to the throne of a kingdom in northeastern India. Within 35 years, the tiny kingdom grew into the giant Maurya (MAH oor yuh) empire. The first king of this empire was Chandragupta (chuhn druh GUP tuh) Maurya.

Chandragupta lived in grand style. A Greek traveler described the impressive sight that greeted him at the king's court. The royal palace was supported by great wooden pillars coated with gold. In the park where the palace stood, fountains sprayed the air and fish splashed in ponds. Scores of servants waited on the king.

Chandragupta enjoyed luxuries from all parts of Asia. When the king appeared before his subjects, he was often seated in a golden chair carried on his servants' shoulders. Sometimes he rode on an elephant covered with jewels.

▼ This complex design shows the skill of Maurya artisans. One figure is part human and part dragon.

The people of India were the first to use elephants in war. During battles, the huge animals fearlessly charged toward men and horses, causing panic and chaos.

Building the Maurya Empire

India was made up of a number of warring states before Chandragupta came to power. Strong and ruthless, he founded the Maurya empire. His armies overthrew kingdoms along the Ganges River. Turning west, his armies advanced into the Indus River Valley. Only a few years later, his power extended over most of north and central India.

Chandragupta was guided by the basic belief that a ruler must have **absolute power,** or complete control over the people. This idea came from a book of advice called *The Science of Material Gain.* The book urged kings to control all their subjects and to maintain an army of spies to inform on them.

Chandragupta commanded a huge army. Thousands of foot soldiers and mounted troops were ready to maintain law and order and to crush any revolts. The army also had 9,000 war elephants, which struck fear into the hearts of opponents.

LINKS ACROSS THE WORLD

Chandragupta and Alexander the Great Chandragupta started life as a slave. One of his masters educated him. Then he met Alexander the Great, the Greek conqueror of the ancient world. Near the time of the meeting, legend says a lion awakened Chandragupta one night by licking his body. Chandragupta thought this meant he would become a great ruler, like Alexander. He made that idea a reality.

Prosperity and Poisoners Under Chandragupta, the empire enjoyed great success. Most of its wealth came from foreign trade. The Maurya empire built up a widespread trade with such faraway places as Greece, Rome, and China.

However, as his rule continued, Chandragupta became fearful for his life. Thinking poisoners were everywhere, he made servants taste his food. To avoid being murdered, he slept in a different room every night. One story says that he finally became a monk in south India. Fasting and praying, he starved himself to death.

Maintaining the Empire Chandragupta did not gain wealth for himself only. Though his rule was harsh, he used his wealth to improve his empire. New irrigation systems brought water to farmers. Forests were cleared, and more food was produced. Government officials promoted crafts and mining. A vast network of roads made it easier for Maurya traders to exchange goods with foreign lands. Chandragupta's leadership brought order and peace to his people.

Asoka: A Father to His People

When Chandragupta died, the empire passed to his son. When the son died, Chandragupta's grandson, Asoka, gained power. Asoka, whose name means "without sorrow," further expanded Chandragupta's empire. By the end of his rule in 232 B.C., Asoka had built the greatest empire India had ever seen.

The Battle of Kalinga   For more than 35 years, Asoka ruled an empire that included much of the subcontinent of India. During the first years of his rule, Asoka was as warlike as his grandfather. He conquered new territories to the east. Early in his rule, Asoka led his army south into the state of Kalinga. He won a bloody battle in 261 B.C. in which more than 100,000 people died. The great slaughter at Kalinga was a turning point in Asoka's life. He was filled with sorrow over the bloodshed. He gave up war and violence. He freed his prisoners and restored their land. Later, he **converted,** or changed his beliefs, to Buddhism.

▼ People believe that this Buddhist monument, the Great Stupa, was begun by Asoka. The massive dome represents heaven encircling the Earth.

Asoka Spreads Buddha's Message   Asoka practiced and preached the teachings of Buddha. He did not allow the use of animals for sacrifices. He gave up hunting, the traditional sport of Indian kings.

Asoka thought of his people as his children. Like a father, he was concerned with their welfare. He had hospitals built throughout his kingdom. He even had wells dug every mile beside the roads so that travelers and animals would not go thirsty.

Asoka was also concerned with his people's moral and spiritual life. To carry Buddha's message throughout his vast empire, Asoka issued writings of moral advice. Some writings urged people to honor their parents. Others asked people not to kill animals. Still others encouraged people to behave with tolerance and with truthfulness. Asoka also issued laws that required people to be treated with humanity. His advice and laws were carved on pillars of stone 30 to 40 feet (9 to 12 meters) high throughout his empire. One pillar bore these words:

> "Both this world and the other are hard to reach, except by great love of the law, great self-examination, great obedience, great respect, great energy."

Asoka's tolerance for others allowed him to accept Hindus. Many of Buddha's teachings became part of Hinduism during Asoka's rule. Buddhism grew under Asoka. He sent missionaries far and wide to

READ ACTIVELY

Connect Think of an event in your life that caused you to make changes or rethink the way you do things. Why did the event make you want to change?

Asoka's Empire

Map Study Animals and other symbols adorned Asoka's pillars. The lions on this pillar have become the emblem of India. **Place** What physical feature formed the northeast boundary of Asoka's empire?

KEY

Asoka's empire about 250 B.C.

Lambert Azimuthal Equal-Area Projection

0   200   400 mi

0   200 400 km

An orange-robed monk teaches the principles of Buddhism to these students in Bangkok, the capital of the modern-day country of Thailand. A gold statue of the Buddha occupies a place of honor.

spread its message. It was missionaries sent by Asoka who spread Buddhism to China. Asoka's sister and brother went to Ceylon—today, the country of Sri Lanka—as Buddhist missionaries. He even sent teachers to Egypt, Greece, and North Africa.

At Asoka's death, India was united as never before. However, the great Maurya empire declined after his death. Without his strong rule, his territories divided. Small states began fighting with one another. Several centuries of invasion and disorder followed. It took almost 600 years before India was united again.

SECTION 4 REVIEW

1. **Define** (a) absolute power, (b) convert.

2. **Identify** (a) Chandragupta, (b) Asoka.

3. How did Chandragupta and Asoka build a great empire?

4. Why could Asoka be called a father to his people?

Critical Thinking

5. **Recognizing Cause and Effect** How did Buddhism in India influence the empire of Asoka?

Activity

6. **Writing to Learn** Asoka wrote many rules of conduct for himself and others to follow. Write down some rules of conduct that you would like to see leaders today follow. Do you think it is possible for today's leaders to follow these rules? Why or why not?

Reading Tables

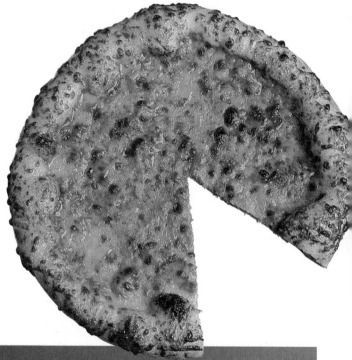

"I want mushroom."

"I think we should have spinach."

"Mmmm, let's get pepperoni!"

The kids in Ms. Frankel's class were trying to figure out what kind of pizza to order for their party day. Ceretha and Ben were in charge of figuring out what to order.

"Wait!" said Ceretha. "We'll never be able to figure this out and remember what everyone wants."

"Let's just get organized," Ben said. "I'll make a table of all this information. That way, we can see at a glance who wants what kind, how many of us want the same kind, and so on."

Get Ready

A chart or table can help you organize and compare information. It is a simple way to arrange facts in columns and rows to make them easy to understand. Charts and tables also provide information in a way that is easy to read and refer to.

Try It Out

To see how a table can work, try making one yourself. Find out what four of your classmates' favorite things are. Fill in a table like the one below.

Classmate	Favorite Food	Favorite TV Show	Favorite Sport
First person			
Second person			
Third person			
Fourth person			

Do several people like the same TV show? How are the first and third persons' favorites alike? How are they different?

Apply the Skill

In this book, you are reading about some of the world's major religions. A good way to understand some information about them is by reading the table below. Follow these steps.

1 **Determine the purpose of the table.** By reading the title and the headings of the columns, you will understand what the table is about. What kinds of information will this table give you?

2 **Use the table.** To locate facts in a table, look across a horizontal row (from left to right) and down a vertical column (from top to bottom) to the spot they intersect, or cross each other. Suppose you want to know where Judaism was founded. What column headings would you read? Which row would you look for? When was Judaism founded? (Remember that the abbreviation *c.* means "about.")

3 **Analyze the information.** Tables are especially useful for comparing information. Which religion was founded most recently? On which continent was each religion founded? Which religions were founded in India?

4 **Use the information.** How might this information be useful to you when reading about ancient history?

Major World Religions		
Religion	When Founded	Where Founded
Buddhism	c. 525 B.C.	India
Christianity	c. A.D. 30	Southwest Asia
Hinduism	c. 1500 B.C.	India
Islam	c. A.D. 622	Southwest Asia
Judaism	c. 1800 B.C.	Southwest Asia

Review and Activities

Reviewing Main Ideas

1. What was the effect of mountains and oceans on the history of India?
2. What made Mohenjo-Daro an advanced city?
3. Explain the connection between early Aryan religion and Hinduism.
4. What do Hindus mean by dharma? What does a person's dharma depend on?
5. Explain the central idea of Buddhism.
6. Explain why Buddha's ideas appealed to so many people.
7. Give three reasons why the Maurya empire was called India's golden age.
8. List four achievements of Asoka and explain their importance in ruling India.

Reviewing Key Terms

Use each key term below in a sentence that shows the meaning of the term.

1. subcontinent
2. monsoon
3. citadel
4. migrate
5. caste
6. reincarnation
7. dharma
8. ahimsa
9. meditate
10. nirvana
11. missionary
12. absolute power
13. convert

Critical Thinking

1. **Drawing Conclusions** Although the language of Mohenjo-Daro is a mystery, its people created a highly organized civilization. How do we know this?
2. **Making Comparisons** How does Gautama's life changing experience with suffering compare to Asoka's?

Graphic Organizer

Copy the chart onto a sheet of paper. Then fill in the empty boxes to complete the chart.

	Achievements	Effect on India's History
Indus Valley People		
Aryans		
Hinduism		
Buddhism		
Maurya Empire		

Map Activity

India

For each place listed below, write the letter from the map that shows its location.

1. Himalaya Mountains

2. Hindu Kush Mountains

3. Indus River

4. Ganges River

5. Mohenjo-Daro

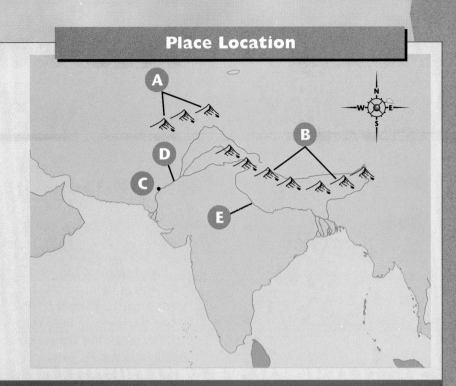

Writing Activity

Writing Inscriptions

Asoka helped spread Buddha's message by inscribing stone pillars with his teachings. Think about the beliefs of Hinduism.

Write inscriptions that could be put on pillars to spread the teachings of Hinduism. Keep in mind the beliefs of Hinduism, and how people worship.

Internet Activity

Use a search engine to find the **Discover India** site. Click on the **Culture** icon. Then select at least four different topics, such as literature, arts, monuments, and festivals, to explore India's culture and history. Use the information you find to write a tour guide of Indian culture or to create a time line of Indian history.

Skills Review

Turn to the Skills Activity. Review the steps for reading a table. Then, briefly explain how a table makes it easy to compare information.

How Am I Doing?

Answer these questions to help you check your progress.

1. Can I describe the main geographic features of India?

2. Do I understand how the civilizations of ancient India compare to other ancient civilizations I've studied?

3. Can I identify historic events or movements that shaped the culture of India?

4. What information from this chapter can I use in my book project?

The Envious Buffalo

A Jataka Story From *The Fables of India*
Retold by Joseph Gaer

BEFORE YOU READ

Reach Into Your Background

Has anyone ever tried to teach you something by telling you a story? Have you ever given advice to a friend by telling an experience you had?

People around the world have always used stories to teach important lessons. The Jataka stories from India teach such lessons. They are part of Buddhism's sacred writings. They tell of the past lives of Buddha, before he was released from the wheel of reincarnation. In his earlier lives, he is called the Bodisat, or the Buddha-to-be. The Bodisat appears in the Jataka stories as a king, teacher, lion, monkey, or other creature.

Many of the Jataka stories are fables, like this one. A fable is a brief story with few characters. It teaches a simple lesson about life called a moral. Fables usually have one or more animal characters.

Questions to Explore
1. What can you learn from this story about the life of farmers in India?
2. Why is this story a good example of the beliefs of Buddhism?

Bubalus (BOO buhl us)
harrow *v.* to break up soil
chaff *n.* the coverings removed from seeds of grain before the grain is ground into flour
husk *v.* to remove the coverings from seeds of grain
millet (MIL it) *n.* a kind of grain

n a small farm in southern India there lived a water buffalo named Big Red Bubalus with his younger brother named Little Red Bubalus. These two brothers did all the hard work on the farm. They plowed and they harrowed; they seeded; and they brought in the harvest for their owner. In between the crops they worked the water wheel which irrigated the farm and the garden; and they turned the pump to supply water for the house and pigpen.

When the crop was in, Big Red Bubalus and Little Red Bubalus were harnessed again to turn the grindstone which milled the flour for the family.

Yet for all their labors they were rarely rewarded. They were seldom allowed to bathe in the stream, which they loved to do. And all they were given to eat was grass and straw, or chaff when the grain was husked.

This same farmer owned a pig who did nothing but eat and wallow in the water pumped up for him by the buffaloes. Yet the hog was fed on rice and millet and was well taken care of by the farmer and his family.

► Again and again the younger buffalo would complain; and each time the older buffalo merely said: "Envy not the pig."

Little Red Bubalus complained to his brother: "We, who do all the hard work, are treated shabbily and our master gives us next to nothing to eat. Most of the time we have to go out into the pasture to find our own food. Yet this lazy pig is fed all the time and never does any work."

"Envy him not, little brother," said Big Red Bubalus (who was the Bodisat in the form of a buffalo). And he would say no more.

Again and again the younger buffalo would complain; and each time the older buffalo merely said:

"Envy not the pig."

One day the farmer's only daughter was engaged to be married. And as the wedding day drew near, the hog was slaughtered and roasted for the wedding feast.

Then Big Red Bubalus said to Little Red Bubalus: "Now do you see why a pig is not to be envied?"

And Little Red Bubalus replied: "Yes, now I understand. It is better to feed on straw and chaff, and to live out our lives, than to be fattened on rice only to end up on a roasting spit."

shabbily *adv.* unfairly, ungenerously

Connect Have you ever envied someone? How did it make you feel?

EXPLORING YOUR READING

Look Back

1. Why does Little Red Bubalus envy the pig?
2. Which character is the Bodisat in this story?

Think It Over

3. From this fable and from what you know about Buddhism, what role do you think the Bodisat might play in other Jataka stories?
4. How are the animals in this story like humans?
5. Why doesn't Big Red Bubalus explain why Little Red Bubalus should not envy the pig?

Go Beyond

6. Restate the moral of this fable in a general way that fits people.

Ideas for Writing: Short Story

7. Think of a lesson about life you think people should be aware of. Using this story as a model, write a fable that teaches the moral you have chosen.

THE ANCIENT WORLD   121

CHAPTER 5

Ancient China

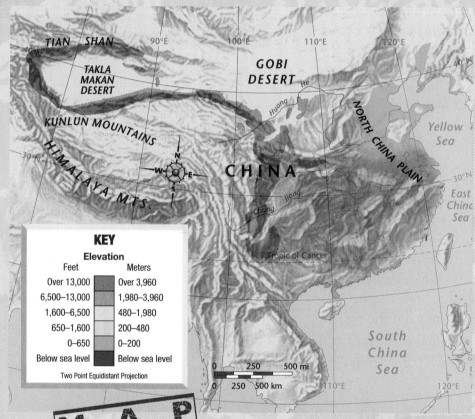

KEY

Elevation

Feet		Meters
Over 13,000		Over 3,960
6,500–13,000		1,980–3,960
1,600–6,500		480–1,980
650–1,600		200–480
0–650		0–200
Below sea level		Below sea level

Two Point Equidistant Projection

Ancient China was the location of one of the world's first civilizations. Get to know this region by completing the following activities.

Study the map
From looking at the map, do you think it was easy or hard for the people of China to make contact with people of other civilizations? Explain your answer.

Choose a place
You know that ancient civilizations in Egypt, Mesopotamia, and India started in river valleys. Pick a place on the map where you think Chinese civilization might have started, and explain your choice.

The Geography of China's River Valleys

▼ This colorful dragon gazes at a statue of the Buddha in the Cave of the Thousand Buddhas in Dunhuang, China.

What words would you use to describe dragons like this one? You may think of these imaginary beasts as being fierce and scary. People of some cultures would agree with you. But to the Chinese people, the dragon is a respected spirit, not a terrible monster. In China, dragons are friendly beasts that bring good luck. They are also connected with the rain that makes the fields fertile.

The Chinese also use this respected spirit to show the importance of their rivers. They traditionally describe their rivers as dragons. The dragon's limbs are the smaller streams. They flow into the dragon's body, or main river. The dragon's mouth is the delta, where the river flows into the sea.

The Geographic Setting of Ancient China

Rivers were important to the development of civilization in China. Other landforms and climate played a role, too.

Muddy River

Large ships cannot travel on the Huang He. Large amounts of loess are deposited on the river's bottom, making it too shallow for safe passage. **Critical Thinking** How could being near a river help people who live in a dry climate?

Visualize Visualize the shape of a river as a dragon.

Contrasting Climate and Landforms Locate the North China Plain on the map on the opening page of this chapter. The climate and vegetation of this northern region of China are very different from those in the south. Monsoons from the South China Sea bring rains to the southern half of China. This area is warm and wet. The monsoon rains don't reach the cooler, northern part of China and the North China Plain. This area doesn't get much rain at other times, either. As a result, the climate is very dry. To survive in this dry land, people have always depended on rivers.

The "Middle Kingdom" Geographic barriers such as mountains and seas cut China off from other lands. As a result, the Chinese knew only of the nomadic peoples to the north and west of them. They had no knowledge of the powerful civilizations half a world away: Egypt, India, Greece, and Rome. In fact, the Chinese did not call their land "China." They were so sure that they lived at the center of the world that they called themselves the "Middle Kingdom."

Rivers, the Birthplace of Civilization Several of the world's earliest civilizations—in Mesopotamia, Egypt, and India—grew up near major rivers. In China, the same forces were at work. Identify on the map the Huang He (hwahng hay) and the Chang Jiang (chahng jee AHNG), sometimes called the Yangzi River. Civilization began in

China along the Huang He and later spread to the wetter south along the Chang Jiang River, the longest river in China.

Like rivers in other parts of the world, China's rivers overflowed their banks each spring. They brought fresh, fertile topsoil to the land. Because of this, China's first farming villages developed along its rivers.

The Huang He, or "Yellow River," begins in the highlands of Tibet. From there, it flows for more than 3,000 miles (4,800 km) until it empties into the Yellow Sea. It is the second-longest river in China.

The Huang He is the muddiest river in the world. In fact, it is called the "Yellow" River because of the **loess** (lehs), or yellow-brown soil, that its waters carry along. When the Huang He floods, it deposits loess on the surrounding plain. After thousands of years and countless floods, the Huang He has carpeted the North China Plain with a thick layer of soil. This makes the land perfect for growing crops, especially a grain called millet. For thousands of years, millet was an important part of the Chinese diet because it grew so well on the northern plain.

China's Sorrow The Chinese people also call the Huang He "China's Sorrow." The river was unpredictable and sometimes dangerous. It brought life to the land. But frequently it also took life away. Destructive floods could come without warning, sometimes as often as

▼ The staircaselike platforms on this hillside above the Huang He are called terraces. These platforms increase the amount of land available for farming. They also prevent soil from washing away during heavy rains.

◀ Today, we have paperback books, but the ancient Chinese read "turtlebacks." Even though the symbols on this turtle shell are about 4,000 years old, they are quite similar to modern Chinese symbols.

LINKS ACROSS TIME

Writing in China The earliest examples of Chinese writing appear on turtle shells and animal bones. These were done by the Shang people between 1750 B.C. and 1120 B.C. Then, each symbol, or character, stood for a thing or idea. Over the years, each character in Chinese writing has come to stand for a word or part of a word. Now there are about 50,000 characters in all! Some characters have been in use for almost 4,000 years.

every two years. Sometimes a flood drowned thousands of people. At times, the river flooded with such force that the water cut an entirely new path over the land. The course of the river could change by hundreds of miles.

To help control the flooding, early Chinese people built dikes along the banks of the Huang He. A **dike** is a protective wall that holds back the waters. But these dikes only worked for a while. As the river water flowed along, some of the loess settled to the bottom. This raised the level of the river. Eventually, the river rose high enough to burst through the dikes, causing even more deadly floods. Despite such dangers, the early Chinese people continued to settle along the banks of the Huang He.

Sowing the Seeds of Civilization

Historians do not know exactly when the first farming settlements developed in the Huang He Valley. Some think it was as early as 5000 B.C. Before that, the people of the North China Plain were probably nomads who moved from place to place to hunt and gather food.

The Shang dynasty was the first known civilization in China. It arose some time after 1700 B.C. The Shang people built China's first cities. Among their many accomplishments is some of the finest bronze work of ancient China.

The Shang people also produced the first Chinese writing. Like Mesopotamia's cuneiform and our own alphabet, the Chinese system of writing could be used for different languages. This was helpful for communications, because China had many regional languages.

The Bonds of Family

The family was the center of early Chinese society. It was far more important than the individual or the nation. For each person, the family was the chief source of well-being. A person's first responsibility was always to the family.

Traditional Families A household in ancient China might contain as many as five generations living together. This meant that small children lived with their great-great-grandparents as well as their parents, uncles and aunts, cousins, brothers and sisters, and so on. These closely related people are called an **extended family.** In rich families, the members might live together in one big home. But most of China's people were poor. In farming villages, members of the extended family might live in separate one-room cottages. The cottages were within easy walking distance from one another.

The status of each person in a Chinese extended family depended on age and sex. The center of authority was usually the oldest man. He had

◀ The elegance of this Chinese family's silk robes shows that they were quite wealthy.

◄ Girls in ancient China rarely received a formal education. Instead, they learned household tasks such as weaving and cooking. At the age of 15, girls took part in special ceremonies during which their hair was pinned up, as in the photograph. This was a sign that they had entered adulthood.

the most privileges and power in the family. He decided who his children and grandchildren would marry. When children were disrespectful, he punished them strictly. After the oldest male died, by tradition all his lands were divided among his sons. Each son then started his own household.

Women's lives were usually governed by men. According to tradition, they obeyed their fathers in youth, their husbands in middle age, and their sons in old age. When a woman married, she left her household and became part of her new husband's family.

Family Names The Chinese were the first people known to use two names. One name was for the family, which was passed down from father to son. The other was for the individual. Of course, people in the United States also use two names. In Chinese society, however, the family name comes first. If this system were used in American society, you would know the first President of the United States as Washington George, not George Washington. Think of other famous people in American history. What would their names be in the Chinese naming style?

The fact that the family name comes first in China shows how important the family is. This tradition in Chinese society dates back to the very earliest times. Centuries later, a great philosopher, Confucius (kuhn FYOO shuhs), added a new meaning to the importance of one's family.

READ ACTIVELY

Connect What would your name be if the Chinese naming system were used in the United States?

SECTION 1 REVIEW

1. Define (a) loess, (b) dike, (c) extended family.

2. Identify (a) North China Plain, (b) Huang He, (c) Chang Jiang.

3. How did the Huang He affect ancient Chinese civilization?

4. How was the early Chinese family household organized?

Critical Thinking

5. Making Comparisons What do you think ancient China might have in common with other great ancient civilizations of Mesopotamia, Egypt, and India?

Activity

6. Writing to Learn Imagine what your life would have been like in an early Chinese household. Write a description.

Confucius and His Teachings

Reach Into Your Background

Why should you do your homework? How should you act toward other people? Must you always obey your parents? Must you always respect the President of the United States? How would you answer these questions? Early Chinese thinkers asked themselves similar questions in an effort to establish a system of rules for their society.

Questions to Explore

1. What values did Confucianism stress?
2. How did Confucius' ideas help shape Chinese society?

Key Terms

philosophy   civil service

Key People

Confucius

One day, the teacher Confucius and his students were walking through the countryside. In the distance they heard a woman crying. As they came around a bend in the road, they saw the woman kneeling at a grave. "Why are you crying?" they asked her. "Because," she answered, "a tiger killed my husband's father. Later, the tiger also killed my husband. Now, the tiger has killed my son as well."

They then asked the woman, "Why do you stay in this place after these terrible things have happened?" The woman answered, "Because there are no cruel rulers here." Confucius turned to his students and said, "Remember this. A cruel ruler is fiercer and more feared than a tiger."

The Life of Confucius

Confucius was the most famous—and important—of the early Chinese thinkers. The Chinese, who regarded Confucius as a great teacher, called him Kong Fu Zi (kahng FOO zuh), or "Master Kong." *Confucius* is the Western version of this name. After his death, Confucius' followers told many stories about him. Most of them were like the story of the woman and the tiger.

▼ Little detail exists about Confucius' life. No one really knows what he looked like. An artist made this portrait more than 1,000 years after Confucius' death.

Confucius was born in 551 B.C. to a noble but poor family of the North China Plain. When he was three years old, his father died. His mother raised him alone. He loved learning and was largely self-taught. Confucius hoped to advance to an important government office, but he never did.

Instead, Confucius decided to try teaching. He charged students a fee to take classes. Many historians think that he was China's first professional teacher. Confucius taught his students his views of life and government. Some of his students went on to hold important government posts.

In Confucius' time, only the rich could afford an education. But Confucius also accepted students who truly wanted to learn, even if they were poor. As he noted:

> "From the very poorest upward . . . none has ever come to me without receiving instruction. I instruct only a student who bursts with eagerness. Only one who bubbles with excitement do I enlighten."

Later in his life, Confucius wandered about North China. He looked for a ruler who would follow his teachings, but was unsuccessful. Confucius returned home a disappointed man. He died in 479 B.C. at the age of 72. By the time of his death, he believed his life had been a failure. He was wrong.

Confucius and His Students

Confucius' complete devotion to teaching and learning is apparent in the following description he gave of himself as "the sort of man who forgets to eat when he engages himself in vigorous pursuit of learning, who is so full of joy that he forgets his worries, and who does not notice that old age is coming on."

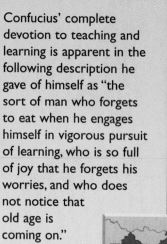

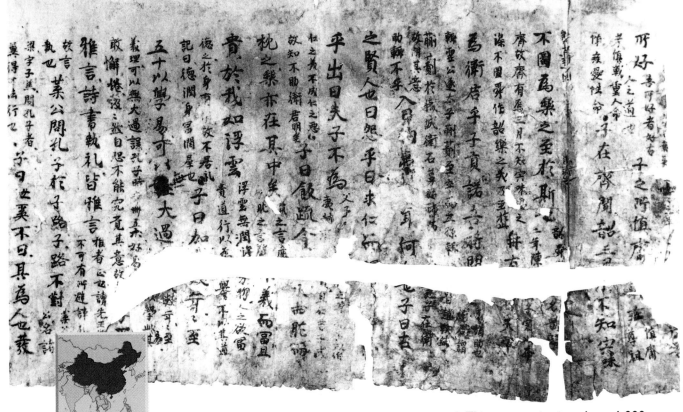

▲ This manuscript is at least 1,000 years old. In it are preserved the teachings of Confucius, known as the *Analects*. The *Analects* formed the basis of Chinese education for more than 2,000 years.

The Teachings of Confucius

Confucius did not claim to be an original thinker. He felt that his role was to pass on the forgotten teachings of wise people from an earlier age. Many of his teachings focused on persuading rulers to reform. He also aimed to bring peace, stability, and prosperity to their kingdoms.

Confucius himself never wrote down his teachings. Instead, his students gathered a collection of his sayings after his death. Together, these writings made up a **philosophy,** or system of beliefs and values. It became known as Confucianism. Confucianism was one of several important philosophies of ancient China. Over time, it began to guide many aspects of life there.

Confucius lived in a period known as the "Time of the Warring States." Powerful rulers of several Chinese states, or kingdoms, fought each other for the control of land. They seemed more interested in getting power than in ruling wisely. Confucius hoped to persuade these rulers to change their ways and bring peace to China.

Confucius' goal was order in society. He believed that if people could be taught to behave properly to one another, order and peace would return. Society would prosper. Confucius said people should know their place in the family and society. They should respect people above and below them. Everyone must treat others justly. He described people in

The Five Classics
Confucianism was based on the Five Classics, which were works of ancient Chinese literature. One, the *Book of Songs*, contains 305 poems. Some were written as early as 1000 B.C. Their subjects include war, love, and loss. In one, a wife speaks fondly of her husband who has gone to war: "My lord is on service;/ How can I not be sad?"

Predict Whom do you think Confucius meant by "those in authority"?

various relationships: ruler and ruled; father and son; husband and wife; older brother and younger brother; and friend and friend. Then he explained how they should behave. Confucius said people in authority—princes or parents—must set a good example. If a ruler was good, his people would follow his example and become good, too. Confucius summarized his ideas about relationships in a simple sentence. It is similar to what Christians and Jews call the Golden Rule: "Do not do to others what you would not want done to yourself."

The Impact of Confucius

Confucius' teachings had a major impact on Chinese government. They became the basic training for members of the civil service. The **civil service** is the group of people who carry out the work of government.

Before Confucius' ideas took hold, government posts were generally given to the sons of important people. Afterward, any male could hold a government post on merit—that is, how well he did his job. People who receive a reward on merit have shown, in some way, that they deserve that reward. Candidates for government jobs had to pass official examinations. To advance, they had to pass more exams. These exams were based on Confucius' teachings.

▶ The lantern this statue holds symbolizes faithfulness. According to Confucianism, wives were to show faith and devotion to their husbands.

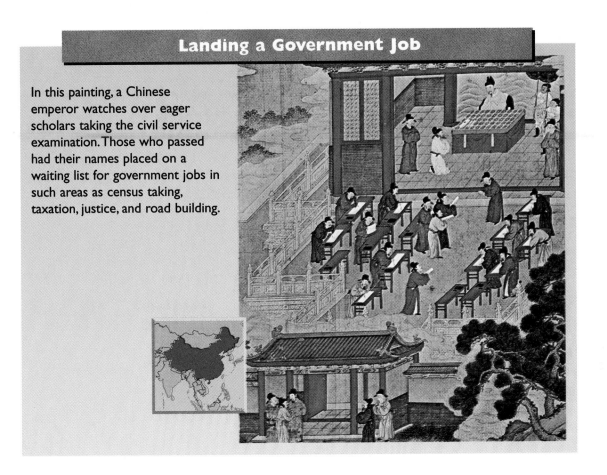

In this painting, a Chinese emperor watches over eager scholars taking the civil service examination. Those who passed had their names placed on a waiting list for government jobs in such areas as census taking, taxation, justice, and road building.

The examination system did bring more able young men into government service. However, it did not open government jobs to everyone. Candidates still had to know how to read. This made it difficult for a poor man to advance. But it was not impossible. Many talented but poor young men rose to high government positions.

Confucius would have been surprised at the impact he had on China. He did not consider himself particularly wise or good. In fact, he felt that he was a failure. But Confucius left his mark on Chinese life as perhaps no one before or after has.

SECTION 2 REVIEW

1. **Define** (a) philosophy, (b) civil service.

2. **Identify** Confucius.

3. What are some basic ideas of Confucianism?

4. How did Confucius' teachings change the way civil servants were chosen in ancient China?

Critical Thinking

5. **Drawing Conclusions** What do you think Confucius would say about government in the United States today? Would he feel that it followed his ideas? Why or why not?

Activity

6. **Writing to Learn** You are a government official in a small state in northern China. One day, a wandering teacher named Confucius comes to your court. Write a journal entry that describes what Confucius said and how your ruler reacted to him.

SECTION 3

Strong Rulers Unite Warring Kingdoms

BEFORE YOU READ

Reach Into Your Background

How would you feel if your government leaders removed many books from the library and burned them? Who do you think is the best judge of what you should read? Why?

Questions to Explore

1. How did the emperor Shi Huangdi help unite China?
2. How did Han rulers build a powerful empire that reunited China for more than 400 years?

Key Terms

currency
warlord

Key People

Shi Huangdi
Liu Bang
Wudi

▼ This life-size, armor-clad, terra-cotta warrior appears ready to defend Shi Huangdi's empire.

In 1974, a group of farmers was digging a well in a grove of trees in northern China. Six feet down, they found some pottery made of a clay-like material called terra cotta. Another five feet down, they unearthed the terra-cotta head of a man. Archaeologists began digging—and discovered more than 8,000 life-sized statues of horses, chariots, and men. It was a terra-cotta army. For more than 2,000 years, these buried soldiers had kept watch at the tomb of the great Chinese emperor, Shi Huangdi (shee hoo ahng DEE).

Today, visitors to the tomb of Shi Huangdi are stunned by the sight of this army. No two statues are identical. Each statue is carefully made, down to the smallest detail of clothing. There are even royal chariots pulled by life-sized terra-cotta horses.

With his underground army, Shi Huangdi planned to rule a second empire in the afterlife. He also had grand plans for the real-life empire he created in China. His dynasty, he boasted, would last for 10,000 generations.

One China, One Ruler

Actually, Shi Huangdi's dynasty lasted for only two generations. But he is still a major figure in Chinese history. He is the ruler who unified China.

The Qin Dynasty   Shi Huangdi's original name was Zheng (juhng). He ruled a fierce people, the Qin (cheen), who lived along China's western edge. A Chinese poet described Zheng this way: "Cracking his long whip, he drove the universe before him. . . . His might shook the four seas."

Marching Across Time

Flakes of paint still cling to some of Shi Huangdi's warriors (below), indicating that they were once brilliantly colored. This kneeling soldier (right) shows the attention to detail artists paid as they made the terra-cotta figures. A craftsman uses ancient techniques to make a model of a terra-cotta soldier (left).

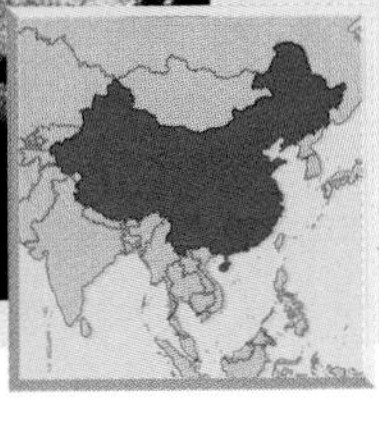

Connect Why do modern people know about other civilizations, even though ancient people did not?

By 221 B.C., Zheng had extended his rule over most of the land that makes up modern-day China. After seizing power, Zheng took his new title of Shi Huangdi, which means "First Emperor." He expected his sons and grandsons would number themselves Second Emperor, Third Emperor, and so on. His dynasty is named after the people of his homeland. It is the Qin dynasty.

Strengthening the Empire

Shi Huangdi set about changing China through strong and harsh rule. One of his first tasks was to protect the new empire from its enemies.

The Great Wall   Throughout history, Chinese rulers had to worry about the nomads that lived along China's huge northern border. Shi Huangdi had a plan to end these border wars. He ordered the largest construction project in Chinese history. It is called the Great Wall of China. Locate the wall on the map on page 138.

▶ The Great Wall has not always looked as it does today. Parts of the Great Wall have been destroyed and rebuilt many times. Further changes were made to meet the military needs of various emperors. For example, one emperor had watchtowers built so that guards could send news of enemy activities with smoke or fire signals. **Regions** What part of his empire did Shi Huangdi hope the Great Wall would protect?

Previous rulers had built walls along the border. Shi Huangdi decided to connect them. He ordered farmers from their fields and merchants from their stores to form an army of 300,000 workers. When it was finished, the wall stretched for 1,400 miles (2,240 km). That is about the distance from Washington, D.C., to Denver, Colorado.

Organizing the Government   To put down rebellions from within the empire, Shi Huangdi put thousands of farmers to work building roads. The new roads enabled his armies to rush to the scene of any uprisings.

The emperor dealt swiftly with local rulers who opposed him by having them killed or put in prison. Shi Huangdi divided all China into areas called districts. Each district had a government run by the emperor's most trusted officials.

Unifying the Culture

Shi Huangdi was not content to unify the government of China. He also wanted the many peoples of these united kingdoms to have one economy and one culture.

READ ACTIVELY

Connect Would you have liked to live in China when Shi Huangdi ruled it? Why or why not?

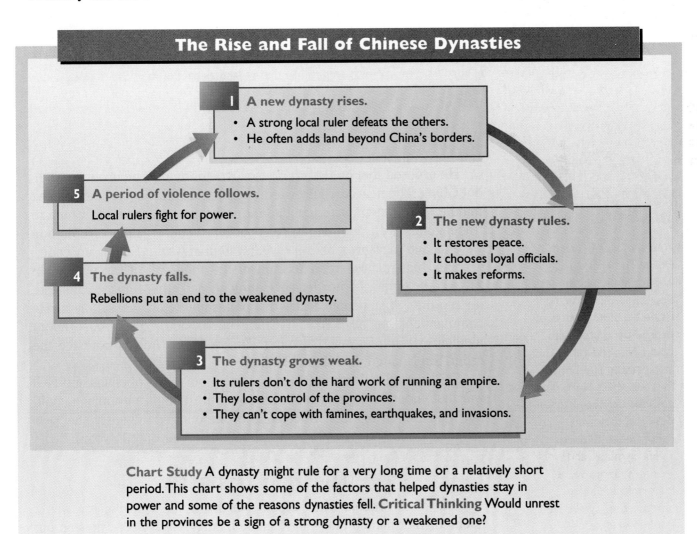

The Rise and Fall of Chinese Dynasties

1 A new dynasty rises.
- A strong local ruler defeats the others.
- He often adds land beyond China's borders.

2 The new dynasty rules.
- It restores peace.
- It chooses loyal officials.
- It makes reforms.

3 The dynasty grows weak.
- Its rulers don't do the hard work of running an empire.
- They lose control of the provinces.
- They can't cope with famines, earthquakes, and invasions.

4 The dynasty falls.
Rebellions put an end to the weakened dynasty.

5 A period of violence follows.
Local rulers fight for power.

Chart Study A dynasty might rule for a very long time or a relatively short period. This chart shows some of the factors that helped dynasties stay in power and some of the reasons dynasties fell. **Critical Thinking** Would unrest in the provinces be a sign of a strong dynasty or a weakened one?

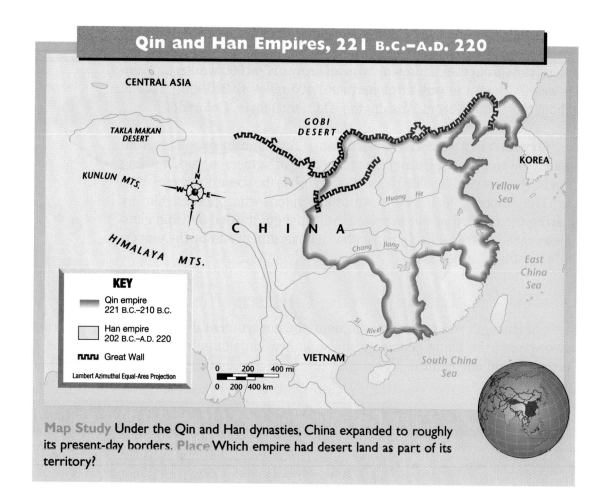

Qin and Han Empires, 221 B.C.–A.D. 220

CENTRAL ASIA

TAKLA MAKAN DESERT

GOBI DESERT

KUNLUN MTS.

KOREA

Yellow Sea

Huang He

C H I N A

HIMALAYA MTS.

Chang Jiang

East China Sea

KEY

Qin empire
221 B.C.–210 B.C.

Han empire
202 B.C.–A.D. 220

Great Wall

Lambert Azimuthal Equal-Area Projection

0   200   400 mi
0   200 400 km

VIETNAM

Si River

South China Sea

Map Study Under the Qin and Han dynasties, China expanded to roughly its present-day borders. **Place** Which empire had desert land as part of its territory?

LINKS TO ART

Han Dynasty Bronze Work The Han dynasty was a time when the arts flourished. Skilled artisans made beautiful objects of bronze decorated with gold, silver, and gems. They also created fine bronze mirrors. These were discs polished on one side. On the back, they were decorated with borders, animal symbols, and writing. Mirrors were important in China because they symbolized self-knowledge.

He ordered that one **currency,** or type of money, be used throughout China. The new currency was a round coin with a square hole in the middle. A common currency made it easier for one region of China to trade goods with another. He also ordered the creation of common weights and measures, an improved system of writing, and a law code.

Shi Huangdi also tried to control the thoughts of his people. In 213 B.C., he outlawed the ideas of Confucius and other thinkers. Instead, he required that people learn the philosophies of Qin scholars. He commanded that all books in China be burned except those about medicine, technology, and farming. Hundreds of scholars protested the order. Shi Huangdi had them all killed.

Shi Huangdi's death in 210 B.C. started four years of chaos and civil war that ended in the murder of his son. Shi Huangdi's grandson could not hold China together. Rebellions broke out. The dynasty that was supposed to last "for 10,000 generations" lasted for only 15 years.

The Han Dynasty

One of the rebels who helped overthrow the Qin dynasty was a talented ruler named Liu Bang (LEE oo bahng). By 202 B.C., he won out over his rivals and became emperor of China. Liu Bang was the first emperor of a new dynasty: the Han (hahn). He was also the first ruler in Chinese history who was born a peasant. Liu Bang created a stable government. His rule was less harsh than Shi Huangdi's.

Stable governments were a feature of the Han dynasty, which lasted for about 400 years. Han rulers realized that they needed educated people to work in the government. So they set up the civil service system based on Confucianism.

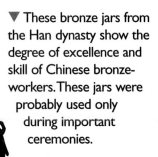

These bronze jars from the Han dynasty show the degree of excellence and skill of Chinese bronze-workers. These jars were probably used only during important ceremonies.

Wudi: The Warrior Emperor   The Han dynasty reached its peak under Wudi (woo dee), Liu Bang's great-grandson. Wudi came to power in 140 B.C., when he was only 14 years old. He remained in power for more than 50 years.

Wudi's main interest was war and military matters. In fact, his name means "Warrior Emperor." He made improvements to Shi Huangdi's Great Wall. He also strengthened the army. By the end of Wudi's reign, Chinese rule stretched west into Central Asia, north into present-day Korea, and south into what today is the country of Vietnam. Locate the Han empire on the map on the opposite page.

The End of the Han Empire   The great emperor Wudi died in 87 B.C. After that, the Han dynasty slowly started to fall apart. The process took more than two centuries. Over time, roads and canals fell into disrepair. **Warlords,** leaders of armed local bands, gained power.

The last Han emperor was kept in power by a warlord who tried to control the empire through him. When that warlord died in A.D. 220, the emperor gave up power. The Han dynasty had ended. China broke up into several smaller kingdoms.

SECTION 3 REVIEW

1. **Define**   (a) currency, (b) warlord.

2. **Identify**   (a) Shi Huangdi, (b) Liu Bang, (c) Wudi.

3. How did Shi Huangdi strengthen the central government of China?

4. Why did the Han dynasty last much longer than the Qin dynasty?

Critical Thinking

5. **Recognizing Bias**   Most information about the emperor Shi Huangdi comes from the writings of Confucian historians who lived during the Han dynasty. Remember, the Han dynasty began when Liu Bang defeated Shi Huangdi's grandson. How might this fact affect what we know about Shi Huangdi?

Activity

6. **Writing to Learn**   The farmers who discovered Shi Huangdi's terra-cotta army made one of the most important archaeological finds in history. You have been called in to examine the find. Write a journal entry about the wonders the farmers have shown you.

Achievements of Ancient China

Reach Into Your Background

What will future historians call the time we live in? Will they think it was a great age? Will they praise its scientific advances, such as the computer and space flight? What do you think?

Questions to Explore

1. What role did Confucianism play in China during the Han dynasty?

2. What important advances in technology were made in China during the Han dynasty?

Key Terms

silk

Key People and Places

Sima Qian
Silk Road

▼ Camels are undoubtedly better equipped than humans to endure a sandstorm. Double rows of protective eyelashes and the ability to close their nostrils help them survive sandstorms.

The caravan slowly plods across the hot sand of the Takla Makan Desert. Weary travelers wearing long robes sway on top of camels. Riderless camels are heaped high with heavy loads.

Suddenly, the camels stop, huddle together, and snarl viciously. An old man riding the lead camel turns around and shouts. No one can hear him because the screaming wind drowns out his words. The man jumps from his camel and quickly wraps a strip of felt around his nose and mouth. The other travelers rush to dismount and cover their faces, too. Just then, the sandstorm hits with full force.

Then, as quickly as it came, the sandstorm is gone. The travelers wipe sand from their eyes and tend to their camels. They have survived just one of the many challenges of traveling on the long and treacherous trade route known as the Silk Road.

The Silk Road:
China Meets the West

Predict What effect do you think the Silk Road had on China?

The Emperor Wudi's conquests in the west brought the Chinese into contact with the people of Central Asia. Trade with these people introduced the Chinese to such new foods as grapes, walnuts, and garlic. This exchange of goods gave rise to a major new trade route. Called the Silk Road, it ran all the way from China to the Mediterranean Sea. Follow the route of the Silk Road on the map below.

The Silk Road was not one continuous road. Rather, it was a series of routes covering more than 4,000 miles (6,400 km), a little less than the distance from Chicago to Hawaii. Travel along the Silk Road was hard and dangerous. The Silk Road began in northern China and went west along the Great Wall of China. Then, it entered a narrow fringe of land between the barren Gobi Desert and the towering Nan Shan, or Southern Mountains. More dangerous land loomed to the west, where the Silk Road edged around the fringes of the dangerous Takla Makan Desert. Here, as you have read, travelers faced the peril of sudden, blinding sandstorms.

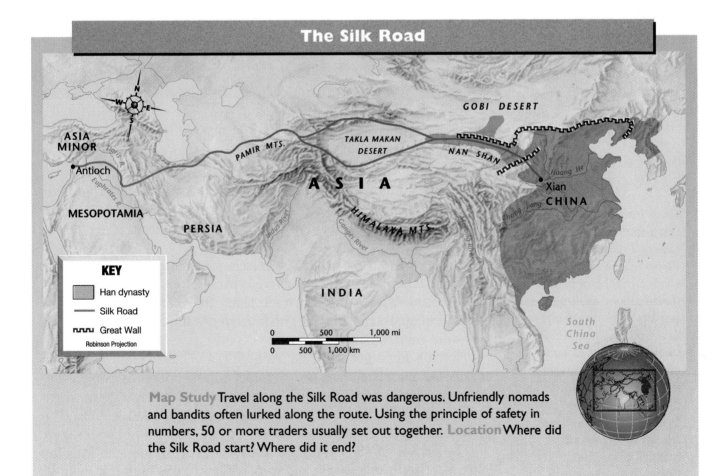

The Silk Road

KEY

Han dynasty

Silk Road

Great Wall

Robinson Projection

Map Study Travel along the Silk Road was dangerous. Unfriendly nomads and bandits often lurked along the route. Using the principle of safety in numbers, 50 or more traders usually set out together. **Location** Where did the Silk Road start? Where did it end?

Fine silk is actually the product of worms (below center) that eat nothing but mulberry leaves. In ancient China, women tended these silkworms until they spun cocoons. Then the women carefully unwound the cocoons and wove the threads into silk cloth. One of the last steps was to pound the silk to soften it—the task shown at the left. Only wealthy people could afford fine silk robes such as the one below.

LINKS TO SCIENCE

Cloth from Caterpillars
Silk is spun by a type of caterpillar called a silkworm. The silkworm winds a cocoon of fine thread around itself. Before the caterpillar can change to a moth, the fine thread—as much as a mile of it—is carefully unwound from the cocoon. This thread is joined with others to form one thick enough to weave into beautiful cloth. The Chinese knew how to make silk by 3000 B.C.

Once the road crossed the Pamir Mountains, travel was easier. The road passed through Persia and Mesopotamia. Finally, it turned north to the city of Antioch (AN tee ahk), in what today is Syria. From here, traders shipped goods across the Mediterranean to Rome, Greece, Egypt, and other lands that bordered the Mediterranean.

A Route for Goods Few travelers journeyed the entire length of the Silk Road. Generally, goods were passed from trader to trader as they crossed Asia. With each trade along the route, the price of the goods went up. By the time the goods arrived at the end of their journey, they were very expensive.

The Silk Road got its name from **silk,** a valuable cloth first made only in China. Han farmers developed new methods for raising silkworms, which made the silk. Han workers found new ways to weave and dye the silk. These methods were closely guarded secrets. The penalty for revealing them was death.

The arrival of silk in Europe created great excitement. Wealthy Romans prized Chinese silk and were willing to pay high prices for it. And wealthy people in China would pay well for glass, horses, ivory, woolens, and linen cloth from Rome.

A Route for Ideas   More than goods traveled the road. New ideas did, too. For example, missionaries from India traveled to China along a section of the road and brought the religion of Buddhism with them. By the time the Han dynasty ended, Buddhism was becoming a major religion in China.

Old Traditions, New Accomplishments

Traditional Chinese ideas flourished during the Han dynasty. Han rulers realized that during troubled times in the past, people had lost respect for tradition. To bring back this respect, rulers encouraged people to return to the teachings of Confucius. It is also why rulers during the Han and later dynasties required members of the civil service to be educated in Confucian teachings.

Language and Literature   Under the Han dynasty, the arts and scholarship flourished. Chinese poets wrote excellent poetry. Chinese scholars put together the first dictionary of the Chinese language. But the greatest advance was in the field of history.

Until the time of the Han, the Chinese people had only a shadowy knowledge of their own history. They knew only myths that had been passed down from generation to generation. But often these stories were in conflict with each other. No one was sure just when Chinese rulers had lived or what they accomplished.

READ ACTIVELY

Predict Why would Han dynasty rulers want to bring back Confucian ideas of respect for authority and tradition?

Han Fine Art

The ceramic head (left) was made during the Han dynasty. The jade carving (below) of a winged beast is also from the Han dynasty. To the Chinese, jade is symbolic of purity and excellence.

The scholar Sima Qian (soo MAH chen) decided to solve the problem. He spent his life writing a history of China from mythical times to the emperor Wudi. His work, called *Historical Records,* is a major source of our information about ancient China. Sima described his work:

> **"I** wish to examine all that encircles heaven and man. I want to probe the changes of the past and present.**"**

Chinese Achievements

Achievements of Ancient China

Technology	Medicine	The Arts
• Paper made from wood pulp	• Acupuncture—treatment of disease using needles	• Silk weaving
• Iron plow for breaking up soil		• Jade carving
• Rudder—a device used to steer ships	• Anesthetics—substances that put patients to sleep for surgery	• Bronze working
• Wheelbarrow		• Temples and palaces
• Compass	• Herbal remedies—discovery of plants useful as medicines	• Poetry and history
	• Circulatory system—discovery that blood travels through the body	

Chart Study This chart shows just a few of the achievements of the ancient Chinese. **Critical Thinking** Which two Chinese inventions were helpful for farmers?

This wheelbarrow allowed one worker to move loads once carried by two. A mixture of chopped plants, water, and other materials was dried on mesh to form sheets of paper. Over 3,000 years ago, the Chinese learned to carve beautiful objects from jade like this ax blade. The Chinese made the first magnetic compasses. Because a compass needle always points north and south, Chinese sailors referred to compasses as "south-pointing fish."

Advances in Technology   During the Han dynasty, China became the most advanced civilization in the world. Its government was stable, so the Chinese could turn their attention to improving their society. Some accomplishments of the Han dynasty are shown in the chart. For example, Chinese artisans began making iron farming tools. These were a great improvement over the stone hoes and plows that farmers had traditionally used. Under Han leadership, workers constructed vast irrigation systems. They developed new ways of farming. They also developed something the world still depends on every day—paper.

Paper   To keep records, Mesopotamians had to carve their cuneiform characters in stone or press them into clay tablets. The Chinese had similar problems. The Chinese used wood scrolls. Later, they wrote messages and even whole books on silk. Then, around A.D. 105, the Chinese made one of their greatest discoveries. They invented paper. The first paper was made from tree bark, hemp, and old rags. It was strengthened with starch and then coated with gelatin, a gooey substance that gave it strength.

This invention influenced learning and the arts in China. After several centuries, the use of paper spread across Asia and into Europe. Eventually paper replaced papyrus from Egypt as the material for scrolls and books.

Other Practical Inventions   During the Han dynasty, the Chinese invented many practical devices that did not reach Europe until centuries later. Among them were the wheelbarrow, the rudder (for steering boats), and the collar and harness that allowed animals to pull heavy loads.

The Han dynasty came to an end in the 200s A.D. But its accomplishments were not forgotten. People in China today call themselves "the children of Han."

SECTION 4 REVIEW

1. **Define** silk.

2. **Identify** (a) Sima Qian, (b) Silk Road.

3. Why did the influence of Confucius grow during the Han dynasty?

4. Name three accomplishments of the Chinese during the Han dynasty.

Critical Thinking

5. **Recognizing Cause and Effect** What do you think was the most important achievement of ancient China? Why?

Activity

6. **Writing to Learn** You are a historian in A.D. 2150. Write a brief description of the accomplishments of the United States in the late 1900s. Use these categories: Trade, Culture, Technology.

Organizing Information

"Chris, what is wrong with your hand?" Chris's mother found him shaking his hand back and forth.

"It hurts, Mom. I've been copying this chapter for hours, taking notes for my report about Confucianism," said Chris.

"Are you really copying every word?" Chris nodded. "Well, you should be writing down only the main ideas and supporting details," she said.

Chris protested. "But it all seems important!"

"I know," said his mother. "But when you read carefully, you will see that some ideas are more important than others. When you figure that out, you will understand the chapter better."

Get Ready

Taking notes is an excellent way to organize information, or arrange facts in a way that makes sense to you.

When you take notes from a book, you should record main ideas and the details that support them. You do this by writing down key words, or the most important words and phrases. It is important to write them in a way that shows how the ideas represented by the key words are related. Usually, you write main ideas as headings and list the details that support them below the headings.

Try It Out

The paragraph in the box on the next page gives information about Confucius. Practice organizing information by reading it carefully and completing the steps that follow.

A. Use key words and phrases to record the main idea. The main idea is often stated in a single sentence. What sentence in the paragraph states the main idea? Using key words, write it down. Don't copy the whole sentence. Write the main idea as a heading.

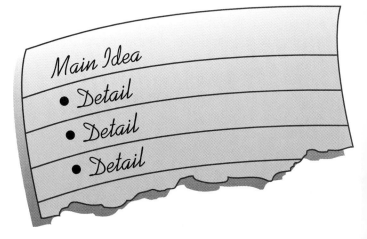

Main Idea
- Detail
- Detail
- Detail

B. Use key words and phrases to record details. Usually, most of the sentences in a paragraph support, or tell more about, the main idea. What details in the passage support the main idea? Record them under the main idea heading, to show that they support it. Remember, you're taking notes, not copying. Use key words and phrases.

Exchange notes with a partner to compare them. Did you identify the same main idea? The same details? Do your notes organize information in a way that is easy to understand? What could you do to improve your work?

Apply the Skill

Look through Section 1 of Chapter 5 in this book. Organize the information in it.

1 **Use key words and phrases to record the main idea of the section.** One helpful hint is to look at the headings within the section.

2 **Use key words and phrases to record details.** How can you identify some of these?

The Chinese philosopher Confucius taught his students to live a life of virtue and respect for wisdom. Three parts of his teachings are especially important. First, he taught people to behave toward others as they would like to be treated themselves. Second, he had many sayings about the 'person with integrity,' and he spoke of this person as a model of virtue for his students. Third, he said that people should respect social rules and treat others according to those rules. Confucius also collected and edited poetry, music, and other writings from a time that he called the golden age. His own teachings and sayings were later written down in a book called the *Analects*.

3 **Double-check your notes.** Compare them to the section. Decide whether your notes give a clear picture of the whole section.

Review and Activities

Reviewing Main Ideas

1. Explain the importance of the extended family in early Chinese life.
2. Why were the early Chinese unaware of other ancient civilizations in Egypt, Mesopotamia, and India?
3. Give two examples of the teachings of Confucius.
4. Describe why Confucius died a disappointed man, but was honored by the Chinese more after his death.
5. Describe three actions the emperor Shi Huangdi took to unite China.
6. Why did the Han dynasty promote the ideas of Confucius?
7. Name two achievements of the Han dynasty, and explain their importance.

Reviewing Key Terms

Match the definitions in Column I with the key terms in Column II.

Column I

1. a kind of money
2. a fine yellow soil
3. protective wall built along rivers to hold back the waters
4. several generations of closely related people
5. a system of beliefs and values
6. a valuable cloth made in China
7. group of people who carry out the government's work
8. local leader of armed bands

Column II

a. extended family
b. dike
c. civil service
d. loess
e. currency
f. philosophy
g. warlord
h. silk

Critical Thinking

1. **Recognizing Cause and Effect** How did the harsh rule of Shi Huangdi help Liu Bang come to power?
2. **Drawing Conclusions** From what you know about the teachings of Confucius, do you think he would approve of the way people live today in the United States? Why or why not?

Graphic Organizer

Copy the chart onto a sheet of paper. Then fill in the empty boxes to complete the chart.

	Qin Dynasty	Han Dynasty
Important Emperors		
Impact of Dynasty on China		

Map Activity

Ancient China
For each place listed below, write the letter from the map that shows its location.

1. Huang He

2. Chang Jiang

3. North China Plain

4. Great Wall of China

5. Silk Road

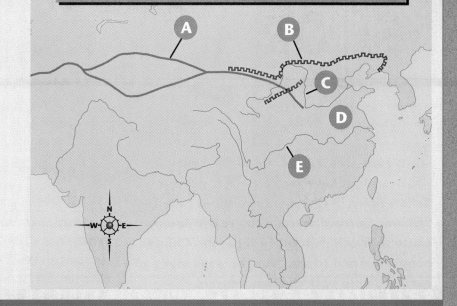

Writing Activity

Creating a Legend
Many legends about Confucius, such as the story about the woman grieving by her son's grave in Section 2, were written by Confucian scholars long after his death. Use what you know about Confucius and China to write a similar brief story. Use his ideas about family or government to write the moral, or lesson, of the story.

Internet Activity

Use a search engine to find **The Ancient China Home Page.** Click on Anthology. Then click on The Analects or The Tao Te Ching and read several chapters. Choose a section of one of the works that relates to your own life and explain the connection. Then make a booklet in which you can collect favorite teachings from different cultures.

Skills Review

Turn to the Skills Activity.
Review the directions for organizing information. Then answer the following: (a) Define key terms. (b) Why should you not copy everything you read as you take notes?

How Am I Doing?

Answer these questions to help you check your progress.

1. Can I describe the important geographic features of ancient China?

2. Do I understand the impact of the teachings of Confucius on Chinese society?

3. Can I name at least two emperors who were important in Chinese history?

4. Can I describe the cultural advances made during the Han dynasty?

5. What information from this chapter can I use in my book project?

Rivers That Flood

I n early history, people had no control over flooding rivers. The Huang He, or Yellow River, in China, is sometimes called "China's Sorrow" because its yearly floods cause so much damage. In time, the Chinese people learned to use dikes, or walls made of earth, to hold back the flood waters.

Purpose

In this activity, you will find out how dikes made from dirt can help protect people and the land from floods.

Materials

- large pan (about 9″ x 13″)
- dirt
- beaker of water
- collection bucket

Procedure

STEP ONE

Set up a flood box like the one shown in the first picture. First, pour dirt in the pan so it is about half full. Pat the dirt into the pan so that it is flat and firm, but not hard. Then, dig a small riverbed in the dirt with your finger. The riverbed should go from one narrow end of the pan to the other.

STEP TWO

Create a model of a river. Put something under one of the narrow ends of the pan so that the pan is on a slight angle. Slowly pour some water into the riverbed at the higher end. This model represents a normally flowing river. Notice how the water is held in place by the sides of the "riverbank." Pour the water out of the pan into a collection bucket. If some of the dirt slips out, rebuild your riverbed.

STEP THREE

Create a model of a flood. Put your pan of dirt on an angle again and refill your beaker of water. Now pour the water quickly into the

STEP ONE

STEP TWO

STEP THREE

riverbed so that some of the water spills over the riverbank. Notice what happens to the low-lying areas surrounding the river. Pour the water out of the pan into a collection bucket.

STEP FOUR

Build dikes out of dirt to contain the flood water. Make small hills out of dirt to run lengthwise along your model river. These dikes will run completely along the river on both sides of the river. Make one row about 1 inch from each side of the river. Make another row about 2 inches from each side of the river (1 inch from the first row you made).

STEP FIVE

See how the dikes can prevent flooding. Create another flood in your river by pouring water quickly into the riverbed. What happens when the water reaches the first dike? Repeat the activity with more water until the first dike is overflowed or washes away.

▲ **Flood Control** These ancient dikes made of earth help prevent flooding in the Hubei province of China.

Observations

1 When the river is running slowly, how well does the riverbank contain the water?

2 What happens to the plains surrounding the river when the river rises above its banks?

3 How did the second dike help protect the land?

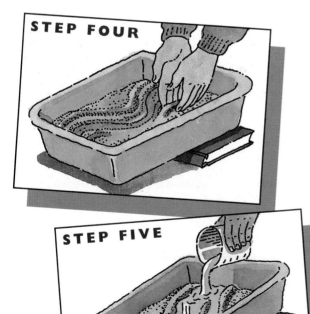

STEP FOUR

STEP FIVE

ANALYSIS AND CONCLUSION

1. How might flooding affect a large civilization living along the banks of a river?

2. How might dikes help civilizations near rivers grow and develop?

CHAPTER 6

Ancient Greece

The land of ancient Greece extended south into the Mediterranean Sea. It was a mountainous land. Ancient Greece also included a large number of islands in the Mediterranean. The ancient Greeks built colonies in places outside of Greece, such as the coast of Asia Minor, or modern-day Turkey. To help you get to know this region, carry out the following activities.

Describe the region
How would you describe the land of Greece? How would you compare the land of Greece to that of the United States?

Think about the people
From the map, make some guesses about how the people of ancient Greece earned their livelihood. What role did the sea probably have in their lives? Why do you think some Greeks left ancient Greece to build cities elsewhere?

The Rise of Greek Civilization

Reach Into Your Background

What makes the community where you live special? What makes it a community? Does it have traditions and customs of its own? What are they? What does your community share with its neighbors?

Questions to Explore

1. How did geography influence the development of civilization in Greece?
2. How did democracy develop in Athens?

Key Terms

peninsula   aristocrat
epic   tyrant
acropolis   democracy
city-state

Key People and Places

Homer
Solon
Troy

First there was nothing. Then came Mother Earth. The gods of Night and Day appeared next, and then starry Sky. Earth and Sky created the Twelve Titans (TYT unz). These great gods rebelled against their father Sky and took away his power. The youngest of the Titans, Cronos, ruled in his father's place. In time, Cronos had six children. The youngest, mighty Zeus (zoos), toppled Cronos from his throne.

With such words, the people of ancient Greece described the struggles of their gods. Like their gods, the people of Greece had to struggle for power and independence. Their struggles began with the land itself.

Greece's Geographic Setting

The land of Greece looks as if the sea had smashed it to pieces. Some pieces have drifted away to form small, rocky islands. Others barely cling to the mainland. Greece is a peninsula made up of peninsulas. A **peninsula** is an area of land surrounded by water on three sides. Look at the map. As you can see, no part of Greece is very far from the sea.

Mountains are the major landform of Greece. Greece's islands are mostly mountain peaks. Mountains wrinkle the mainland, so there are only small patches of farmland. Only about one fifth of Greece is good for growing crops. No wonder the Greeks became traders and sailors. At times, they even left Greece to found colonies far away.

What was life like for people living in Greece 3,000 years ago? In a way, the ancient Greeks were all islanders. Some lived on real islands completely surrounded by water or on small peninsulas. Others lived on

▼ The sea was an important part of life in ancient Greece. It inspired an artist to decorate this clay pot with soldiers riding dolphins.

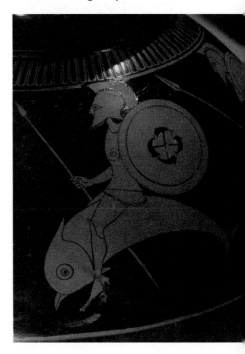

▶ Several typical geographic features appear in this picture of the northwestern coast of Greece. These features include a rocky coastline and rugged mountains. **Critical Thinking** How did the geographic features shown affect the way ancient people lived in this area?

Predict What effect do you think the geography of Greece had on the kind of communities that developed?

"land islands." Mountains cut off these small communities from each other. The geography of Greece made it hard for people from different communities to get together.

For this reason, it is no surprise that ancient Greek communities thought of themselves as separate countries. Each one developed its own customs and beliefs. Each believed its own land, traditions, and way of life were the best. And each was more than ready to go to war to protect itself. In fact, for most of their history, the Greeks were so busy fighting among themselves that it is easy to forget that they shared a common heritage, spoke the same language, and worshipped the same gods.

Greek Beginnings

All Greeks shared a wealth of stories and myths about their origins. The myths explained the creation of the universe and the features of nature. They described the adventures of Greek heroes and gods. Various stories told how cities and traditions came to be.

The most important stories told about the Trojan War, a long struggle between Greece and the city of Troy on the west coast of Asia Minor. All the great heroes from both regions joined in the war.

The Trojan War   The story of the Trojan War has everything a story should have—great battles, plots and schemes, loyalty and betrayal. According to the myths, a prince named Paris, from the wealthy city of Troy, was the guest of a Greek chieftain named Menelaus (men uh LAY us). Breaking the law of the gods, Paris kidnapped Menelaus' wife, Helen, and took her to Troy. To get Helen back, the Greek chieftains sent a huge army to attack Troy.

For ten long years, the war dragged on. Many heroes on both sides perished. At last, the Greeks conquered Troy by a trick—the Trojan Horse. The Greeks burned and looted Troy and then returned home.

Two **epics,** or long poems, about the Trojan War survive today. They are the *Iliad* and the *Odyssey.* The *Iliad* tells about a quarrel between Greek leaders in the last year of the war. The *Odyssey* describes the adventures of the hero Odysseus (oh DIS ee us) as he struggles to return to his homeland from Troy.

These epics may have been composed by many people, but they are credited to a poet called Homer. The poems were important to the Greeks. They taught them what their gods were like and how the noblest of their heroes behaved. Today, people think these poems came from stories memorized by several poets and passed down by word of mouth through many generations. Homer may have been the last and greatest in this line of poets who told about the Trojan War.

Ask Questions What would you like to know about the Trojan War?

Trojan Horse

Sissy Pachiadaki
age 12
Greece

This picture shows how the Trojan Horse helped the Greeks conquer Troy. Greek warriors hid inside a huge wooden horse. The horse was rolled to the city gates. The Trojans thought it was a gift to the gods, so they brought it into their city. During the night, the Greek soldiers climbed out of the horse and let the rest of their army into Troy.

◄These warriors decorate a vase from the 500s B.C. The background is the natural color of the baked clay. The black figures were painted on.

The Dark Ages of Greece Not long after the end of Troy, civilization in Greece collapsed. No one knows exactly why. Life went on, but poverty was everywhere. People no longer traded for food and other goods beyond Greece. They had to depend on what they could raise themselves. Some were forced to move to islands and to the western part of Asia Minor. The art of writing disappeared.

These years, from the early 1100s B.C. to about 750 B.C., have been called Greece's Dark Ages. Without writing, people had to depend on word of mouth to keep their traditions and history alive. Old traditions were remembered only in the myths that were told and retold.

Greece's Dark Ages were not completely bleak, however. During this time, families gradually began to resettle in places where they could grow crops and raise animals. Some of these family farms may have developed into villages. When they chose places to build their farms, people favored places near rocky, protected hills where they would be safe from attack. The name for such a place was **acropolis,** meaning "high city."

Governing the City-States

Sometime around 750 B.C., villages in a small area probably joined together to form a city in the shadow of an acropolis. At that time, each city began to develop its own traditions and its own form of government and laws. Each one was not only a city, but also a separate independent state. Today, we call these tiny nations **city-states.** Each included a city and the villages and fields surrounding it. Hundreds of Greek city-states grew up, each more or less independent.

Troy Discovered Over the years, people came to believe that Troy and the Trojan War were fiction. An amateur archaeologist, Heinrich Schliemann, disagreed. In the late 1800s he used clues in the *Iliad* to pinpoint the location of Troy. When he and later archaeologists dug there, they found nine layers of ruins from ancient cities. One was possibly the Troy of the *Iliad* and the *Odyssey*.

156   THE ANCIENT WORLD

Aristocracy: Nobles Rule The earliest rulers of city-states were probably chieftains or kings who were military leaders. By the end of Greece's Dark Ages, most city-states were ruled by **aristocrats,** members of the rich and powerful families. Aristocrats controlled most of the good land. They could afford horses, chariots, and the best weapons to make themselves stronger than others.

A New Type of Ruler As the Greeks sailed to foreign ports trading olive oil, marble, and other products, the city-states became richer. A middle class of merchants and artisans developed. They wanted some say in the government of their cities. These people could not afford to equip themselves with horses and chariots for war. However, they could afford armor, swords, and spears. With these weapons, large groups of soldiers could fight effectively on foot. Gradually, military strength in the cities shifted from aristocrats to merchants and artisans.

As a result of these changes, aristocratic governments were often overthrown and replaced by rulers called tyrants. A **tyrant** was a ruler who seized power by force. Tyrants were usually supported by the middle and working classes. Today, we think of tyrants as being cruel and violent. That was true of some Greek tyrants, but others ruled wisely and well.

Democracy: Rule by the People Eventually, the people of many city-states overthrew tyrants who were too harsh. A few cities moved to a form of government called **democracy.** In a democracy, citizens govern themselves. The city-state in which democracy was most fully expressed was Athens.

▼ The Acropolis in Athens was known for its beautiful temples. It was also a fortress. During wartime, people moved to the Acropolis where the enemy could not easily reach them.

Symbols of Democracy

In this carving (right), the woman stands for democracy. She is crowning a man seated on a throne. He stands for the Athenian people. The carving reminded the people of Athens of their duty to take part in government. Greek citizens served on juries at trials. Bronze plates like this one (below) were used to identify and choose members of juries.

Connect Would you like to have lived under the democracy in Athens? Why or why not?

About 594 B.C., a wise Athenian leader called Solon won the power to reform the laws. Solon was well known for his fairness. His laws reformed both the economy and the government of Athens. One of his first laws canceled all debts and freed citizens who had been enslaved for having debts. Another law allowed any male citizen of Athens aged 18 or older to have a say in debating important laws. These laws and others allowed Athens to become the leading democracy of the ancient world.

However, not everyone living in ancient Athens benefited from democracy. Only about one in five Athenians was a citizen. Some of the people living in Athens were enslaved. These people did not take part in democracy. Nor did women and foreigners. But the men who were citizens of Athens were free and self-governing.

SECTION 1 REVIEW

1. **Define** (a) peninsula, (b) epic, (c) acropolis, (d) city-state, (e) aristocrat, (f) tyrant, (g) democracy.

2. **Identify** (a) Homer, (b) Solon, (c) Troy.

3. Describe the three kinds of governments that developed in the Greek city-states after the Dark Ages.

4. What group of Athenians benefited most from democracy? Why?

Critical Thinking

5. **Recognizing Cause and Effect** How did the mountains in Greece contribute to the rise of city-states?

Activity

6. **Writing to Learn** Describe conditions in Greece during the period between the 1100s B.C. and the 700s B.C. Why are these years referred to as Greece's Dark Ages?

Greek Religion, Philosophy, and Literature

Reach Into Your Background

Think about the things that make the United States a good place to live. What do you like about living here? How would you describe life in the United States to someone from another country? What would you say were the most important achievements of the United States?

Questions to Explore

1. What were some accomplishments of the Golden Age?

2. How did Greek philosophers try to understand the world?

Key Terms

tribute   philosopher
immortal   tragedy

Key People and Places

Pericles
Parthenon
Socrates

> **"O**ur constitution does not copy the laws of neighboring states. We are a pattern to other cities rather than imitators. Our constitution favors the many instead of the few. That is why it is called a democracy. If we look at the laws, we see they give equal justice to all . . . . Poverty does not bar the way, if a man is able to serve the state. . . . In short, I say that as a city we are the school for all Greece.**"**

These are the words of the Athenian leader Pericles (PEHR ih kleez). He was reminding the citizens that Athens was special. Pericles' words had special meaning: They were spoken during the first year of a war with Sparta, another Greek city-state. Eventually, it was Sparta that ended Athens' Golden Age of accomplishment.

▶ Pericles led the Athenians in peace and war. The helmet he wears reminds us that he was a skilled general.

Predict Why do you think the years from 479 B.C. to 431 B.C. are called the Golden Age?

The Golden Age of Athens

The years from 479 B.C. to 431 B.C. are called the Golden Age of Athens. During the Golden Age, Athens grew rich from trade and from silver mined by slaves in regions around the city. **Tribute,** or payments made to Athens by its allies, added to its wealth.

Athenians also made amazing achievements in the arts, philosophy, and literature. And democracy reached its high point. For about 30 years during the Golden Age, Pericles was the most powerful man in Athenian politics. This well-educated and intelligent man had the best interests of his city at heart. When he made speeches to the Athenians, he could move and persuade them.

Pericles was a member of an aristocratic family, but he supported democracy. Around 460 B.C., he became leader of a democratic group. He introduced reforms that strengthened democracy. The most important change was to have the city pay a salary to its officials. This meant that poor citizens could afford to hold public office.

The Flourishing Arts

Today, Pericles is probably best known for making Athens a beautiful city. In 480 B.C., during one of the city's many wars, the Acropolis of Athens had been destroyed. Pericles decided to rebuild the Acropolis

In Honor of Athena

and create new buildings to glorify the city. He hired the Greek world's finest architects and sculptors for the project.

Magnificent Architecture The builders of the new Acropolis brought Greek architecture to its highest point. Their most magnificent work was the Parthenon, a temple to the goddess Athena. The temple was made of fine marble. Rows of columns surrounded it on all four sides. Within the columns was a room that held the statue of Athena, made of wood, ivory, and gold. The statue rose 40 feet (12 m), as high as a four-story building.

Lifelike Sculpture The great statue of Athena disappeared long ago. However, much of the sculpture on the inside and outside of the temple still exists. Many of the scenes that decorate the Parthenon have three important characteristics. First, they are full of action. Second, the artist carefully arranged the figures to show balance and order. Third, the sculptures are lifelike and accurate. However, they are ideal, or perfect, views of humans and animals. These characteristics reflect the goal of Greek art. This goal was to present images of human perfection in a balanced and orderly way. Real people and animals would not look like these sculptures.

The Golden Rectangle Greek architects based the design of their buildings on a figure called the Golden Rectangle. A Golden Rectangle is one with the long sides about one and two thirds times the length of the short sides. The Greeks thought Golden Rectangles made buildings more pleasing to look at. Modern architects have also used the Golden Rectangle.

It took the Athenians 15 years to build the Parthenon (left), considered the home on Earth of the goddess Athena. Its beauty still crowns the city of Athens. The graceful riders (far left, on facing page) are part of a sculptured procession. They were carved on the inner wall of the Parthenon.

The Search for Knowledge

Greeks worshipped a family of gods and goddesses called the Twelve Olympians. Each ruled different areas of human life. The chart on the next page gives you more information about the Olympians.

Greek Religion   Wherever the Greeks lived, they built temples to the gods. Since the gods had human forms, they also had many human characteristics. The main difference between gods and humans was that the gods were perfect in form and had awesome power. Also, the gods were **immortal,** which meant they lived forever.

In addition to the 12 great gods led by Zeus, the Greeks worshipped many lesser ones. They also honored mythical heroes like Achilles (uh KIL eez), who had done great deeds during the Trojan War. The story of Achilles is told in the *Iliad*.

Greek Science and Philosophy   Most Greeks believed that their gods were the source of all natural events. But a few thinkers disagreed. About 150 years before the Golden Age of Athens, some people thought about ways besides myths to understand the world.

These people came to be called **philosophers.** They believed that people could use the power of mind and reason to understand natural events. One of the first philosophers, Thales (THAY leez), believed that water was the basic material of the world. Everything was made from it. Over the years, other philosophers had other ideas about the universe. They did not do experiments. But they were careful observers and good thinkers. Democritus (dih MAHK ruh tus), who lived in the 400s B.C., thought that everything was made of tiny particles he called atoms. More than 2,000 years later, science showed he was right.

During the Golden Age and later, several important philosophers taught in Athens. One was a man called Socrates (SOCK ruh teez). People in the market-place of Athens could not help but notice this sturdy, round-faced man. He was there at all hours of the day, eagerly discussing wisdom and goodness.

Socrates wanted people to consider the true meaning of qualities such as justice and courage. To do this, he asked

Predict What kind of gods do you think the Greeks worshipped?

► The ancient Greeks worshipped many gods. One of them was Athena, the goddess of wisdom.

A Family of Gods

God or Goddess	Description
Zeus (zoos)	King of the gods and goddesses. Ruler of the sky and storms. Lord of the thunderbolt. Protector of the law.
Hera (HIR uh)	Wife and queen to Zeus. Goddess of marriage and women.
Apollo (uh PAHL oh)	Son of Zeus. Handsome young god of poetry and music.
Athena (uh THEE nuh)	Zeus' wise daughter. Goddess of crafts. War goddess who defended her cities, including Athens.
Poseidon (poh SY duhn)	Zeus' brother. Ruler of the sea and cause of earthquakes. Lord of horses.

Chart Study The Greeks considered these five gods to be the most powerful of the Twelve Olympians. **Critical Thinking** Which of these gods were concerned with the way people lived? Which were related to natural events?

▼ This bronze statue of the god Poseidon was made about 460 B.C.

questions that made others think about their beliefs. Sometimes they became angry, because Socrates often showed them that they didn't know what they were talking about. "Know thyself," was his most important lesson.

Socrates' questions frightened many Athenians. This man challenged all the values of Athens. In 399 B.C., Socrates was brought to trial. The authorities accused him of dishonoring the gods and misleading young people. He was condemned to death. Friends visited Socrates in prison and urged him to flee. He replied that escape would be unacceptable behavior. He calmly drank poison and died.

READ ACTIVELY

Connect How would you feel toward Socrates if he questioned your values?

Greek Drama

What do today's plays, movies, and television shows have in common with Athens? The answer is surprising. The Athenians were the first people to write dramas. Among the city's greatest achievements were the plays written and produced there in the 400s B.C., during the Golden Age. These plays soon became popular all over the Greek world.

Tragedy Some of the most famous Greek plays were tragedies. A **tragedy** is a serious story that usually ends in disaster for the main character. Often, tragedies told of fictional humans who were destroyed when forced to make impossible choices. A Greek tragedy consisted of several scenes that featured the characters of the story. Between the scenes, a chorus chanted or sang poems. In most plays, the author used the chorus to give background information, comment on the events, or praise the gods.

Performances of tragedies were part of contests held during religious festivals. At the main festival at Athens in the spring, three playwrights entered four plays apiece in the contest. The city chose wealthy citizens to pay the bills for these dramatic contests.

Comedy Comic writers also competed at the dramatic festivals. During the 400s B.C. in Athens, these poets wrote comedies that made fun of well-known citizens and politicians and also made jokes about the customs of the day. Because of the freedom in Athens, people accepted the humor and jokes.

▶ **Theater at Epidaurus** This is the most famous of ancient Greek theaters. The seating area, which held 14,000 people, is built into a hillside. The round space, or orchestra, was where the action took place and the chorus danced and sang. The theater is still used for plays today. It is so well constructed that everyone can easily hear the words of the play.

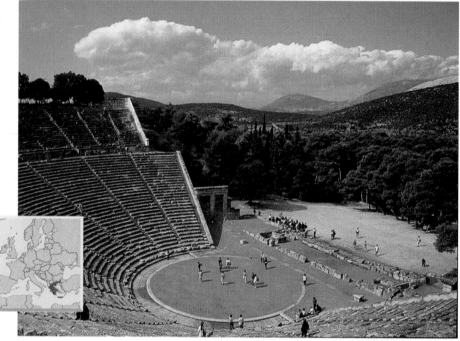

SECTION 2 REVIEW

1. Define (a) tribute, (b) immortal, (c) philosopher, (d) tragedy.

2. Identify (a) Pericles, (b) Parthenon, (c) Socrates.

3. What part did religion play in Athenian achievements during the Golden Age?

4. According to Greek philosophers, how could people understand natural events?

Critical Thinking

5. Drawing Conclusions Why do you think Pericles called Athens "the school of all Greece"?

Activity

6. Writing to Learn Write a brief essay describing the achievements that Athenians made during the Golden Age.

Daily Life of the Ancient Greeks

BEFORE YOU READ

Reach Into Your Background

Ask yourself the following questions about your daily life at home and at school. How does the climate of your region affect your daily life? Who does the work in your home to keep things running?

Questions to Explore

1. What was life like during the Golden Age of Greece?
2. What was the difference between the daily lives of men, women, and slaves in Athens?

Key Terms
agora

Key Places
Athens

The light from the courtyard was still gray when the young boy awoke. The boy sat up on his hard bed and felt the air on his face. He had to get up for school. The boy swallowed his breakfast, pulled his cloak around him, and left the house. Others inside were just beginning to stir. Soon, the household would be starting the day's weaving and other chores.

On the way to school, the boy met other students. All were carrying wooden tablets covered with wax. They would write their lessons on the tablets. They talked about their lesson, a long passage of history that they had to memorize.

The best part of the day came after school. Then, the boy spent the afternoon at the training ground. All the boys exercised and practiced wrestling and throwing a flat plate called a discus. They might watch older athletes training to compete in the Olympic Games, held in honor of Zeus.

In the Marketplace

On their way to school, the boys passed through the Agora (AG uh ruh) of Athens. The Acropolis was the center of Athens' religious life, and the Agora was the center of its public life. It was not far from the Acropolis, which rose in splendor above it. All Greek

▼ This statue captures a Greek athlete as he throws a discus. This event is still part of the Olympic Games.

READ ACTIVELY

Visualize Try to visualize people talking and carrying on their business in the Athenian Agora.

cities had **agoras,** or public market and meeting places. Athens' Agora was probably the busiest and most interesting of them all.

In the morning, many Athenian men wandered to the Agora. They liked being outdoors. The mild climate of Athens made it possible to carry on business in the open. In the Agora, the men talked of politics and philosophy. Sometimes they just gossiped.

As they talked, they heard the cries of vendors, or sellers of goods, and the haggling over prices. Some people came eager to find bargains. The streets were lined with shops. Farmers and artisans also sold their

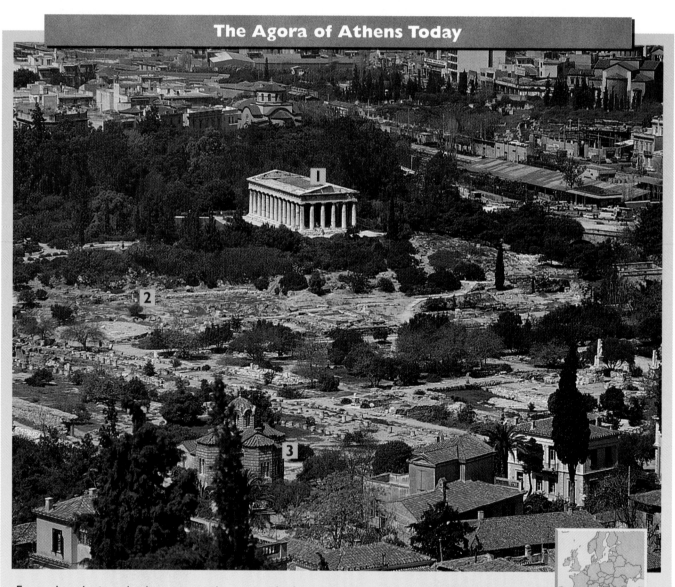

The Agora of Athens Today

For archaeologists, the Agora is a rich source of information about ancient Athens.
1. The temple of Hephaistos, god of metalworking
2. Buildings important to Athenian democracy. They include the Bouleterion, where laws were written, and the round Tholos, the workplace for citizens who ran the government.
3. The Middle Stoa. Stoae (STOH eye) were long buildings lined with columned walkways. Behind the columns were shops and offices.

wares from stands set up under shady trees. Just about any food an Athenian would want could be found in the Agora. Everyday goods were also for sale—sheep's wool, pottery, hardware, cloth, and books.

Temples and government buildings lined the Agora. One building was headquarters for Athens' army. Another was a prison. A board displayed public notices such as new laws and upcoming court cases.

Life at Home

The splendor of public buildings in Athens contrasted with the simplicity of people's houses, even in the Golden Age. Throughout Greece, private homes were plain. Made of mud bricks, they consisted of rooms set around an open courtyard hidden from the street. The courtyard was the center of the household. Other rooms might include a kitchen, storerooms, a dining room, and bedrooms. Some homes even had bathrooms. But water had to be carried from a public fountain.

Like homes, Greek food was simple. Breakfast might be just bread. For midday meals, the Athenian might add cheese or olives to the bread. Dinner would be a hot meal that was more filling. It might consist of fish and vegetables followed by cheese, fruit, and even cakes sweetened with honey. Most Athenians ate little meat. Even wealthy families only ate meat during religious festivals.

Slavery in Ancient Greece

It was the job of Greek women to spin thread and weave it into cloth. If these women were wealthy, they owned slaves to help them. Slaves did a great deal of work throughout the city-states of Greece. No one knows for sure, but historians

Greek Vase Painting The Athenians were known for their beautiful pottery. They decorated vases, jars, and cups with black or reddish-tan figures. Many scenes were mythological, but others showed Athenian daily life.

▶ In this school scene, a teacher holds a scroll showing the first words of the *Odyssey*. The boy may be reciting them from memory.

estimate that as many as 100,000 slaves may have lived in Athens. That is almost one third of the population. Today, we consider slavery a crime. But almost no one questioned it in ancient times, even in democratic Athens.

Many free people became enslaved when they were captured by armies during war or by pirates while traveling on ships. Some slaves were the children of slaves. A large number in Greece were foreigners, because some Greeks were uncomfortable owning other Greeks. Enslaved people did many kinds of work. Some provided labor on farms. Others dug silver and other metals in the mines. Still others assisted artisans by making pottery, constructing buildings, or forging weapons and armor. Most Greek households could not run without slaves. They cooked and served food, tended children, and wove cloth.

It is hard to make general statements about how enslaved people were treated. Household slaves may have had the easiest life. Often they

Connect If you were a ruler, how would you change Greek society so everyone had equal rights?

▶ This carved grave marker, or stele, shows Hegeso, an Athenian woman, choosing a jewel from a box held by an enslaved girl.

were treated like members of the family. The slaves who worked in the mines suffered the most. The work was not only physically tiring, but also extremely dangerous. Slaves in the mines did not live long.

Women in Athens

If you had walked through the Agora, you might have been surprised to see that most of the people there were men. If you had asked where the women were, an Athenian man might have replied, "At home."

Home was where most Athenian women spent their days. They had almost none of the freedom their husbands, sons, and fathers took for granted. They could not take any part in politics. Nor could they vote. They could not own property. About the only official activity allowed them was to be priestesses in religious groups.

Running the home and family was the job of women. In some wealthy families, men and women had completely separate quarters. Women organized the spinning and weaving, looked after supplies of food and wine, and cared for young children. They also kept track of the family finances. If a family was wealthy enough to have slaves, they were the woman's responsibility as well. She directed them, trained them, and cared for them when they were sick.

Women throughout Greece did important work. No Greek man would have denied it. Yet women were expected to be almost invisible. As Pericles said: "The greatest glory will belong to the woman who is least talked about by men, whether they praise her or find fault with her."

▼ Making clothing for the family was the job of the Greek wife and her enslaved servants. The women wove woolen cloth on large standing looms like the one pictured on this vase from the 500s B.C.

SECTION 3 REVIEW

1. **Define** agora.

2. **Identify** Athens.

3. What place was the center of activity for men during the Golden Age?

4. How did the lives of men, women, and slaves in Athens differ?

Critical Thinking

5. **Identify Central Issues** What do you think was the most important aspect of life in Athens? Why?

Activity

6. **Writing to Learn** Write a journal entry about your day at school that covers the same events as those discussed in this section. Discuss who wakes you up, what you eat for breakfast, and what you do after school. How does your day compare with that of the Greek boy you read about at the beginning of this section?

Athens and Sparta

TWO CITIES IN CONFLICT

Reach Into Your Background

All people are different. Because of their backgrounds, people place different values on different things. How are some of your values different from those of some of your friends?

Questions to Explore

1. How did Athens differ from Sparta?
2. What was the result of the war between Athens and Sparta?

Key Terms

plague
blockade

Key Places

Sparta
Persia
Marathon

▶ This mysterious bronze warrior from Sparta is wrapped in a cloak and wears a helmet that hides his face.

The boy stood still and straight beside his companions as their trainer approached. "You," the trainer barked. "Are you sick? Don't think you'll get out of sword practice—and why are you holding your belly? Hiding something?"

The trainer gave the boy's cloak a sharp tug. It fell to the ground, freeing a fox that streaked off into the underbrush. The boy sank down to the ground, shaking. His cloak was a crimson red. His side was shredded with deep cuts and bites. The boy had stolen the fox and hidden it beneath his cloak.

Later, the boy died from his wounds. The people of his city, Sparta, celebrated his life. He had endured terrible pain without giving any sign of his distress. To the Spartans, this was the sign of true character.

A Spartan Life

This Spartan story of the boy and the fox may be true or not. Yet it tells us much about the people of Sparta, a city-state in southern Greece.

If the life of the citizens of Athens was free and open, the life of the citizens of Sparta was the opposite. Life in Sparta was harsh and even cruel. The Spartans themselves were tough, silent, and grim. Sparta's army easily equaled Athens' in the 400s B.C. However, Sparta never came close to equaling Athens' other achievements.

Like the warrior on the previous page, Sparta's sheer mountains sometimes wear a cloak of mystery. The city lies in a fertile valley with mountains on three sides. Sparta spent its money and energy on its army instead of fine buildings. Today, few ruins remain to tell us about this important city-state.

A Different Kind of City   In its early days, Sparta seemed to be developing as the other Greek cities were. Then, in the 600s B.C., wars inside and outside the city led to changes in government and the way people lived. The changes turned Sparta into an awesome war machine. The city-state made one basic rule: Always put the city's needs above your own.

Early in its history, the Spartans conquered the land around their city. They turned the conquered people into helots, or slaves. Helots (HEL uts) did all the farm work on the land owned by Spartan citizens. This left the Spartans free to wage war. However, the helots far outnumbered the Spartans. Living in fear of a helot revolt, the Spartans turned their city into an armed camp. They treated the helots very harshly.

Growing Up in Sparta   The life of every Spartan was in the hands of the government from the first moment of life. Only the healthiest children were raised. This was because the Spartans wanted only the healthiest males as its soldiers. Training began early. At seven, a Spartan boy left his mother to live in barracks with other boys. His training continued for the next 13 years.

By the age of 12, a boy had spent long hours practicing with swords and spears. He had only one cloak and a thin mat to sleep on. He could hardly live on the food he was given, so he was urged to steal. This was to help him learn how to live off the land during a war. However, if the boy was caught, he was severely punished. After all, if a soldier was caught stealing, he would probably be killed. Boys were expected to bear pain, hardship, and punishment in silence.

CITIZEN HEROES

Working Together In one of the wars against the Persians, some 6,000 Greeks had to defend a mountain pass leading into southern Greece. They faced almost 200,000 Persians. Most of the Greeks retreated, but 300 Spartan soldiers stood their ground. All died in the battle. They didn't hold back the Persians. But they earned undying praise for their brave sacrifice.

Like their brothers, girls also trained and competed in wrestling and spear throwing. No one expected the girls to become soldiers. But Spartans did believe that girls who grew up strong and healthy would have strong, healthy children. Spartan women had a somewhat better life than women in other Greek city-states. They were allowed to own land and even take some part in business.

Spartan life lacked the beauty and pleasures found in Athens and some other Greek cities. But Spartan warriors were known for their skill and bravery. The Spartan fighting force played a key role in the Greek wars against the Persians, a people who lived across the Aegean Sea, east of Greece.

The Persians Invade

Much of the history of the Greeks tells of wars they fought among themselves. But near the beginning of the 400s B.C., a new threat loomed. This was the growing might of Persia. By 520 B.C., the Persians had already gained control of the Greek colonies on the west coast of Asia Minor.

In the fall of 490 B.C., a huge force of thousands of Persians landed in Greece itself. They gathered at Marathon, about 25 miles (40 km) north of Athens. The Athenians hastily put together a small army. The Persians outnumbered them by at least two to one. For several days the armies stared tensely at each other across the plain of Marathon.

Then, without warning the Athenians rushed the Persians, who were overwhelmed by the furious attack. By the time the battle was over, the Athenians had killed 6,400 Persians and lost only 192 soldiers themselves. In a few hours, this tiny state had defeated the giant that had come to destroy it.

◀ A Persian duels with a Greek warrior (left) on this vase from the 500s B.C. To the left is the hand of another Persian raising a bow.

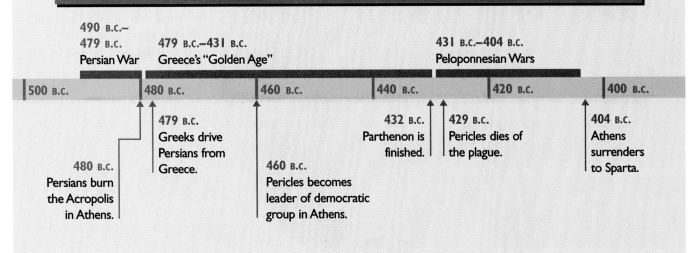

Classical Greece, 500 B.C. to 400 B.C.

490 B.C.– 479 B.C. Persian War

479 B.C.–431 B.C. Greece's "Golden Age"

431 B.C.–404 B.C. Peloponnesian Wars

| 500 B.C. | 480 B.C. | 460 B.C. | 440 B.C. | 420 B.C. | 400 B.C. |

479 B.C. Greeks drive Persians from Greece.

480 B.C. Persians burn the Acropolis in Athens.

460 B.C. Pericles becomes leader of democratic group in Athens.

432 B.C. Parthenon is finished.

429 B.C. Pericles dies of the plague.

404 B.C. Athens surrenders to Sparta.

▲ The time line shows important events in the 400s B.C., the high point in ancient Greece's history.

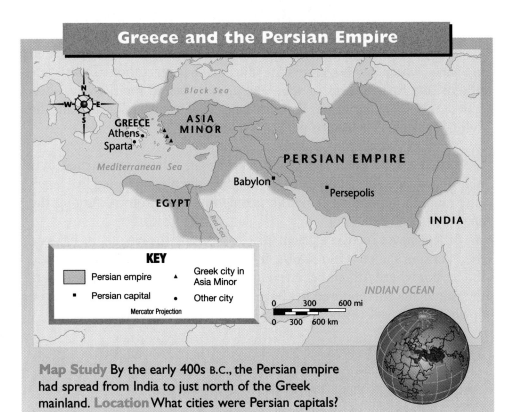

Greece and the Persian Empire

KEY

Persian empire ▲ Greek city in Asia Minor

■ Persian capital ● Other city

Mercator Projection

0   300   600 mi
0   300   600 km

Map Study By the early 400s B.C., the Persian empire had spread from India to just north of the Greek mainland. **Location** What cities were Persian capitals?

LINKS ACROSS TIME

A Run from Marathon
After Marathon, the Athenians sent their fastest runner to tell the people of Athens of the victory. His chest heaving, the runner covered the distance to the city and shouted to the people "Rejoice! We have won." Then he dropped dead. This valiant run is still honored today every time anyone runs the 26.2 miles of a marathon race.

After Persia: Athenian Empire

After several more battles, the Persians were finally defeated. The influence of Athens spread over much of eastern Greece. Athens joined itself with other city-states and supported democratic groups within them. In time, these cities became more like subjects than allies.

◀ The Athenians put great faith in their fleet of warships. These ships played a huge role in defeating Persia.

Sparta and Athens at War Athens may have been a democracy at home. But it began to act unfairly toward the other city-states. At first the allies had paid tribute to Athens for protection in case the Persians caused more trouble. But later Athens used this money for the Parthenon and other projects. In response, the people of these city-states began to fear and resent Athens' power. They looked to Sparta, which had not joined the alliance, to protect them. In 431 B.C., Athens and Sparta went to war. The conflict lasted for 27 years. It is called the Peloponnesian War, because Sparta was located in the Peloponnesus, or southern part of Greece.

The Fall of Athens Early in the war, Athens was struck by a plague, or widespread disease. By the time the plague ended five years later, about one third of Athens's people had died from it. Among the dead was Pericles.

Athens never recovered from its losses during the plague. In 405 B.C., the Spartans staged a blockade, in which they surrounded and closed the harbor where Athens received food shipments. Starving and beaten, the Athenians surrendered in 404 B.C. The victorious Spartans knocked down Athens' walls. Athens never again dominated the Greek world.

READ ACTIVELY

Connect If you lived in another city-state, how would you feel about the power of Athens? Why?

SECTION 4 REVIEW

1. **Define** (a) plague, (b) blockade.
2. **Identify** (a) Sparta, (b) Persia, (c) Marathon.

3. How was the life of citizens of Athens more free and open than the life of citizens of Sparta?
4. What events led to the war between Athens and Sparta?

Critical Thinking
5. **Recognizing Cause and Effect** How did the attitude of the people of Athens lead to their own downfall?

Activity
6. **Writing to Learn** Pretend you are the trainer in the story that begins this section. Write a report explaining the event to other Spartan officers. Be sure to write the story from the Spartan point of view.

The Spread of Greek Culture

Reach Into Your Background

Who are your heroes? Are there people living today or in the past whom you admire? Why are they your heroes?

What can you do to become more like them?

Questions to Explore

1. What role did the conquests of Alexander the Great play in spreading Greek culture?
2. What advances in science did the Greeks make after Alexander's death?

Key Terms

barbarian
assassinate
Hellenistic

Key People and Places

King Philip
Macedonia
Alexander the Great
Alexandria
Euclid
Archimedes

King Philip of Macedonia (mas uh DOH nee uh) had not wasted the money he spent on Greek tutors for his son. Young Alexander was a fine student— and an eager one. The boy wanted to learn as much as he could, especially about the ideas and deeds of the Greeks.

The kingdom of Macedonia lay just north of Greece. Alexander thought of himself as Greek and spoke the Greek language. But people who lived to the south in such cities as Athens and Sparta did not really accept the Macedonians as Greeks. They thought the Macedonians were **barbarians,** or wild, uncivilized people.

Alexander's tutor was the Greek philosopher Aristotle (AIR uh staht ul). Aristotle taught the boy Greek literature, philosophy, and science. Aristotle also passed on his strong feelings that the Greeks were far better than other people and, therefore, deserved to rule.

Alexander loved his tutor, but his role model was Achilles, the warrior hero of the *Iliad*. One day, Alexander vowed, he would visit the site of Troy and lay a wreath on the tomb of his hero.

◄▼ This carving of King Philip of Macedonia (left), illustrates his strength and energy. The silver coin (below) is stamped with a portrait of his son, Alexander.

Alexander Builds an Empire

Before King Philip seized power in 359 B.C., Macedonia was poor and divided. Philip united Macedonia and built an army even stronger than Sparta's. With such an army and with his talent for waging war, Philip captured one Greek city-state after another. By 338 B.C., Philip controlled all of Greece. No one had ever done this.

Alexander Comes to the Throne Philip then planned to attack Persia. But in 336 B.C., before he could carry out his plan, he was **assassinated,** or murdered, by a rival. At just 20 years old, Alexander became king. This was his chance to be as great as his hero Achilles.

Alexander the Great One of Alexander's first actions was to invade the Persian Empire. Within 11 years, he had conquered Persia, Egypt, and lands extending beyond the Indus River in the east. He earned the right to be called "Alexander the Great."

Alexander's energy and military genius helped him succeed. He drove himself and his army hard, advancing across vast lands at lightning speed. His soldiers grumbled, but they obeyed him. Wherever

Ask Questions Think of some things you would like to know about Alexander the Great and his deeds.

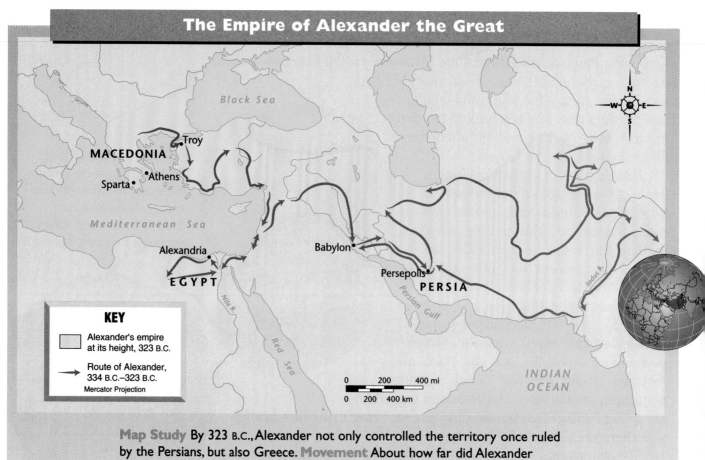

The Empire of Alexander the Great

KEY

Alexander's empire at its height, 323 B.C.

Route of Alexander, 334 B.C.–323 B.C.

Mercator Projection

0   200   400 mi
0   200   400 km

Map Study By 323 B.C., Alexander not only controlled the territory once ruled by the Persians, but also Greece. **Movement** About how far did Alexander travel when he traveled back to Babylon from the Indus River?

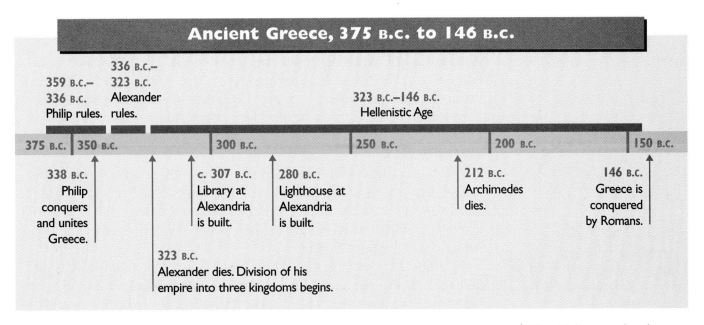

Ancient Greece, 375 B.C. to 146 B.C.

359 B.C.–336 B.C. Philip rules.

336 B.C.–323 B.C. Alexander rules.

323 B.C.–146 B.C. Hellenistic Age

375 B.C. | 350 B.C. | 300 B.C. | 250 B.C. | 200 B.C. | 150 B.C.

338 B.C. Philip conquers and unites Greece.

323 B.C. Alexander dies. Division of his empire into three kingdoms begins.

c. 307 B.C. Library at Alexandria is built.

280 B.C. Lighthouse at Alexandria is built.

212 B.C. Archimedes dies.

146 B.C. Greece is conquered by Romans.

▲ The Hellenistic Age began with the death of Alexander. How long did it last?

Alexander went, he established cities. Many of them he named after himself. Even today, there are numerous cities named Alexandria or Alexandropolis throughout western Asia. Alexander never stayed very long in his cities. He quickly pushed on. He never lost a battle.

At last, not far beyond the Indus River, his weary troops refused to go another step east. Alexander was angry, but he turned back. Alexander got as far as Babylon, where he came down with a fever. In 323 B.C., only 13 years after he came to the throne, Alexander died. Like the legendary warrior Achilles, he had died young. But he had gone far beyond the deeds of his hero. He had conquered practically all of the known world.

Greek Culture Spreads

Alexander's death spelled death for his empire. Within 50 years, the empire had broken into three main kingdoms. Each one was ruled by a family descended from one of his commanders. Although the empire broke apart, Greek culture remained alive and well in these new kingdoms.

The Hellenistic Kingdoms When Alexander took control of lands, he tried not to destroy the cultures of the defeated people. Instead, he hoped that in his new cities the local cultures would mix with Greek culture. Unfortunately, this did not happen in the three Hellenistic kingdoms, as they came to be called. Hellenistic comes from the word Hellas—the name Greeks gave their land.

The cities of the Hellenistic world were modeled after Greek cities. Greek kings ruled, and Greeks held the most important jobs. There were Greek temples and agoras. Citizens gathered at large theaters for performances of old Greek tragedies. The Greek language was spoken in the cities, though people in the countryside spoke local languages.

Hellenism in Egypt The greatest of all Hellenistic cities was Alexandria in Egypt. Alexander had founded this city in 332 B.C. at the edge of the Nile delta. Alexandria became the capital of Egypt. Over the years, it grew famous as a center for business and trade. Its double harbor was dominated by a huge lighthouse that rose about 350 feet (106 m) in the air. The tower was topped by a flame that guided ships safely into port.

The important Hellenistic cities were centers of learning. But Alexandria was greater than any of the rest. It boasted the largest library in the world, with half a million book rolls. Alexandria was the learning capital of the Greek world. Scholars and writers from all over came to use the huge library.

Mathematics and science also flourished at Alexandria. Around 300 B.C., a mathematician named Euclid (YOO klid) developed the branch of mathematics called geometry. He started with accepted mathematical laws. Then, he wrote carefully thought out, step-by-step proofs of mathematical principles. The proofs helped explain the qualities of such figures as squares, cubes, angles, triangles, and cones. Mathematicians today still use Euclid's system.

Visualize Try to visualize the huge, scroll-filled library at Alexandria.

▶ The great lighthouse at Alexandria, called the Pharos, was considered one of the Seven Wonders of the World.

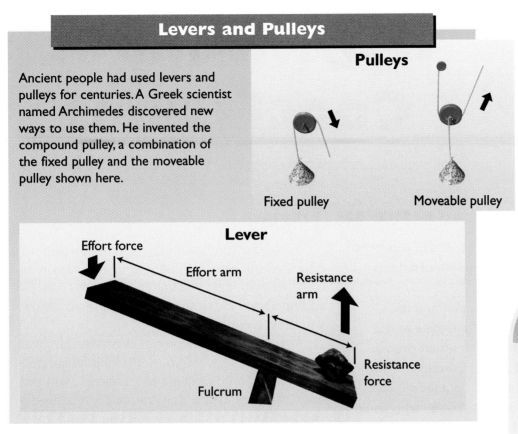

Levers and Pulleys

Ancient people had used levers and pulleys for centuries. A Greek scientist named Archimedes discovered new ways to use them. He invented the compound pulley, a combination of the fixed pulley and the moveable pulley shown here.

Pulleys

Fixed pulley

Moveable pulley

Lever

Effort force

Effort arm

Resistance arm

Resistance force

Fulcrum

The Earth and the Sun One scientist of the 200s B.C. rejected the idea that the Earth was the center of the universe. Aristarchus of Samos believed that the sun is at the center and that the Earth revolves around it. His idea did not catch on. Astronomers continued to base their work on an Earth-centered universe until the A.D. 1500s.

Have you ever heard that people of Christopher Columbus' time believed the Earth was flat? This is not accurate. In Hellenistic times, many scientists knew the Earth was round. A scientist named Eratosthenes (ehr uh TAHS thuh neez) even calculated the distance around the Earth. His answer, 24,662 miles (39,679 km), was very close.

Probably the greatest scientist of the times was Archimedes (ar kuh MEE deez). Archimedes discovered that people can use pulleys and levers to lift very heavy objects. One story says that he hoisted up a loaded ship with these devices. Once he boasted: "Give me a lever long enough and a place to stand on, and I will move the Earth."

SECTION 5 REVIEW

1. **Define** (a) barbarian, (b) assassinate, (c) Hellenistic.
2. **Identify** (a) King Philip, (b) Macedonia, (c) Alexander the Great, (d) Alexandria, (e) Euclid, (f) Archimedes.
3. What features of Greek culture could be seen in the Hellenistic kingdoms?
4. Describe the contributions of Euclid, Eratosthenes, and Archimedes.

Critical Thinking
5. **Identifying Central Issues** Why do you think Alexander the Great named so many cities after himself?

Activity
6. **Writing to Learn** Think of someone you consider a hero or a role model. Write a description of that person. Is he or she more like King Philip and Alexander or like Aristotle and Archimedes? Explain your answer.

Drawing Conclusions

The teacher looked right at Lisa when she asked, "How did the people of Athens feel about drama?"

Lisa swallowed hard. She had read the assignment, but there wasn't anything in the book about how Athenians felt about drama. She did remember a few facts, though. "They had a lot of theaters and put on a lot of plays. Sometimes they had contests to see who could write the best plays." Lisa hoped her answer was good enough.

"And so from all of that, can you tell how they felt about drama?" her teacher asked.

Lisa took a shot. "Well, I guess if they had so much of it they must have liked it ."

"Right! Good!"

Lisa breathed a sigh of relief. Of course the Athenians felt drama was important. And Lisa felt good about herself, having answered a tough question—about something that wasn't even in the book.

Get Ready

Lisa could answer the question because she drew a conclusion from what she read. Drawing conclusions means learning something more from what you read than just what is written. Drawing conclusions is a skill that will help you get the most from your schoolwork or any reading you do.

You draw conclusions by making intelligent, educated guesses. You base your conclusion on clues, or evidence, you find in what you read. By adding these clues to what you already know, you draw a conclusion.

You draw conclusions in everyday life, too. For example, suppose you see a long line of people waiting to buy tickets to a concert. You can draw the conclusion that the singer giving the concert is very popular, even if you do not know anything else about that performer.

Try It Out

Practice drawing a conclusion from this sentence.

All Spartan men served in the army.

You can draw the conclusion that the military was a central part of Spartan society. Notice that this conclusion is directly related to what you read, even though it is not stated in the sentence. The conclusion goes beyond what is written. You use what you already know to add to what you read. You already know that if half the population of a society does something, it must be an important part of that society.

Clues from what you read + What you already know = Conclusions about what you read

Apply the Skill

Read again the part of Section 1 in this chapter that tells about the Trojan War. Draw some conclusions.

1 Look for clues. The first sentence of the part about the war says, "The story of the Trojan War has everything a story should have—great battles, plots and schemes, loyalty and betrayal."

2 Think about what you already know. Think about stories you like to read or watch in the movies or on television.

3 Draw a conclusion based on what you read and what you already know. Why has the history of the Trojan War been so interesting to so many people through the years?

Explain how the conclusion you drew was based on clues in what you read plus what you already know. What other conclusions can you draw about the Trojan War?

The clue in this sentence tells me that the story of the Trojan War is about great battles.

I already know that I like stories about great battles.

What's my conclusion?

Review and Activities

Reviewing Main Ideas

1. What role did the sea and mountains play in the development of ancient Greece?
2. Explain the difference between aristocracy, tyranny, and democracy in ancient Greece.
3. List two ideas that governed Greek religions.
4. From what you have read about Greek art, history, religion, and philosophy, how would you describe the Greek attitude towards the achievements of human beings?
5. What was everyday life like in the Golden Age of Athens?
6. Describe the roles of women and slaves in Athenian life.
7. How did life in Sparta keep this city-state from achieving the kinds of things Athens achieved?
8. Describe the relationship of Athens to Sparta after their long war.
9. How did Greek culture spread from Greece to parts of Europe, Africa, and Southwest Asia?
10. Describe some advances made in science during the Hellenistic period.

Reviewing Key Terms

Use each key term below in a sentence that shows the meaning of the term.

1. peninsula
2. epic
3. acropolis
4. city-state
5. aristocrat
6. tyrant
7. democracy
8. tribute
9. immortal
10. philosopher
11. tragedy
12. agora
13. plague
14. blockade
15. barbarian
16. assassinate
17. Hellenistic

Critical Thinking

1. **Identifying Central Issues** What did the Greek city-states have in common? What kept them separate?
2. **Making Comparisons** Compare the way most ancient Greeks would have explained their world to the way the philosophers did.
3. **Cause and Effect** Athenians were proud of their culture and their city. How do you think that view was influenced by Athens' defeat by the Spartans?

Graphic Organizer

Copy the chart onto a separate sheet of paper. Then fill in the boxes to complete the chart.

Important Wars and Their Results	
Important People and What They Did	
Governments	
Culture/Literature/ Art/Science	

Map Activity

The Greek World

For each place listed below, write the letter from the map that shows its location.

1. Athens

2. Sparta

3. Macedonia

4. Marathon

5. Troy

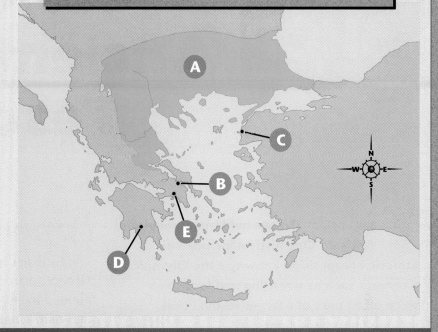

Writing Activity

Writing a Dialogue
Imagine that the Athenian boy from Section 3 met the Spartan boy from Section 4. The time is the Golden Age of Athens. Write a dialogue, or conversation, between them. Have each young man tell the other about how he was raised and educated. Have each defend the way of life and form of government in his own city.

Internet Activity

Use a search engine to find **The Ancient Greek World** site. Click on the links at the bottom of the page to explore the land, daily life, economy, and religion of the ancient Greeks. Write a report or give a presentation describing what life was like in ancient Greece. Be sure to include geographic and economic information.

Skills Review

Turn to the Skills Activity. Think again about the steps for drawing conclusions. Why is it important to consider what you already know as you are reading?

How Am I Doing?

Answer these questions to help you check your progress.

1. Do I understand how the geographical features of Greece affected life there in ancient times?

2. Can I describe ancient Greek religion, types of government, and cultural achievements?

3. Can I identify some events that shaped the history of the ancient Greek world?

4. What information from this chapter could I use in my book project?

Hold an Ancient Greek Festival

The ancient Greeks held many religious festivals. One festival included an athletic competition known as the Olympics. Contests such as wrestling and footraces were often part of a larger festival that included plays and feasts.

Purpose

To learn more about the culture of ancient Greece, plan a festival to share information about ancient Greek games, food, drama, art, and mathematical and scientific discoveries.

Plan a Festival

Read the five festival presentations described here and divide into groups to organize them.

PUT ON A PLAY

Act out an ancient Greek myth such as the story of Perseus and Medusa or Orpheus and the underworld. To tell the story, you might choose a narrator as well as actors. Introduce your performance with background information on each character in the myth.

PRESENT AN ART SHOW

Collect pictures of ancient Greek art. Find out what people or events the pictures represent. If possible, also find out how each kind of art was made. Write a caption for each picture and hang the picture in a "gallery" on your classroom wall.

DISCOVER ANCIENT KNOWLEDGE

Ancient Greeks contributed many ideas to the fields of math and science. Find out what kind of math they helped invent. Also, research one of their scientific ideas. For example, you might find out what the Greek astronomer Ptolemy thought about the universe. Create a poster that shows your findings in a way that people can understand. Add the poster to your classroom's gallery.

PLAN A FEAST

Write a menu for an ancient meal that includes some of the foods the Greeks might have eaten. How were each of the foods on your menu grown or produced in ancient Greece? Who grew the food? Who prepared it?

Links to Other Subjects

Performing a scene
from a Greek drama . . . . . . **Language Arts**

Researching Greek art . . . . **Art**

Explaining contributions
from ancient Greek
mathematicians or
scientists . . . . **Math, Science**

SPEAK ABOUT THE OLYMPICS

Research the Olympic Games in ancient Greece. Here are a few of the questions you should answer: Why were the Olympics held? What games did the spectators see? Could anyone compete in the games? Brainstorm for some other questions to answer. Then give a presentation about what you have learned. You can give your presentation by yourself or with a group.

ANALYSIS AND CONCLUSION

Write a summary describing what you learned from the festival. Be sure to answer the following questions in your summary.

1. What was the most interesting idea or fact you learned from each presentation?

2. Did the festival make you think of any new questions about ancient Greek drama, art, math, science, food, or athletic competitions? Think of at least three questions.

The Sirens

A GREEK MYTH
FROM *THE ADVENTURES OF ULYSSES*
RETOLD BY BERNARD EVSLIN

BEFORE YOU READ

Reach Into Your Background

Do television commercials make you want to buy the things they advertise? Have you ever been persuaded to do something because someone made it sound fun or exciting? Sometimes messages like this can make things appear better than they are.

Such messages can lead people in the wrong direction.

The Sirens (SY ruhnz) in this myth are creatures who use their songs to lead sailors to destruction. The hero Ulysses (yoo LIS eez) is warned about the Sirens as he tries to sail to his island home in Greece after the Trojan War. The clever and curious Ulysses had expected an easy journey home. Instead, he was delayed by adventures that tested his mind and spirit.

The tale of Ulysses and the Sirens comes from Homer's *Odyssey*. Ulysses is the name

the Roman people gave to the Greek hero Odysseus. Like Homer himself and other storytellers, Bernard Evslin has retold the ancient story of the Sirens in his own words. The events are the same as those in the *Odyssey*. But the author has added many details to make the story his own.

Questions to Explore

1. What does this story tell you about the technology of the Greeks?
2. What can you learn about the Greek idea of a hero from this story?

I n the first light of morning Ulysses awoke and called his crew about him.

"Men," he said. "Listen well, for your lives today hang upon what I am about to tell you. That large island to the west is Thrinacia, where we must make a landfall, for our provisions run low. But to get to the island we must pass through a narrow strait. And at the head of this strait is a rocky islet where dwell two sisters called Sirens, whose voices you must not hear. Now I

shall guard you against their singing, which would lure you to shipwreck, but first you must bind me to the mast. Tie me tightly, as though I were a dangerous captive. And no matter how I struggle, no matter what signals I make to you, *do not release me,* lest I follow their voices to destruction, taking you with me."

Thereupon Ulysses took a large lump of the beeswax that was used by the sail mender to slick his heavy thread and kneaded it

Thrinacia (thrih NAY shee uh) *n.* mythological island that might have been Sicily
strait *n.* narrow ocean passage between two pieces of land
islet *n.* small island

This Siren is part of a scene on a Greek vase made about 470 B.C. She flies over Ulysses' ship while he is tied to the mast.

in his powerful hands until it become soft. Then he went to each man of the crew and plugged his ears with soft wax; he caulked their ears so tightly that they could hear nothing but the thin pulsing of their own blood.

Then he stood himself against the mast, and the men bound him about with rawhide, winding it tightly around his body, lashing him to the thick mast.

They had lowered the sail because ships cannot sail through a narrow strait unless there is a following wind, and now each man of the crew took his place at the great oars. The polished blades whipped the sea into a froth of white water and the ship nosed toward the strait.

Ulysses had left his own ears unplugged because he had to remain in command of the ship and had need of his hearing. Every sound means something

upon the sea. But when they drew near the rocky islet and he heard the first faint strains of the Sirens' singing, then he wished he, too, had stopped his own ears with wax. All his strength suddenly surged toward the sound of those magical voices. The very hair of his head seemed to be tugging at his scalp, trying to fly away. His eyeballs started out of his head.

For in those voices were the sounds that men love:

Happy sounds like birds railing, sleet hailing, milk pailing. . . .

Sad sounds like rain leaking, trees creaking, wind seeking. . . .

Autumn sounds like leaves tapping, fire snapping, river lapping. . . .

Quiet sounds like snow flaking, spider waking, heart breaking. . . .

caulk *v.* to stop up and make tight
strain *n.* tune
surge *v.* to rise or swell suddenly
rail *v.* to scold
lap *v.* to splash in little waves

READ ACTIVELY

Predict How will Ulysses keep his men from hearing the voices of the Sirens?

READ ACTIVELY

Predict What do you think Ulysses will do when he hears the Sirens' song?

purl v. to make a soft murmuring sound like a flowing stream

spume n. foam

hawser (HAW zur) n. a large rope

▶ The rocky shore of Sicily where Greek myths said the Sirens lived.

It seemed to him then that the sun was burning him to a cinder as he stood. And the voices of the Sirens purled in a cool crystal pool upon their rock past the blue-hot flatness of the sea and its lacings of white-hot spume. It seemed to him he could actually see their voices deepening into a silvery, cool pool and must plunge into that pool or die a flaming death.

He was filled with such a fury of desire that he swelled his mighty muscles, burst the rawhide bonds like thread, and dashed for the rail.

But he had warned two of his strongest men—Perimedes (pehr ih MEE deez) and Eurylochus (yoo RIHL uh kus)—to guard him close. They seized him before he could plunge into the water. He swept them aside as if they had

been children. But they had held him long enough to give the crew time to swarm about him. He was overpowered—crushed by their numbers—and dragged back to the mast. This time he was bound with the mighty hawser that held the anchor.

The men returned to their rowing seats, unable to hear the voices because of the wax corking their ears. The ship swung about and headed for the strait again.

Louder now, and clearer, the tormenting voices came to Ulysses. Again he was aflame with a fury of desire. But try as he might he could not break the thick anchor line. He strained against it until he bled, but the line held.

The men bent to their oars and rowed more swiftly, for they saw the mast bending like a tall tree in a heavy wind, and they

feared that Ulysses, in his fury, might snap it off short and dive, mast and all, into the water to get at the Sirens.

Now they were passing the rock, and Ulysses could see the singers. There were two of them. They sat on a heap of white bones—the bones of shipwrecked sailors—and sang more beautifully than senses could bear. But their appearance did not match their voices, for they were shaped like birds, huge birds, larger than eagles. They had feathers instead of hair, and their hands and feet were claws. But their faces were the faces of young girls.

When Ulysses saw them he was able to forget the sweetness of their voices because their look was so fearsome. He closed his eyes against the terrible sight of these bird-women perched on their heap of bones. But when he closed his eyes he could not see their ugliness, then their voices maddened him once again, and he felt himself straining against the bloody ropes. He forced himself to open his eyes and look upon the monsters, so that the terror of their bodies would blot the beauty of their voices.

But the men, who could only see, not hear the Sirens, were so appalled by their aspect that they swept their oars faster and faster, and the black ship scuttled past the rock. The Sirens' voices sounded fainter and fainter and finally died away.

When Perimedes and Eurylochus saw their captain's face lose its madness, they unbound him, and he signaled to the men to unstop their ears. For now he heard the whistling gurgle of a whirlpool, and he knew that they were approaching the narrowest part of the strait, and must past between Scylla and Charybdis.

appall *v.* to horrify
aspect *n.* the way something looks
Scylla (SIL uh) *n.* a monster who ate sailors passing through the Straits of Messina between Italy and Sicily
Charybdis (kuh RIB dis) *n.* a monster in the form of a deadly whirlpool near Scylla

READ ACTIVELY

Visualize Try to picture the Sirens on their rocky islet.

EXPLORING YOUR READING

Look Back

1. What does Ulysses fear will happen if he is not tied to the mast and his companions do not have wax in their ears?

Think It Over

2. Do you think Ulysses is a good leader? Why or why not?

3. Ulysses "left his own ears unplugged" so he could still be in command. What do you think might be another reason that he listened to the Sirens?

4. Why do you think that the Sirens are birds with human faces?

Go Beyond

5. What do you think people mean when they describe something as a Siren song?

Ideas for Writing: Retelling in a Different Form

6. "The Sirens" is in the form of a short story. Use another form of writing to retell it. You might choose to make it into a poem. Or you could write a play or movie script, with dialogue, stage directions, and descriptions of the scenes. You might even want to draw it as a comic strip.

CHAPTER 7

Ancient Rome

MAP ACTIVITIES

The Roman Empire was huge. It set boundaries, built cities, and gave names to places that are used today. To get to know the effect of the Roman Empire on the modern world, complete the following activities.

What city is it today?
Look at the major cities of the Roman Empire at its height. Check the location of the cities against the maps of Europe, Asia, and Africa in the Atlas. Study the names of the cities. Compare the locations and names. What are the names of these cities today?

Name that country
Study the same maps, and tell which of today's countries match the following areas ruled by Rome: Gaul, Numidia, Judea, Syria, Asia Minor, Thrace, and Dacia.

The Roman Republic

Reach Into Your Background

Remember when you started the school year? What did it feel like to be in a new class, perhaps in a new school, and to begin new subjects? Was it exciting? Was it scary? What is it like to face a new world, with new challenges and new responsibilities?

Questions to Explore

1. Why did the early Romans form a republic?
2. Why did the Roman Republic collapse?

Key Terms

republic	consul
patrician	veto
plebeian	dictator

Key People and Places

Romulus and Remus
Etruscans
Julius Caesar   Italy
Octavian   Carthage
Tiber River   Gaul
Rome

▼ This bronze statue honors the wolf that rescued and cared for Romulus and Remus in the legend of Rome's founding.

Americans learn about the founding of their nation as young people. They read about the 13 British colonies, the battles of Lexington and Concord, and the leadership of George Washington. They learn about the final victory of the new nation, the United States of America.

In ancient times, young Romans also learned about the founding of their state. But it was a story that mixed a little fact with a great deal of legend. The main characters in the story were twin brothers, Romulus and Remus. They were the children of a princess and Mars, the Roman god of war. A jealous king feared that the twins would someday seize power from him. He ordered them to be drowned. However, the gods protected the infants. A female wolf rescued them. Then a shepherd found the twins and raised them as his own. The twins grew up, killed the king, and went off to build their own city. At a place where seven hills rise above the Tiber River, they founded the city of Rome.

Rome's Geographic Setting

Predict From the story of Romulus and Remus, what do you think the Roman people valued?

We can learn much from the story of Rome's founding—even if it is mostly legend. We learn that the Romans valued loyalty and justice. People who broke the law would be severely punished, just as the king was punished. We also learn that the Romans believed that the favor of the gods was important.

The first settlers on Rome's seven hills were not thinking about building a great empire. They chose that site because it seemed to be a good place to live. The hills made it easy to defend. The soil was fertile. There was a river. But as centuries passed, the people of Rome discovered that the location of their city gave them other advantages. Rome was at the center of the long, narrow peninsula we now call Italy. Italy was at the center of the Mediterranean Sea. And the Mediterranean Sea was at the center of the known Western world.

Ancient Italy About 600 B.C.

Map Study Look at the map. Notice that Roman civilization arose on the Italian peninsula in southern Europe. The fertile soil of Italy's countryside (below) supported the olive trees and grape vines that fed a growing population. **Location** Which of Italy's coasts is Rome closest to?

Rome

ITALY

Adriatic Sea

Tyrrhenian Sea

Mediterranean Sea

0   100   200 mi
0   100   200 km
Albers Equal-Area Conic Projection

Rome's Beginnings

We know very little about the people who actually founded Rome. However, we do know that their first settlements date from about the 900s B.C. Rome grew slowly, as the Romans fought their neighbors for land.

About 600 B.C., a mysterious people, the Etruscans (ee TRUHS kuhnz), took power in Rome. They spoke a language totally unlike any other in Italy. Although we have many examples of their writing, we can read very little of it. Where had they come from? Even today, no one is sure. For a time, Etruscans ruled as kings of Rome. However, in 509 B.C., the Romans revolted and drove the Etruscans from power.

Although the Romans defeated the Etruscans, the victors adopted Etruscan ideas. For example, many of the Roman gods were originally Etruscan. The Romans also borrowed the Greek alphabet that the Etruscans used. The Roman garment called the toga came from the Etruscans.

The Roman Arch Roman architects made great use of the curved structure called the arch. Arches span openings in buildings. An arch can hold great weight above it. The Romans probably learned about arches from the Etruscans. Beginning in the 300s B.C., Romans used arches for water channels, bridges, and later for monuments.

◀ Time has faded the painted colors but not the grace of this Etruscan tomb sculpture, which was made around 510 B.C.

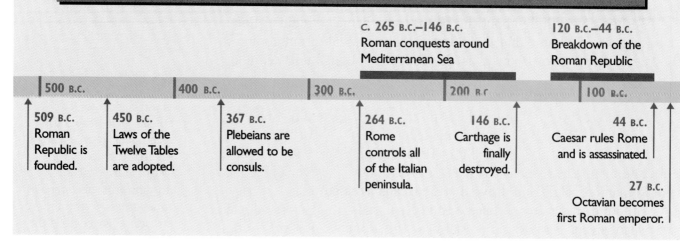

The Roman Republic

c. 265 B.C.–146 B.C.
Roman conquests around
Mediterranean Sea

120 B.C.–44 B.C.
Breakdown of the
Roman Republic

| 500 B.C. | 400 B.C. | 300 B.C. | 200 B.C. | 100 B.C. |

509 B.C.
Roman
Republic is
founded.

450 B.C.
Laws of the
Twelve Tables
are adopted.

367 B.C.
Plebeians are
allowed to be
consuls.

264 B.C.
Rome
controls all
of the Italian
peninsula.

146 B.C.
Carthage is
finally
destroyed.

44 B.C.
Caesar rules Rome
and is assassinated.

27 B.C.
Octavian becomes
first Roman emperor.

▲ The Roman Republic lasted for almost 500 years. By what year did Rome control all of the Italian peninsula?

Ask Questions What would you like to know about the differences between patricians and plebeians?

Rome Becomes a Republic

After driving the last Etruscan king from the throne, the Romans vowed never again to put so much trust in kings. They created a new form of government, a republic. In a **republic**, citizens who have the right to vote select their leaders. The leaders rule in the name of the people.

In the Roman Republic, the most powerful part of the government was a group called the senate. At first, the senate was made up only of 300 upper-class men called **patricians.** Ordinary citizens were known as **plebeians.** In the early republic, plebeians could not hold office or be senators. The government was led by two men called **consuls.** Before 367 B.C., plebeians could not be consuls. The senate advised the consuls on foreign affairs, laws, and finances, among other things.

Consuls almost always did what the senate wanted. Consuls ruled for one year only. Power was divided equally between them. Both had to agree before the government could take any action. If only one consul said "Veto" ("I forbid it"), the matter was dropped. Today, we use the word **veto** to mean the rejection of a bill by the President.

The Romans knew that their government might not work if the two consuls disagreed in an emergency. For this reason, Roman law held that a dictator could be appointed to handle an emergency. A **dictator** was an official who had all the powers of a king but could hold office for only six months.

Patricians Versus Plebeians Through wars of conquest, the Roman Republic extended its control across Italy. Within about 250 years, Rome had conquered almost all of Italy. This caused growing troubles between patricians and plebeians.

Patricians and plebeians had different attitudes. Patricians thought of themselves as leaders. They fought hard to keep control over the government. Plebeians believed they had a right to be respected and treated fairly. Plebeians did not trust the actions of the patrician senate.

They felt the senate was often unfair to the plebeians. Therefore, plebeians formed their own groups to protect their interests.

Many patricians grew wealthy because of Rome's conquests. They took riches from defeated people. Then, they bought land from small farmers and created huge farms for themselves. Plebeians did not work on these farms. Rather, the work was done by slaves brought back from conquests. Many plebeian farmers found themselves without work. The cities, especially Rome, were filled with jobless plebeians.

Eventually, angry plebeians refused to fight in the Roman army. Then the patricians gave in to one of their main demands. This was a written code of laws called the Laws of the Twelve Tables. The Twelve Tables applied equally to all citizens. They were hung in marketplaces so everyone could know what the laws were. Despite this victory, the plebeians never managed to gain power equal to the patricians.

Master of the Mediterranean While patricians and plebeians fought for power in Rome, Roman armies were conquering new territories. Roman armies invaded the North African empire of the city of Carthage. After a series of bloody wars, they destroyed the empire of Carthage. They also seized control of Spain. Other Roman armies conquered Greece. Then, the Romans turned their attention to the warlike tribes of Gaul, which is now France.

▼ Carthage had a formidable weapon—the elephant. War elephants easily smashed through enemy lines. They also terrified enemy soldiers. Little wonder, then, that the powerful Roman army took so long to conquer Carthage.

The End of the Republic

Even though it ruled a large area, by 120 B.C. Rome was in trouble. Some leaders tried to break up estates and give land to the plebeians. The patricians fought back, and plebeian leaders were murdered.

In the next 75 years, a number of the most successful generals gathered private armies around them and fought for power. Consuls no longer respected each other's veto power. Rome dissolved into civil war, with private armies roaming the streets and murdering their enemies. As Rome seemed about to break up, Julius Caesar arose as a strong leader.

▶ Julius Caesar was a powerful dictator of the Roman Empire. Later Roman leaders adopted his name as a title. In time, *Caesar* came to mean "emperor."

The Rise of Julius Caesar Caesar was a smart leader, eager for power. From 58 B.C. to 51 B.C., he led his army in conquering Gaul. He killed, enslaved, and uprooted millions of Gauls. He captured huge amounts of gold. His strong leadership won him the loyalty of his troops. They would follow him anywhere—even back to Rome to seize power. In 49 B.C., Caesar returned to Italy. War broke out between Caesar and the senate. Caesar won the war and became dictator of the Roman world in 48 B.C.

The Death of a Dictator For four years, Caesar took over important public offices. In 45 B.C., he became the only consul. In 44 B.C., he became dictator for life. Caesar took many useful steps to reorganize the government. But it seemed to many senators that Rome once again had a king. They hated this idea.

On March 15, 44 B.C., Caesar attended a meeting of the senate. His wife had urged him not to go, fearing danger. But Caesar insisted on going. At the meeting, a group of senators gathered around Caesar. Suddenly, they pulled out knives and began stabbing him. He fell to the ground, dead. Caesar had been a great leader. However, many Romans felt that he had gone too far, too fast, in gathering power.

Civil war followed Caesar's death. When war ended 13 years later, Caesar's adopted son, Octavian, held power. In 27 B.C., the senate awarded Octavian the title Augustus, which means "highly respected." He was the first emperor of Rome.

SECTION 1 REVIEW

1. **Define** (a) republic, (b) patrician, (c) plebeian, (d) consul, (e) veto, (f) dictator.

2. **Identify** (a) Romulus and Remus, (b) Etruscans, (c) Julius Caesar, (d) Octavian, (e) Tiber River, (f) Rome, (g) Italy, (h) Carthage, (i) Gaul.

3. Why did the Romans want the republic to have two leaders rather than one?

4. What factors enabled Julius Caesar to come to power?

Critical Thinking

5. **Drawing Conclusions** Why would the Roman senate be likely to lead the opposition to Caesar's growing power?

Activity

6. **Writing to Learn** You are sitting in the senate on March 15, 44 B.C., when Julius Caesar enters the chamber. Write a journal entry noting what happened next, including the reasons for the action.

The Roman Empire

Reach Into Your Background

This section might have been called "The Glory of Rome." What do you think that means? What makes a country "glorious"?

Questions to Explore

1. How did the Romans establish sound government to rule their empire?
2. What advances did the Romans make in the fields of architecture, technology, and science?

Key Terms

province   aqueduct

Key People and Places

Augustus   Greece
Hadrian   Colosseum

❝Then the captured weapons passed. There were bronze helmets, shields, . . . and glittering steel swords piled on wagons. Then followed 3,000 men carrying 750 trays heaped with silver coins. . . . Next came the king's small children, now slaves, and the king himself in a dark robe. Some in the crowd wept for the children, but not for the king. Suddenly our great consul himself, in a golden chariot. . . . The crowd broke into a roar. . . . It was he who brought all this wealth and glory to Rome.❞

Rome's armies brought much wealth and glory to Rome in the years after Augustus came to power. When these armies returned to Rome, they were greeted with a magnificent parade, known as a "triumph."

Ruling an Empire

When Augustus came to power after Caesar's death, Roman control had already spread far beyond Italy. Under Augustus and the emperors who followed, Rome gained an even greater empire. Look at the map at the

▼ The Arch of Constantine, erected in Rome about A.D. 315, honors Constantine, the first emperor of Rome to legalize Christianity. In the background stands the Colosseum, Rome's huge stadium.

beginning of this chapter. The Roman Empire stretched from Britain to Mesopotamia. Rome controlled all the lands around the Mediterranean. This gave the Romans great pride. In fact, they called the Mediterranean *mare nostrum* (MAH ray NOHS truhm), or "our sea."

Augustus, the Senate, and the People Augustus was an intelligent ruler. When he was struggling for power, he often ignored the senate and its laws. But after he won control, he changed his manner. He showed great respect for the senate and was careful to avoid acting like a king. He did not want to have the same fate as Julius Caesar. Augustus often said that he wanted to share power with the senate. He even said he wanted to restore the republic.

What really happened, however, was quite different. The senate and the people were so grateful for Rome's peace and prosperity that they gave Augustus as much power as he wanted.

▼ Augustus ruled the Roman Empire from 27 B.C. to A.D. 14. He issued new coins to promote trade, and he set up a postal service. He also ordered a census, or population count, to improve tax collection.

Governing Conquered Peoples The Romans treated conquered peoples wisely. The Romans took some slaves after a conquest, but most of the conquered people remained free. To govern, they divided their empire into areas called **provinces.** Each province had a Roman governor supported by an army. Often, the Romans built a city in a new province to serve as its capital.

Generally, the Romans did not force their way of life on conquered peoples. They allowed these people to follow their own religions. Local rulers were allowed to run the daily affairs of government. As long as there was peace, Roman governors did not interfere in conquered peoples' lives. Rather, they kept watch over them. Rome wanted peaceful provinces that would supply it with the raw materials it needed. It also wanted the conquered people to buy Roman goods and to pay taxes. Many of the conquered people adopted Roman ways. Many learned to speak Latin, the language of the Romans, and to worship Roman gods.

The Five Good Emperors

Augustus died in A.D. 14. For 82 years after his death, Roman history was a story of good, bad, and terrible emperors. Two of the worst were Caligula (kuh LIG yuh luh) and Nero. They both may have been insane. Caligula

◀ Marcus Aurelius was the last of the five "good emperors." In this stone sculpture, he pardons the barbarians whose attacks weakened the Roman Empire.

proclaimed himself a god and was a cruel, unfair ruler. Nero murdered his half-brother, his mother, and his wife.

In A.D. 96, Rome entered what is called the age of the five "good emperors." Only the last of these emperors had a son. Each of the others adopted the best young man he could find to be the next emperor.

Perhaps the greatest was the emperor Hadrian (HAY dree uhn). He worked hard to build a good government. His laws protected women, children, and slaves. He issued a code of laws so that all laws were the same throughout the empire. Hadrian reorganized the army so that soldiers were allowed to defend their home provinces. This gave them a greater sense of responsibility. Hadrian also encouraged learning.

READ ACTIVELY

Predict How does the civilization of Rome compare to that of Greece?

The Greek Influence on Rome

The Romans had long admired Greek achievements. People said that Hadrian spoke Greek better than he spoke Latin. The last of the "good emperors," Marcus Aurelius (aw REE lee uhs), wrote a famous book of philosophy in Greek. Many Romans visited Greece to study Greek art, architecture, and ideas about government.

There was a major difference between Greek and Roman views of learning. The Greeks were interested in ideas. They sought to learn truths about the world through reason. They developed studies such as mathematics, philosophy, and astronomy, which is the study of the stars and planets. The Romans were more interested in using these studies to build things. Under the Romans, architecture and engineering blossomed. With these skills, they built their empire.

Architecture and Technology

Early Roman art and architecture copied the Etruscans. Later, the Romans studied and copied Greek sculpture and architecture. However, Roman statues and buildings were heavier and stronger in style than those of the Greeks. Using arches, Romans were able to build larger structures. They could create large open spaces inside buildings with wide arched ceilings supported by heavy walls.

The Pantheon in Rome

Built during the reign of Emperor Hadrian, the Pantheon was first used to hold statues of the Roman gods. Later, it became a Christian church. Now it serves as the burial place of many famous Italians. At its highest point, the Pantheon's majestic dome rises 71 feet (22 m) above the floor. Light streams in from the opening at the top of the dome.

Most large buildings were built of bricks covered with thin slabs of white marble. However, one important development was a new building material—concrete. Concrete was a mix of stone, sand, cement, and water that dried as hard as a rock. Concrete helped the Romans put up buildings that were far taller than any built before.

The greatest Roman building was the Colosseum, a giant arena that held 50,000 spectators. Its walls were so well built that the floor of the arena could be flooded for mock naval battles using real people in real boats. Stairways and ramps ran through the building. There were even elevators to carry wild animals from dens below the floor to the arena.

Roman engineers built roads from Rome to every part of the empire. This road system covered a distance equal to twice the distance around the Earth at the Equator. Do you know the saying, "All roads lead to Rome"? In Roman times, it was true. No matter what road travelers started out on, they would eventually arrive in Rome.

A Roman Road

EXPLORING TECHNOLOGY

Roman roads were built to allow the speedy movement of troops and communication around the empire. The first road built was the Appian Way. Begun in 312 B.C., it connected Rome with southern Italy. Roman roads were built as straight as possible and sometimes included tunnels. These roads were rugged and strong—some even have survived to today. The diagram below shows a typical Roman road.

Milestones were placed along Roman roads. Each was marked with the number of miles to Rome. A Roman mile was 1,000 paces. Each pace was two steps long, about 5 feet.

1 After surveyors laid out the road, workers dug parallel ditches. These ditches were lined with a row of curbstones.

5 The road was paved with tightly fitted flat stones. The surface was higher in the center to allow rainwater to run off into the side ditches.

4 Then came a layer of gravel, sand, and mortar about 1 foot thick.

2 Workers dug a deep ditch between the two rows of curbstones. They added a layer of broken flat stones 10 to 24 inches deep.

3 The next layer, about 9 inches thick, was made up of smaller stones mixed with lime mortar.

THE ANCIENT WORLD **201**

Romans were famous for their **aqueducts,** structures that carried water over long distances. The aqueducts were huge lines of arches, often many miles long. A channel along the top carried water from the countryside to the cities. Roman aqueducts tunneled through mountains and spanned valleys. Some are still being used today.

Roman Law

Roman law followed Roman roads throughout the empire. The great Roman senator Cicero (SIS uh roh) expressed Roman feeling about law.

> **W**hat sort of thing is the law? It is the kind that cannot be bent by influence, or broken by power, or spoiled by money.

A later ruler named Justinian (juh STIHN ee uhn) used Roman law to create a famous code of justice. Here are a few laws from that code.

> **N**o one suffers a penalty for what he thinks. No one may be forcibly removed from his own house. The burden of proof is upon the person who accuses. In inflicting penalties, the age and inexperience of the guilty party must be taken into account.

Connect From what you know about law in the United States, how is it similar to Roman law?

Roman law continued to be passed down to other cultures, including our own. Think of our Bill of Rights. Do any of Justinian's laws appear there? Other Roman ideas of justice are also basic to our system of laws. For example, persons accused of crimes had the right to face their accusers. If there was doubt about a person's guilt, he or she would be judged innocent.

SECTION 2 REVIEW

1. **Define** (a) province, (b) aqueduct.
2. **Identify** (a) Caligula, (b) Hadrian, (c) Greece, (d) Colosseum.
3. Why did the Romans give Augustus so much power?

4. Why is Roman law important to us today?

Critical Thinking
5. **Drawing Conclusions** The "good emperor" Marcus Aurelius chose his son Commodus to follow him. Commodus was one of the worst emperors in Roman history. Why do you think a good emperor might make such a bad choice?

Activity
6. **Writing to Learn** Write down a few ideas for guidelines that you would give to every new governor of a Roman province. How should the governor treat the people of the province? What should the governor do about the religion and existing government of the conquered people?

Daily Life Among the Romans

BEFORE YOU READ

Reach Into Your Background

How would you describe your daily life? Have you ever thought that people in earlier times might have lived very differently? How do you think a person from another period in history would describe your life? What would they think was strange? What might be familiar?

Questions to Explore

1. How were the lives of the rich and the poor different in ancient Rome?

2. How were slaves treated in ancient Rome?

Key Terms
circus

Key People
Martial
Seneca

At the height of its glory, Rome had the most beautiful monuments and public buildings in the world. Wealth and goods flowed into Rome from all parts of the empire. Tourists and merchants flocked to the city. Its marketplaces and shops had more goods than any other city. Not everyone was thrilled with the excitement. One Roman complained of narrow streets "jammed with carts and their swearing drivers." Another writer, the poet Martial (MAR shuhl), complained of the noise:

> "Before it gets light, we have the bakers. Then it's the hammering of the artisans all day. There's no peace or quiet in this city!"

▼ A scene from daily life in ancient Rome is shown in this faded 2,000-year-old fresco—a painting on a plaster wall. It shows customers buying fresh bread in a bakery.

The Rich, the Poor, and the Slaves

Roman society was made up of the few rich people, the many poor people, and the slaves. Most citizens had nothing like the luxuries of the wealthy. In fact, there was a huge difference between the lives of rich and poor. A majority of Romans were not only poor, they were jobless. Most of these survived only by handouts from the government.

LINKS ACROSS TIME

New Hairdo or Old?
People today are not the first to use makeup and to style their hair. The Romans and earlier people spent time and money on their looks. Rich Roman women used powdered minerals to paint their faces, make up their eyes, and redden their lips. Fancy hairdos were created with curling irons, dyes, and the work of slaves.

▼ Wealthy Roman families lived in villas like this one. In this drawing, the roof is cut away to show the inside. Find the dining room. Notice how the wealthy ate while lying on couches.

A Life of Luxury The rich often had elegant homes in the city. They also had country estates called villas. Some wealthy families had huge estates in the provinces where much of the food for the empire was grown. Wealthy Romans were famous for overdoing things, especially concerning food. A Roman historian describes the eating habits of Aulus Vitellius (OW luhs vuh TEL ee uhs), emperor for only six months in A.D. 69.

> "He used to have three, or four, heavy meals a day. . . . He had himself invited to a different house for each meal. The cost to the host was never less than 400,000 coins a time."

Of course, few Romans could afford to eat like an emperor. Still, the wealthy were known for their feasts. Often they served game, perhaps partridge or wild boar. For very special occasions, they might also serve exotic dishes such as flamingo or ostrich. A special treat was dormouse cooked in honey. Roman feasts often had entertainment, including musicians, dancers, and performers reciting poems.

Atrium

Study

Dining room

Bedroom

Open courtyard

Kitchen

A Roman cook might have heated honey sauce in this saucepan (left). The cake pan (right) looks about right for muffins.

Another Way of Life for the Poor   The world of the poor was a far cry from the feasts of the wealthy. In Rome, most people lived in poor housing. Many lived in tall apartment houses with no running water, toilets, or kitchens. All food and drink had to be carried up the stairs. Rubbish and human waste had to be carried down, or—as frequently happened—dumped out the window. Because most houses were made of wood, fires were frequent and often fatal. The worst, in A.D. 64, destroyed most of the city.

Bread and Circuses   Poor citizens needed wheat to survive. When wheat harvests were bad, or when grain shipments from overseas were late, the poor often rioted. To prevent this, the emperors provided free grain to the poor. They also provided spectacular shows. They were held in the Colosseum or in arenas called **circuses,** so the shows came to be called circuses, too.

The circuses could be violent. Romans, rich and poor, packed the arenas to watch the events. These included animals fighting other animals, animals fighting humans, and humans fighting humans. Clowns might also entertain, or there might even be a public execution of a criminal. The highlights of the day were the fights between gladiators, men who fought to the death. Most gladiators were slaves who had been captured in battle. However, a few were free men—and some women—who enjoyed the fame and fortune they could gain.

READ ACTIVELY

Visualize Visualize a feast at the home of a rich Roman. Then visualize a meal with poor Romans.

▼▶ In this gladiator battle (right), two chariot drivers crash into one another. Gladiators wore helmets (below) for protection.

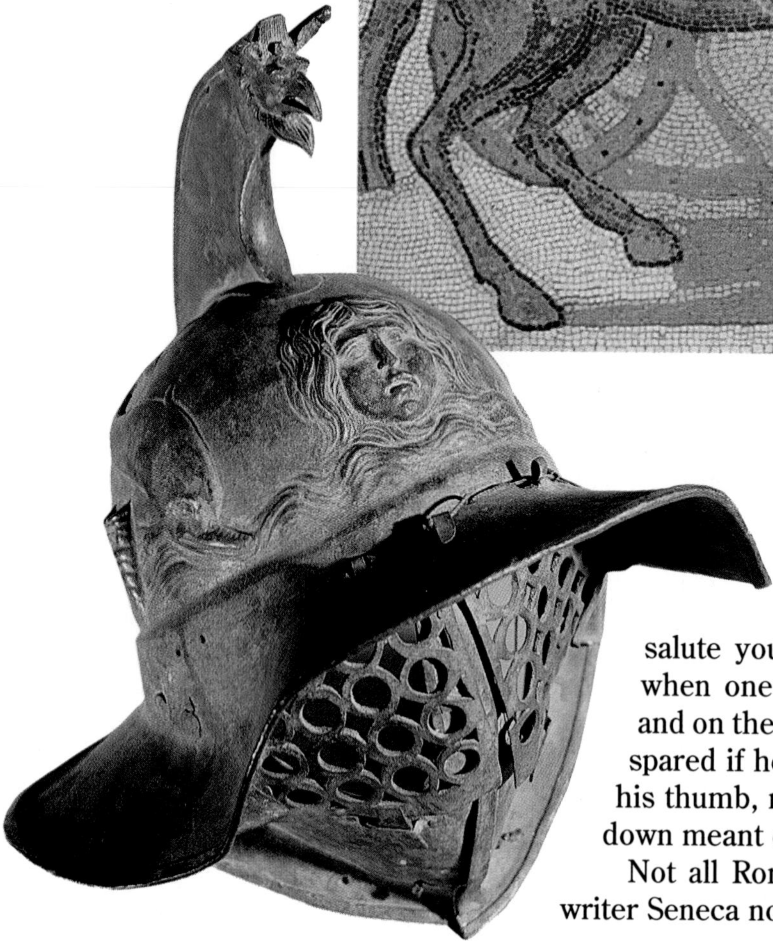

Before the battles, the gladiators paraded onto the floor of the arena. Approaching the emperor's box, they raised their arms in salute and shouted "Hail Caesar! We who are about to die salute you." Then the battles began. The end came when one gladiator was dead or dying, or disarmed and on the ground. A wounded gladiator's life might be spared if he had fought well. The emperor would raise his thumb, meaning "spare the loser." A thumb pointed down meant death.

Not all Romans approved of these brutal sports. The writer Seneca noted:

> **❝I**t's sheer murder. In the morning, men are thrown to the lions or bears. At noon, they are thrown to the spectators.**❞**

Roman Family Life

Despite these brutal sports, many Romans had a strong sense of values. Most of all, they valued family life. Roman writings are filled with stories of happy families and dedication and love.

The Roman government rewarded parents who had many children. Under Roman law, the father had absolute power over the entire household. He owned the household—wife, children, slaves, and furniture. In the early days, he could sell a son or daughter into slavery. Later, this power was reduced.

The amount of freedom a woman in ancient Rome enjoyed depended on her husband's wealth and status. Wealthy women had a great deal of independence. Women had a strong influence on their families, and some wives of famous men became famous themselves. The mothers or wives of some Roman emperors gained great political power.

Ask Questions What do you want to know about the status of women and slaves in Rome?

Slavery in Rome

Slavery was common in ancient Rome. Almost every wealthy family owned slaves. Even poor families might own one. While few owners paid slaves for their work, they often took good care of household slaves. Slaves had almost no rights. Yet relationships between household slaves and their owners were sometimes trusting and tender. These slaves helped raise children and provided companionship. Sometimes they rose to important positions in the households of wealthy owners.

Household slaves were more fortunate. Other kinds of slaves often led short, brutal lives. Slaves who worked on farms sometimes worked chained together during the day and slept in chains at night. Slaves in copper, tin, and iron mines worked in terrible conditions. Gladiators risked death every time they fought. Roman warships were powered by slaves trained as rowers.

Some slaves were able to save tips or wages and buy their freedom. These might be slaves with very special skills, such as chariot racers. These sports heroes sometimes became famous and wealthy.

SECTION 3 REVIEW

1. **Define** circus.

2. **Identify** (a) Martial, (b) Seneca.

3. How were the lives of rich and poor Romans different?

4. What was the difference in the treatment a household slave and a mine slave received?

Critical Thinking

5. **Recognizing Cause and Effect** How do you think abolishing slavery would have affected Roman family life?

Activity

6. **Writing to Learn** In this section, you read the reaction of the writer Seneca to a circus. Write a journal entry telling of your reactions to what you might have seen at a Roman circus.

A New Religion: Christianity

BEFORE YOU READ

Reach Into Your Background
How would you feel if people teased or criticized you for a belief that you held? What would you do? Would you defend your belief? If so, how would you do this?

Questions to Explore
1. What ideas did Jesus teach?
2. How did the Roman government attack Christianity? How did the religion finally triumph?

Key Terms
messiah
disciple
Gospel
epistle
martyr

Key People and Places
Jesus
Paul
Nero
Judea

▼ In this Roman sculpture, Jesus restores sight to a blind man. Belief in Jesus' powers helped early Christians face cruel persecution.

"Blessed are the poor in spirit, for theirs is the kingdom of heaven.

Blessed are those who mourn, for they shall be comforted.

Blessed are the lowly, for they shall inherit the earth.

Blessed are those who hunger and thirst for what is right, for they shall be satisfied.

Blessed are the merciful, for they shall be treated with mercy.

Blessed are the pure in heart, for they shall see God.

Blessed are the peacemakers, for they shall be called children of God.

Blessed are those who are persecuted in the cause of right, for theirs is the kingdom of heaven."

—*The Sermon on the Mount, Matthew 5:1–10*

According to the Bible, Jesus, a Jewish religious teacher, spoke these words to his followers and others in the first century A.D. These words are an important part of the religion called Christianity. In the beginning, its followers were mainly the poor and slaves. Roman rulers tried to stamp out Christianity by killing its followers. But over time, it spread throughout the entire Roman Empire.

The Beginnings of Christianity

Christianity was one of many religions in the vast Roman Empire. The empire contained many lands with different languages, customs, and religions. The Romans were tolerant toward the people in these lands. They allowed them to follow their own religions. But the conquered people had to show loyalty to Roman gods and to the emperor.

The Romans conquered the Jewish homeland of Judea in 63 B.C. At first, they respected the Jews' right to worship their God. But, many Jews resented foreign rule. Some believed that a **messiah,** or savior, would come to bring justice and freedom to the land. As opposition to Roman rule grew, the Romans struck back with harsh punishment. In 37 B.C., the Roman senate appointed a new ruler of Judea named Herod (HAIR uhd). It was during Herod's reign that Jesus was born in the Judean town of Bethlehem.

Most of what we know about Jesus' life is found in the New Testament, a part of the Christian Bible. After Jesus died, his **disciples,** or followers, told stories about his life and teaching. Between 40 and 70 years after his death, four stories of his life were written from these oral traditions. People came to believe that four disciples—Matthew, Mark, Luke, and John—had each written one story. These writings are called the **Gospels.**

We know little of Jesus' childhood and youth except that he grew up in Nazareth. He learned to be a carpenter and began teaching when he was about 30 years old. For three years, Jesus traveled from place to place, preaching to Jews who lived in the countryside. Much of what he taught was part of the Jewish tradition into which he had been born. Like all Jewish teachers, Jesus preached that there was only one true God.

According to the Gospels, Jesus taught that God was loving and forgiving. He said that a person had the responsibility to "love the Lord your God with all your heart and your neighbor as yourself." Jesus also said he

READ ACTIVELY

Ask Questions What questions do you have about Jesus and his beliefs?

▼ This scene, painted on a wall of a catacomb in Rome, shows Jesus with his disciples.

was the Son of God and the Messiah. He promised that people who believed in him and followed his teachings would have everlasting life.

Jesus' teachings alarmed many people. Some complained to the Romans that Jesus was teaching that God was greater than the emperor. The Romans feared that he would lead an armed revolt against Roman rule, so the Roman governor condemned Jesus to death. He was crucified, or put to death by being nailed to a large wooden cross. According to the Gospels, Jesus rose from the dead and spoke to his disciples, telling them to spread his teachings.

Christianity Spreads

The Greek equivalent of the word *messiah* was *christos*. Many educated people of that day spoke Greek. As these people accepted Jesus' teachings, they began calling him Christ. After his death, his followers, called Christians, spread the new religion from Jerusalem to Antioch in Syria, and finally to Rome itself.

One of Jesus' most devoted disciples was a Jew named Paul. Paul was well educated and spoke both Greek and Latin. According to the

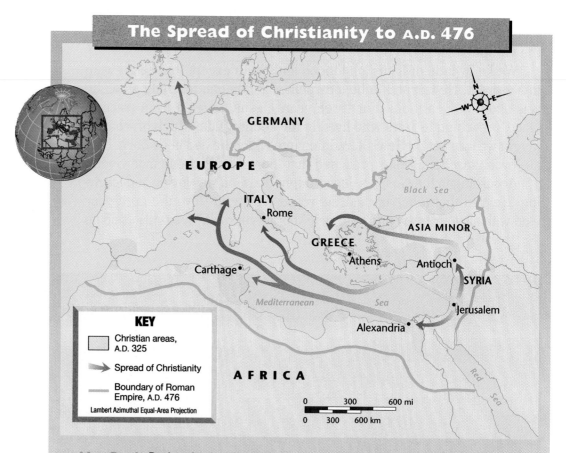

The Spread of Christianity to A.D. 476

KEY
☐ Christian areas, A.D. 325
→ Spread of Christianity
— Boundary of Roman Empire, A.D. 476
Lambert Azimuthal Equal-Area Projection

0   300   600 mi
0   300   600 km

Map Study Paul and other apostles carried the Christian message to far-flung places. From its beginning in Jerusalem, the new religion eventually extended throughout the Roman Empire. **Location** Christianity spread out from Jerusalem. To which North African cities did it spread? To which Italian city did it spread?

Gospels, Paul at first rejected the Christian message. One day as he approached the Syrian city of Damascus, he had a vision that Jesus spoke to him. After this experience, Paul decided to travel to spread the word of Jesus. He persuaded Jesus' followers that his teachings should be spread to Greeks and Romans, and not just to Jews. Paul carried Christianity to the cities around the Mediterranean.

Paul's writings also helped turn the Christian faith into an organized religion. Paul wrote many epistles (ee PIS uhlz), or letters, to Christian groups in distant cities. Many of these epistles became a part of the Christian Bible.

The fast-growing new religion soon alarmed the Roman government. Christians refused to worship the Roman gods or the emperor. Many Roman officials began to view them as enemies of the empire. Under the emperor Nero, the first official campaign against the Christians began in A.D. 64. One night, a fire started in some shops in Rome. The fire burned for nine days and left much of the city in ruins.

Nero blamed the Christians. He watched with pleasure as Christians were sent to their deaths. Some were forced to fight wild animals in the Colosseum. Others were soaked with oil and burned alive. Others were crucified or, like the disciple Paul, beheaded.

LINKS TO LANGUAGE ARTS

Sign of the Fish A secret sign that Christians used to identify one another was a simple image of a fish. How did a fish come to be an early Christian symbol? Each letter of the Greek word for fish, *ichthys*, was the first letter of a word in a Greek phrase. The phrase meant "Jesus Christ, Son of God, Savior."

Christian Catacombs

Hidden deep underground, in passageways called catacombs (right), early Christians buried their dead and worshipped in secret. They decorated the tombstones with Christian symbols such as the fish and cross-shaped anchor (left).

◀ Statues and paintings showing Jesus as a shepherd borrowed a popular pre-Christian symbol for gentleness and charity.

The Romans tormented Christians off and on for another 250 years. During these years, the Roman Empire began to lose its power. To explain the decline, Romans looked for people to blame. They found them among the followers of the new religion. As one Roman wrote:

"If the Tiber River reaches the walls, if the Nile fails to rise to the fields, if the sky doesn't move or the Earth does, if there is famine or plague, the cry is at once: "The Christians to the Lions.**"**

Still, Christianity spread throughout the empire. Its message of hope for a better life after death appealed to many. The help that Christian communities gave to widows, orphans, and the poor also attracted people. Not even the emperor Diocletian (dy uh KLEE shuhn) could stop its growth. Diocletian outlawed Christian services, imprisoned Christian priests, and put many believers to death.

However, these actions did the opposite of what Diocletian wanted. Many Romans admired the Christians. They saw them as martyrs and heroes. **Martyrs** are people who choose to die for a cause they believe in. By the A.D. 300s, about one in every ten Romans had accepted the Christian faith.

SECTION 4 REVIEW

1. **Define** (a) messiah, (b) disciple, (c) Gospel, (d) epistle, (e) martyr.

2. **Identify** (a) Jesus, (b) Paul, (c) Nero, (d) Judea.

3. What ideas of Jesus attracted followers?

4. Why did Christianity seem threatening to the Roman government?

Critical Thinking

5. **Drawing Conclusions** Why do you think the Christians refused to worship the Roman gods and the emperor?

Activity

6. **Writing to Learn** You are a Roman official at the time of Jesus. Write a journal entry that describes your feelings about the new religion.

The Fall of Rome

SECTION 5

BEFORE YOU READ

Reach Into Your Background

Have you ever thought about what you would do if you had all the money you could want?

Would you spend it wisely? Would you help others? Would you save some, or would you spend until the money began to run out?

Questions to Explore

1. Why did Rome begin to lose its power?
2. How did Constantine try to restore Rome's greatness?

Key Terms

mercenary
inflation

Key People and Places

Constantine
Diocletian
Constantinople

One day in the year A.D. 312, the emperor Constantine (KAHN stuhn teen) stood with his troops under a cloudy sky near a bridge across the Tiber River. He was filled with doubts. A battle was about to begin. His enemies were waiting on the other side of the river.

While Constantine was hoping for victory, the sun broke through the clouds. According to Constantine, the sun had a cross on it. And above the cross was written in Latin: "Under this sign you will conquer!"

The next morning, Constantine had his artisans put the Christian symbol of the cross on his soldiers' shields. In the battle, they won an overwhelming victory. Constantine believed that the victory had come from the Christian God. Constantine vowed to become a Christian.

Historians today debate whether this event ever happened. But we know that as emperor from A.D. 312 to A.D. 337, Constantine strongly encouraged the spread of Christianity throughout the Roman Empire. As he lay dying, he may have converted to Christianity.

◀ This statue of Emperor Constantine originally towered over 30 feet (9 m). Today, only the head remains.

The Empire Crumbles

Ask Questions What questions do you have about the fall of Rome?

The Christian Church provided comfort and authority at a time when the mighty Roman Empire was on the edge of disaster. By the time Constantine took power, he could do little to stop the empire's fall.

The trouble started 125 years before. That's when the last of the "good emperors"—Marcus Aurelius—died. The emperor, known for his wisdom, left his son Commodus in power in A.D. 180. Commodus was not a wise choice. He was a savage ruler who loved the bloodshed of the gladiators. He ruled by bribing the army to support him.

The rule of Commodus began the decline of the Roman Empire. Historians do not agree on any one cause for this decline. Generally, they believe that the following problems together led to Rome's end.

Weak, Corrupt Rulers   After Commodus, emperors were almost always successful generals and not politicians. They often stole money from the treasury. They used the money to enrich themselves and pay off the soldiers. Under these emperors, the government and the economy fell to pieces. The senate lost its power. During this time, even emperors were not safe. Between A.D. 180 and A.D. 284, Rome had 29 emperors. Most were murdered.

▼ These time line entries show the decline and collapse of the Roman Empire.

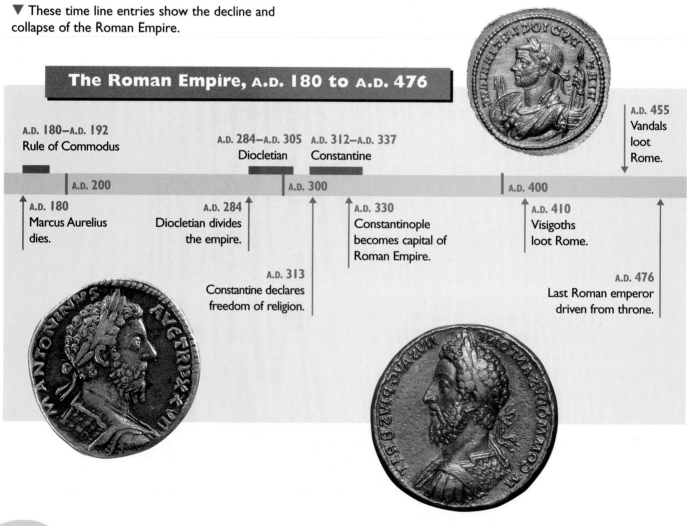

The Roman Empire, A.D. 180 to A.D. 476

A.D. 180–A.D. 192
Rule of Commodus

A.D. 284–A.D. 305
Diocletian

A.D. 312–A.D. 337
Constantine

A.D. 455
Vandals loot Rome.

A.D. 200

A.D. 300

A.D. 400

A.D. 180
Marcus Aurelius dies.

A.D. 284
Diocletian divides the empire.

A.D. 330
Constantinople becomes capital of Roman Empire.

A.D. 410
Visigoths loot Rome.

A.D. 313
Constantine declares freedom of religion.

A.D. 476
Last Roman emperor driven from throne.

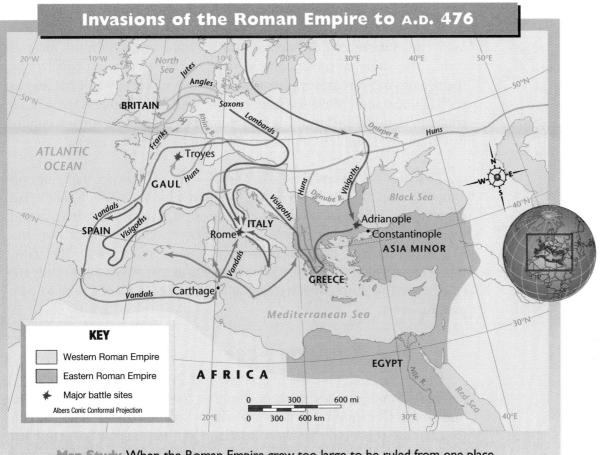

Map Study When the Roman Empire grew too large to be ruled from one place, the emperor Diocletian divided it into western and eastern parts. The eastern empire would survive the fall of the western empire by 1,000 years. Movement Trace the routes of foreign invasions of the Roman Empire. In which part did most occur?

A Mercenary Army Once, the Roman army had been made up of citizen soldiers ready to defend their land. Now the army was filled with **mercenaries,** foreign soldiers who serve only for pay. The problem with mercenaries is that they do not fight for any cause. They often switch sides if it is to their personal advantage. Rome's strength depended on a strong army loyal to the nation. Such an army was now just a memory.

The Size of the Empire The Roman Empire had grown too big to be ruled from one place. All over the empire, in Asia, Africa, and northern Europe, the enemies of Rome attacked. Tribes that the Romans had earlier conquered now poured over the empire's borders. This caused the empire to shrink.

Serious Economic Problems When Rome stopped conquering new lands, no new sources of wealth were available. This meant that taxes grew heavier. Further, the resources of the empire were being drained to pay an army that often would not fight. There was severe unemployment throughout the empire.

Predict How did Diocletian try to stop the decline of the Roman Empire?

Food was scarce. That made the price of food go up. To pay for this food, the government decided to produce more money in the form of coins. The value of those coins depended on the amount of silver in them. But since the government did not have much silver, it put less in each coin. So there was more money, but the money had less value. This situation is called **inflation.** If inflation is not controlled, money continues to buy less and less. Roman coins soon became worthless.

Trying to Stop the Decline Some emperors made strong efforts to stop the steady decline of the Roman Empire. While Diocletian persecuted Christians, he also worked to strengthen Rome. He enlarged the army and built new forts at the borders. He also improved the system of collecting taxes. This brought in more money to pay the army. Diocletian divided the empire into two parts to make it easier to rule. He ruled over the more wealthy east and appointed a co-emperor to rule over the west.

The Romans Accept Christianity

Diocletian and his co-emperor retired in A.D 305. A struggle for power followed. For seven years, generals fought each other for power until one—Constantine—came out the winner. As you read earlier, Constantine reported that the Christian God had helped his army win the battle for the control of Rome. A year later, Constantine declared Christianity the religion of the empire, outlawing the persecution of Christians and granting them freedom of worship. Christianity soon became the official religion of the Roman Empire.

During Constantine's 25 years as emperor, he worked to strengthen the Christian church. In 330, Constantine moved his capital to the city of Byzantium (biz AN tee uhm). In his honor, the city was renamed Constantinople.

▼ This shows a Roman-style viaduct in Constantinople, the capital of the eastern Roman Empire. Today Constantinople is known as Istanbul, Turkey.

The Fall of Rome

Constantine had struggled to keep the empire together. But the forces pulling it apart were too great. After his death, invaders swept across Rome's borders and overwhelmed the empire. The invaders belonged to tribes from the north. Today, we call them Germanic tribes. The Romans called them barbarians. In the past, the Roman army had been able to defeat these

The Anglo-Saxons who invaded Roman England buried their kings in ships. At a site discovered in England in 1939, the ancient ship had rotted. Yet many solid gold items, including this helmet, remained.

Vandals Today, we call someone who destroys property and valuable things a *vandal*. The Vandals were one of the Germanic tribes that invaded the Roman Empire. They looted Rome in A.D. 455. They were no worse than the other Germanic tribes. But their name came to be connected to this kind of damaging behavior.

tribes. Now, however, they could not stop the northerners. In the 400s, the Germanic tribes overran the empire. They captured and looted Rome in 410 and 455. The Roman emperor was almost powerless.

The last Roman emperor was 14-year-old Romulus Augustulus. His name recalled more than 1,000 years of Roman glory. But the boy emperor did not win glory for himself. In 476, a German general took power and sent him to work on a farm. After Romulus Augustulus, no emperor ruled over Rome and the western part of the empire.

However, even after Rome fell, the eastern part of the empire remained strong. Its capital, Constantinople, remained the center of another empire, the Byzantine empire, for another thousand years.

SECTION 5 REVIEW

1. **Define** (a) mercenary, (b) inflation.

2. **Identify** (a) Constantine, (b) Diocletian, (c) Constantinople.

3. Why did Roman money finally become worthless?

4. What did Diocletian do to make governing the Roman Empire easier?

Critical Thinking

5. **Expressing Problems Clearly** Summarize in two or three sentences the causes of the fall of the Roman Empire.

Activity

6. **Writing to Learn** Today, we think of the fall of the western Roman Empire in A.D. 476 as a great turning point in history. However, some historians think most people in those days hardly noticed any change. Why do you think that might be true?

SKILLS ACTIVITY

Reading Actively

Joji loved to read mystery stories. He was halfway through one when he thought to himself, "I want to know why this guy is going to the haunted house alone. What does he think he'll find there? Why doesn't he take someone with him?"

As he continued to read the story, Joji got excited again. "Wow!" he thought. "I bet the police will be there when the robber turns the corner. I can just see that robber's face when he gets caught. It will be just like that movie I saw once."

Get Ready

Joji was reading actively. He was enjoying what he was reading because he was actively participating in the story as he read. You can learn to do that, too. You can do it with everything you read, not just stories. You have been reading actively as you read this book, especially if you have paid attention to the hints in the margins labeled Read Actively.

Try It Out

Here are some strategies you can use to read actively.

A. Ask questions while you read. Joji did this when he asked himself why the hero was going into the haunted house alone. That helped Joji read to find out the answer. If you are reading a textbook, you might turn the headings into questions to ask yourself what you will find out as you read.

B. Connect what you read to your own life. Think about similar experiences you have had that can help you understand what you are reading. Joji's book reminded him of a movie he had seen. You can connect what you have read about ancient history in this book to your own life because you know something about what people need and how they act. And maybe you have read myths or stories or seen movies about the same topics.

C. Predict what you will find out. As you read, predict what will happen and why. Or think ahead to figure out how you think one fact you are reading might affect something else. See how your predictions match what you find out. What did Joji predict?

D. Visualize what things look like. As you read, form pictures in your mind. You can think about the expression on someone's face, as Joji did. You can also extend this strategy to think about how something smells or sounds or feels. This strategy can help you feel as though you are part of what you are reading.

Apply the Skill

Now practice by reading actively the boxed paragraphs about daily life in the streets of Rome. Use the strategies.

The streets of Rome were very narrow and difficult to walk through, but that did not stop people from gathering there. Shops and their customers spilled out onto the streets. Butchers chopped meat and barbers shaved their customers right out in the open.

Many Romans spent most of the day on the streets, rather than stay in their tiny, uncomfortable apartments. Children recited their lessons. People chatted with their friends and ran their businesses. Countless noises filled the air. Anyone walking through had to struggle with heavy crowds, full of shoving people.

1 **Ask questions.** Right after you read the first sentence, you might ask yourself why people could not succeed if they tried to hurry through the streets of Rome. What other questions did you ask yourself as you read?

2 **Connect.** What did you read in the paragraphs that made you think of something you have experienced or read about? Perhaps you have been in a crowd where you felt pushed from all sides.

3 **Predict.** Did you predict that the busy Roman streets would also be very noisy? What other predictions did you make? How did your predictions match what the paragraphs said?

4 **Visualize.** What would this street scene look like? What would it sound like? How might it smell?

Review and Activities

Reviewing Main Ideas

1. How did the experience with kings shape Romans' attitudes toward their republic?
2. Why was the Roman Empire successful?
3. List three major Roman advances in the field of technology. Then, choose one of them and describe its importance.
4. Give two examples of the way poor people lived in ancient Rome.
5. How were household slaves treated differently from other slaves?
6. (a) What were some teachings of Jesus?
   (b) What did Jesus promise to his followers?
7. Why did the Romans persecute the early Christians?
8. What did mercenaries have to do with the decline of the Roman Empire?
9. Describe two possible reasons why the Roman Empire declined in power.
10. How was the division of Rome into two parts an attempt to restore its greatness?

Reviewing Key Terms

Use each key term below in a sentence that shows the meaning of the term.

1. republic
2. patrician
3. plebeian
4. consul
5. veto
6. dictator
7. province
8. aqueduct
9. circus
10. messiah
11. disciple
12. Gospel
13. epistle
14. martyr
15. mercenary
16. inflation

Critical Thinking

1. **Recognizing Cause and Effect** What good and bad effects resulted from the great size of the Roman Empire?
2. **Drawing Conclusions** Why did poor Romans and slaves find Christianity appealing?

Graphic Organizer

Copy the chart onto a sheet of paper. Then fill in the empty boxes to complete the chart.

	Roman Republic	Roman Empire	Christianity	Fall of Rome
Events				
People				
Achievements				

Map Activity

Place Location

The Roman World
For each place listed below, write the letter from the map that shows its location.

1. Rome

2. Mediterranean Sea

3. Gaul

4. Judea

5. Britain

6. Greece

7. Constantinople

Writing Activity

Writing a Short Story
Write a two-page fictional short story on one of the episodes that you read about in this chapter. Make your leading character a participant in the event you choose.

Skills Review

Turn to the Skills Activity. Then complete the following: (a) List the Read Actively strategies that can help you understand better what you read. (b) Briefly explain how to use each strategy.

Internet Activity

Use a search engine to find **Exploring Ancient World Cultures.** Click on the **Rome** link at the bottom of the page. Click on **Chronology.** Choose a time period and click on it. Use the Chronological Space/Time Index to travel to ancient Rome. Choose **Rome** from the pull-down menu and type a date into the box. Press **Go.** When you are finished exploring, return to the **Rome** page and click **Roman Emperors Quiz** to test your knowledge of the Roman emperors.

How Am I Doing?

Answer these questions to help you check your progress.

1. Can I describe how Rome's central location helped make it a powerful force in ancient times?

2. Do I understand something about the achievements of the ancient Romans?

3. Can I identify some events that shaped the history of the ancient Roman world?

4. Do I understand something about the beliefs of Christianity?

5. What information from this chapter could I use in my book project?

THE ANCIENT WORLD
PROJECT POSSIBILITIES

The chapters in this book have some answers to these important questions.

☞ **What methods do people use today to try to understand cultures of the past?**

☞ **How did physical geography affect the growth of ancient civilizations?**

☞ **How did the beliefs and values of ancient civilizations affect the lives of their members?**

☞ **How did civilizations develop a government and an economic system?**

☞ **What accomplishments is each civilization known for?**

Doing projects is another way of answering the Guiding Questions in this book. Show what you know about the ancient world!

GEO CLEO

Project Menu

Now it's time for you to find your own answers by doing projects on your own or with a group. Here are some ways to make your own discoveries about the ancient world.

Ancient World Travel Guide As you study each civilization in this book, write a chapter for a travel guide to the world of ancient times. Create a map for each place, and write about its geography and history.

Include a picture of a special place or interesting feature of each civilization that travelers "must see." When you have finished all of the chapters, combine them to make a book.

From Questions to Careers

ARCHAEOLOGIST

Sometimes it seems amazing that we know so much about people and places that existed long ago. Since there were no cameras, no one took pictures of how it was back then. Often, there is no written record, either. The bits and pieces that we find out are like a jigsaw puzzle. Archaeologists are people who specialize in solving these puzzles.

Archaeologists study the past. They hunt for artifacts, such as pottery and tools. They examine very old, large structures like buildings and bridges. Archaeologists also study the natural objects that are found around these items such as bones, stones, and seeds. These ancient natural objects are called ecofacts.

Archaeologists may find artifacts and ecofacts in a variety of places. Some places, or sites, are easy to find, such as pyramids. Others are underground, underwater, or in caves.

Archaeologists make careful records of the items they find on a site. Often, they test the items to see how old they are.

Archaeologists study archaeology, history, languages, mathematics, and sciences. They work in excavation sites; in schools, teaching and researching; in museums; and in government jobs.

The Hall of Ancient Heritage Many ancient customs and activities such as games, sports, or celebrations still exist today. Choose one custom or activity from three or four civilizations in this book. Compare it with a modern custom or activity that seems similar to you. How are the versions alike? How are they different? What might be some reasons for those differences? To share your findings, create a poster with pictures and captions. Display this poster by itself or with others in a "Hall of Ancient Heritage" in your school.

Ancient Debate Which of the civilizations in this book made the greatest contributions to the modern world? Stage a debate with representatives from each civilization. To prove why your civilization is the best, you might research its form of government, art, inventions, language, science, literature, and other accomplishments. Visual aids such as pictures and posters could make your arguments more convincing. Rehearse your debate before presenting it to the class.

Life in the Ancient World Organize and hold an Ancient World Fair. Represent each of the civilizations in this book in your fair. You might have booths where students sell baked or fresh foods that represent each civilization. Other students can enact drama or sports that were popular in these civilizations. Include an art table, where visitors can make artwork or jewelry like that of the civilization. Other students can make or collect costumes for the participants to wear that look like the clothing of these civilizations.

WORLD EXPLORER

Reference

TABLE OF CONTENTS

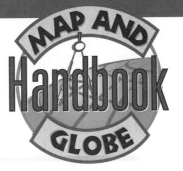

MAP AND GLOBE Handbook

This Map and Globe Handbook is designed to help you develop some of the skills you need to be a world explorer. These can help you whether you explore from the top of an elephant in India or from a computer at school.

You can use the information in this handbook to improve your map and globe skills. But the best way to sharpen your skills is to practice. The more you practice, the better you'll get.

GEO CLEO and GEO LEO

Table of Contents

Five Themes of Geography

Studying the geography of the entire world can be a huge task. You can make that task easier by using the five themes of geography: location, place, human-environment interaction, movement, and regions. The themes are tools you can use to organize information and to answer the where, why, and how of geography.

1 Location answers the question, "Where is it?" You can think of the location of a continent or a country as its address. You might give an absolute location such as "22 South Lake Street" or "40°N and 80°W." You might also use a relative address, telling where one place is by referring to another place. "Between school and the mall" and "eight miles east of Pleasant City" are examples of relative locations.

2 Place identifies the natural and human features that make one place different from every other place. You can identify a specific place by its landforms, climate, plants, animals, people, or cultures. You might even think of place as a geographic signature. Use the signature to help you understand the natural and human features that make one place different from every other place.

1. Location
Chicago, Illinois, occupies one location on the Earth. No other place has exactly the same absolute location.

2. Place
Ancient cultures in Egypt built distinctive pyramids. Use the theme of place to help you remember features that exist only in Egypt.

3 Human-Environment Interaction focuses on the relationship between people and the environment. As people live in an area, they often begin to make changes to it, usually to make their lives easier. For example, they might build a dam to control flooding during rainy seasons. Also, the environment can affect how people live, work, dress, travel, and communicate.

4 Movement answers the question "How do people, goods, and ideas move from place to place?" Remember that, often, what happens in one place can affect what happens in another. Use the theme of movement to help you trace the spread of goods, people, and ideas from one location to the next.

5 Region is the last geographic theme. A region is a group of places that share common features. Geographers divide the world into many types of regions. For example, countries, states, and cities are political regions. The people in these places live under the same type of government. Other features can be used to define regions. Places that have the same climate belong to a particular climate region. Places that share the same culture belong to a cultural region. The same place can be found in more than one region. The state of Hawaii is in the political region of the United States. Because it has a tropical climate, Hawaii is also part of a tropical climate region.

3. Human-Environment Interaction
Peruvians have changed steep mountain slopes into terraces suitable for farming. Think how this environment looked before people made changes.

PRACTICE YOUR WORLD EXPLORER SKILLS

1. What is the absolute location of your school? What is one way to describe its relative location?

2. What might be a "geographic signature" of the town or city you live in?

3. Give an example of human-environment interaction where you live.

4. Name at least one thing that comes into your town or city and one that goes out. How is each moved? Where does it come from? Where does it go?

5. What are several regions you think your town or city belongs in?

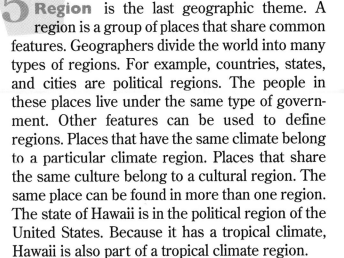

4. Movement
Arab traders brought not only goods to Kuala Lumpur, Malaysia, but also Arab building styles and the Islamic religion.

5. Regions
Wheat farming is an important activity in Kansas. This means that Kansas is part of a farming region.

Understanding Movements of the Earth

Planet Earth is part of our solar system. The Earth revolves around the sun in a nearly circular path called an orbit. A revolution, or one complete orbit around the sun, takes 365 1/4 days, or a year. As the Earth revolves around the sun, it is also spinning around in space. This movement is called a rotation. The Earth rotates on its axis—an invisible line through the center of the Earth from the North Pole to the South Pole. The Earth makes one full rotation about every 24 hours. As the Earth rotates, it is daytime on the side facing the sun. It is night on the side away from the sun.

The Earth's axis is tilted at an angle. Because of this tilt, sunlight strikes different parts of the Earth at certain points in the year, creating different seasons.

Earth's Revolution and the Seasons

Summer On June 21 or 22, the sun's direct rays are over the Tropic of Cancer. The Northern Hemisphere receives the greatest number of sunlight hours. It is the beginning of summer there.

Spring On March 20 or 21, the sun's rays shine strongest near the Equator. The Northern and Southern Hemispheres each receive almost equal hours of sunlight and darkness. It is the beginning of spring in the Northern Hemisphere.

Autumn On September 22 or 23, the sun's rays shine strongest near the Equator. Again, the Northern and Southern Hemispheres each receive almost equal hours of sunlight and darkness. It is the beginning of fall in the Northern Hemisphere.

Winter Around December 21, the sun is over the Tropic of Capricorn in the Southern Hemisphere. The Northern Hemisphere is tilted away from the sun and it is the beginning of winter there.

▲ **Location** This diagram shows how the Earth's tilt and orbit around the sun combine to create the seasons. Remember, in the Southern Hemisphere the seasons are reversed.

1 What causes the seasons in the Northern Hemisphere to be the opposite of those in the Southern Hemisphere?

2 During which two months of the year do the Northern and Southern Hemispheres have about equal hours of daylight and darkness?

Maps and Globes Represent the Earth

Globes

A globe is a scale model of the Earth. It shows the actual shapes, sizes, and locations of all the Earth's landmasses and bodies of water. Features on the surface of the Earth are drawn to scale on a globe. This means a smaller unit of measure on the globe stands for a larger unit of measure on the Earth.

Because a globe is made in the true shape of the Earth, it offers these advantages for studying the Earth.

- The shape of all land and water bodies are accurate.
- Compass directions from one point to any other point are correct.
- The distance from one location to another is always accurately represented.

However, a globe presents some disadvantages for studying the Earth. Because a globe shows the entire Earth, it cannot show small areas in great detail. Also, a globe is not easily folded and carried from one place to another. For these reasons, geographers often use maps to learn about the Earth.

Maps

A map is a drawing or representation, on a flat surface, of a region. A map can show details too small to be seen on a globe. Floor plans, mall directories, and road maps are among the maps we use most often.

While maps solve some of the problems posed by globes, they have some disadvantages of their own. Maps flatten the real round world. Mapmakers cut, stretch, push, and pull some parts of the Earth to get it all flat on paper. As a result, some locations may be distorted. That is, their size, shape, and relative location may not be accurate. For example, on most maps of the entire world, the size and shape of the Antarctic and Arctic regions are not accurate.

PRACTICE YOUR WORLD EXPLORER SKILLS

1. What is the main difference between a globe and a map?

2. What is one advantage of using a globe instead of a map?

Global Gores

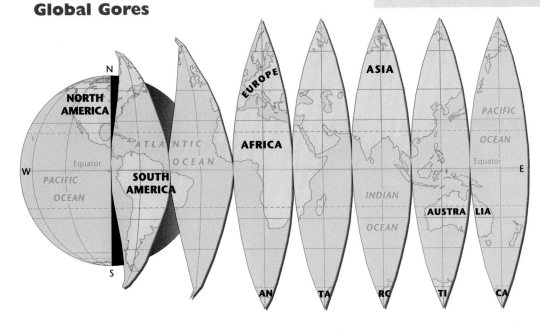

◀ **Location**
When mapmakers flatten the surface of the Earth, curves become straight lines. As a result, size, shape, and distance are distorted.

The Hemispheres

Another name for a round ball like a globe is a sphere. The Equator, an imaginary line halfway between the North and South Poles, divides the globe into two hemispheres. (The prefix *hemi* means "half.") Land and water south of the Equator are in the Southern Hemisphere. Land and water north of the Equator are in the Northern Hemisphere.

Mapmakers sometimes divide the globe along an imaginary line that runs from North Pole to South Pole. This line, called the Prime Meridian, divides the globe into the Eastern and Western Hemispheres.

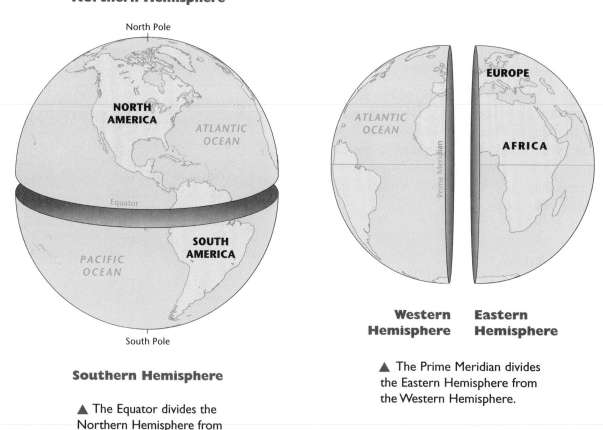

Northern Hemisphere

North Pole

NORTH AMERICA

ATLANTIC OCEAN

Equator

SOUTH AMERICA

PACIFIC OCEAN

South Pole

Southern Hemisphere

▲ The Equator divides the Northern Hemisphere from the Southern Hemisphere.

EUROPE

ATLANTIC OCEAN

Prime Meridian

AFRICA

Western Hemisphere **Eastern Hemisphere**

▲ The Prime Meridian divides the Eastern Hemisphere from the Western Hemisphere.

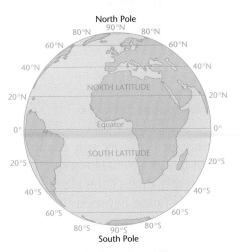

Parallels of Latitude

The Equator, at 0° latitude, is the starting place for measuring latitude or distances north and south. Most globes do not show every parallel of latitude. They may show every 10, 20, or even 30 degrees.

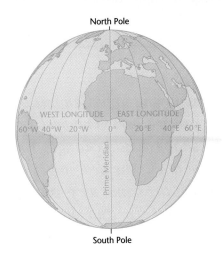

Meridians of Longitude

The Prime Meridian, at 0° longitude, runs from pole to pole through Greenwich, England. It is the starting place for measuring longitude or distances east and west. Each meridian of longitude meets its opposite longitude at the North and South Poles.

The Global Grid

Two sets of lines cover most globes. One set of lines runs parallel to the Equator. These lines, including the Equator, are called *parallels of latitude*. They are measured in degrees (°). One degree of latitude represents a distance of about 70 miles (112 km). The Equator has a location of 0°. The other parallels of latitude tell the direction and distance from the Equator to another location.

The second set of lines runs north and south. These lines are called *meridians of longitude*. Meridians show the degrees of longitude east or west of the Prime Meridian, which is located at 0°. A meridian of longitude tells the direction and distance from the Prime Meridian to another location. Unlike parallels, meridians are not the same distance apart everywhere on the globe.

Together the pattern of parallels of latitude and meridians of longitude is called the global grid. Using the lines of latitude and longitude, you can locate any place on Earth. For example, the location of 30° north latitude and 90° west longitude is usually written as 30°N, 90°W. Only one place on Earth has these coordinates—the city of New Orleans, in the state of Louisiana.

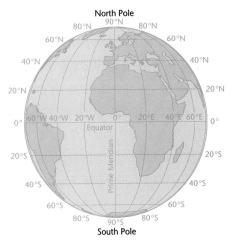

The Global Grid

By using lines of latitude and longitude, you can give the absolute location of any place on the Earth.

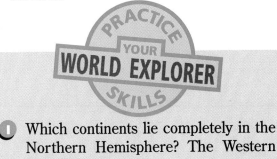

1. Which continents lie completely in the Northern Hemisphere? The Western Hemisphere?

2. Is there land or water at 20°S latitude and the Prime Meridian? At the Equator and 60°W longitude?

Imagine trying to flatten out a complete orange peel. The peel would split. The shape would change. You would have to cut the peel to get it to lie flat. In much the same way, maps cannot show the correct size and shape of every landmass or body of water on the Earth's curved surface. Maps shrink some places and stretch others. This shrinking and stretching is called distortion—a change made to a shape.

To make up for this disadvantage, mapmakers use different map projections. Each map projection is a way of showing the round Earth on flat paper. Each type of projection has some distortion. No one projection can accurately show the correct area, shape, distance, and direction for the Earth's surface. Mapmakers use the projection that has the least distortion for the information they are studying.

Same-Shape Maps

Some map projections can accurately show the shapes of landmasses. However, these projections often greatly distort the size of landmasses as well as the distance between them.

One of the most common same-shape maps is a Mercator projection, named for the mapmaker who invented it. The Mercator projection accurately shows shape and direction, but it distorts distance and size. In this projection, the northern and southern areas of the globe appear stretched more than areas near the Equator. Because the projection shows true directions, ships' navigators use it to chart a straight line course between two ports.

Mercator Projection

Equal-Area Maps

Some map projections can show the correct size of landmasses. Maps that use these projections are called equal-area maps. In order to show the correct size of landmasses, these maps usually distort shapes. The distortion is usually greater at the edges of the map and less at the center.

Robinson Maps

Many of the maps in this book use the Robinson projection. This is a compromise between the Mercator and equal-area projections. It gives a useful overall picture of the world. The Robinson projection keeps the size and shape relationships of most continents and oceans but does distort size of the polar regions.

Azimuthal Maps

Another kind of projection shows true compass direction. Maps that use this projection are called azimuthal maps. Such maps are easy to recognize—they are usually circular. Azimuthal maps are often used to show the areas of the North and South Poles. However, azimuthal maps distort scale, area, and shape.

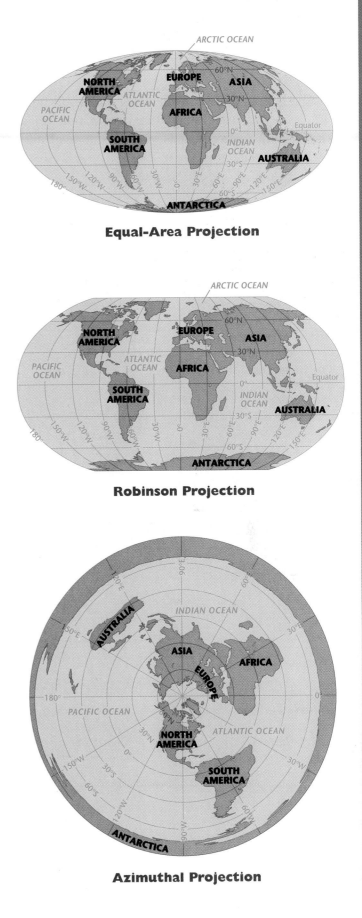

Equal-Area Projection

Robinson Projection

Azimuthal Projection

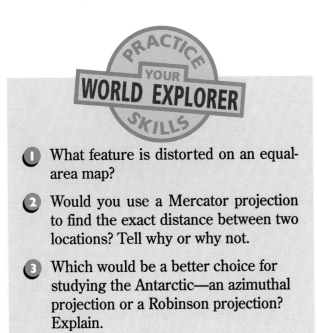

PRACTICE YOUR WORLD EXPLORER SKILLS

1. What feature is distorted on an equal-area map?

2. Would you use a Mercator projection to find the exact distance between two locations? Tell why or why not.

3. Which would be a better choice for studying the Antarctic—an azimuthal projection or a Robinson projection? Explain.

Parts of a Map

Mapmakers provide several clues to help you understand the information on a map. As an explorer, it is your job to read and interpret these clues.

Compass

Many maps show north at the top of the map. One way to show direction on a map is to use an arrow that points north. There may be an N shown with the arrow. Many maps give more information about direction by displaying a compass showing the directions, north, east, south, and west. The letters N, E, S, and W are placed to indicate these directions.

Title

The title of a map is the most basic clue. It signals what kinds of information you are likely to find on the map. A map titled *West Africa: Population Density* will be most useful for locating information about where people live in West Africa.

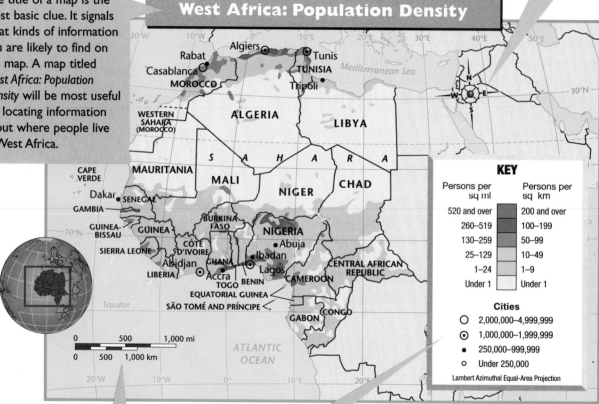

West Africa: Population Density

KEY

Persons per sq ml	Persons per sq km
520 and over	200 and over
260–519	100–199
130–259	50–99
25–129	10–49
1–24	1–9
Under 1	Under 1

Cities

○ 2,000,000–4,999,999
◉ 1,000,000–1,999,999
• 250,000–999,999
○ Under 250,000

Lambert Azimuthal Equal-Area Projection

Scale

A map scale helps you find the actual distances between points shown on the map. You can measure the distance between any two points on the map, compare them to the scale, and find out the actual distance between the points. Most map scales show distances in both miles and kilometers.

Key

Often a map has a key, or legend, that shows the symbols used on the map and what each one means. On some maps, color is used as a symbol. On those maps, the key also tells the meaning of each color.

PRACTICE YOUR WORLD EXPLORER SKILLS

1. What part of a map tells you what the map is about?

2. Where on the map should you look to find out the meaning of this symbol? •

3. What part of the map can you use to find the distance between two cities?

Comparing Maps of Different Scale

ere are three maps drawn to three different scales. The first map shows Moscow's location in the northeastern portion of Russia. This map shows the greatest area—a large section of northern Europe. It has the smallest scale (1 inch = about 900 miles) and shows the fewest details. This map can tell you what direction to travel to reach Moscow from Finland.

Find the red box on Map 1. It shows the whole area covered by Map 2. Study Map 2. It gives a closer look at the city of Moscow. It shows the features around the city, the city's boundary, and the general shape of the city. This map can help you find your way from the airport to the center of town.

Now find the red box on Map 2. This box shows the area shown on Map 3. This map moves you closer into the city. Like the zoom on a computer or camera, Map 3 shows the smallest area but has the greatest detail. This map has the largest scale (1 inch = about 0.8 miles). This is the map to use to explore downtown Moscow.

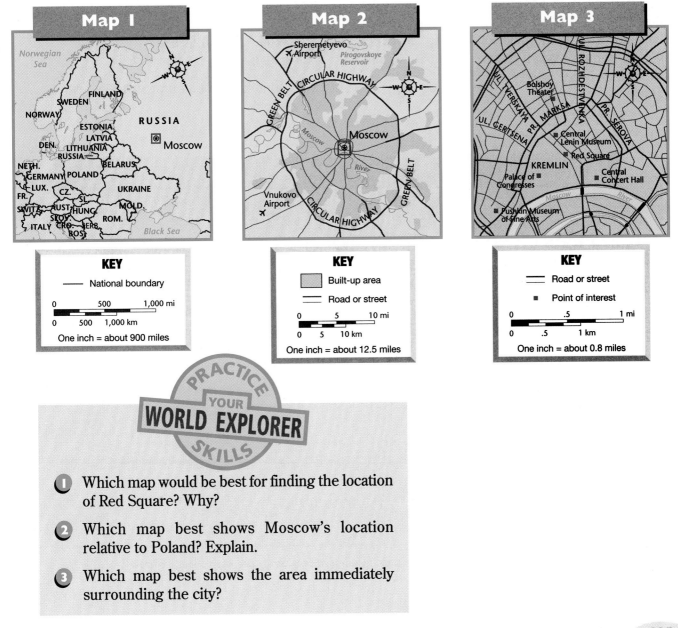

PRACTICE YOUR WORLD EXPLORER SKILLS

1. Which map would be best for finding the location of Red Square? Why?

2. Which map best shows Moscow's location relative to Poland? Explain.

3. Which map best shows the area immediately surrounding the city?

Political Maps

apmakers create maps to show all kinds of information. The kind of information presented affects the way a map looks. One type of map is called a political map. Its main purpose is to show continents, countries, and divisions within countries such as states or provinces. Usually different colors are used to show different countries or divisions within a country. The colors do not have any special meaning. They are used only to make the map easier to read.

Political maps also show where people have built towns and cities. Symbols can help you tell capital cities from other cities and towns. Even though political maps do not give information that shows what the land looks like, they often include some physical features such as oceans, lakes, and rivers.

Political maps usually have many labels. They give country names, and the names of capital and major cities. Bodies of water such as lakes, rivers, oceans, seas, gulfs, and bays are also labeled.

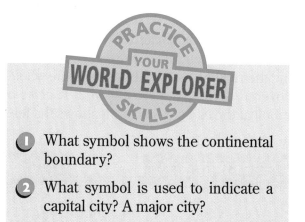

PRACTICE YOUR WORLD EXPLORER SKILLS

1. What symbol shows the continental boundary?

2. What symbol is used to indicate a capital city? A major city?

3. What kinds of landforms are shown on this map?

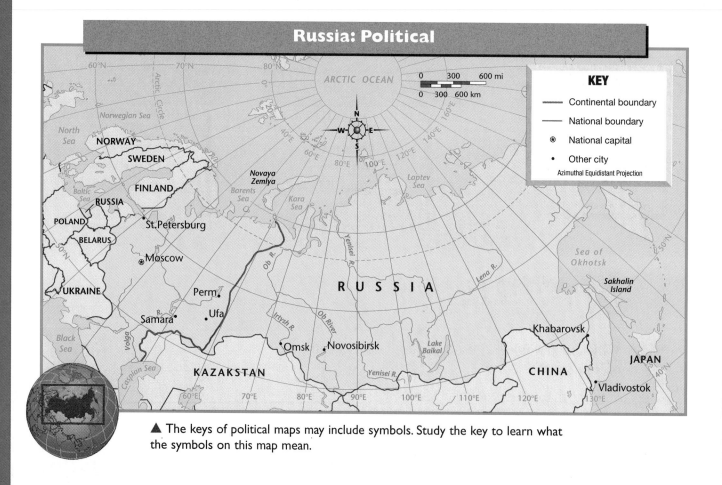

Russia: Political

KEY
— Continental boundary
— National boundary
⊛ National capital
• Other city
Azimuthal Equidistant Projection

▲ The keys of political maps may include symbols. Study the key to learn what the symbols on this map mean.

Physical Maps

Like political maps, physical maps show country labels and labels for capital cities. However, physical maps also show what the land of a region looks like by showing the major physical features such as plains, hills, plateaus, or mountains. Labels give the names of features such as mountain peaks, mountains, plateaus, and river basins.

In order to tell one landform from another, physical maps often show elevation and relief.

Elevation is the height of the land above sea level. Physical maps in this book use color to show elevation. Browns and oranges show higher lands while blues and greens show lands that are at or below sea level.

Relief shows how quickly the land rises or falls. Hills, mountains, and plateaus are shown on relief maps using shades of gray. Level or nearly level land is shown without shading. Darkly shaded areas indicate steeper lands.

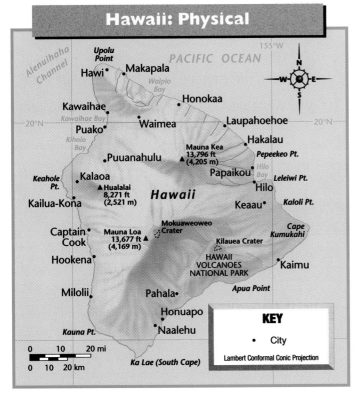

Hawaii: Physical

▲ On a physical map, shading is sometimes used to show relief. Use the shading to locate the mountains in Hawaii.

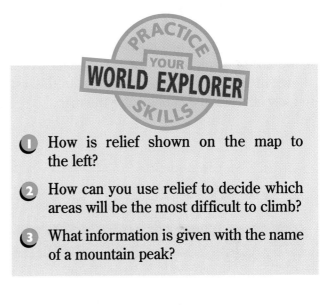

PRACTICE YOUR WORLD EXPLORER SKILLS

1. How is relief shown on the map to the left?

2. How can you use relief to decide which areas will be the most difficult to climb?

3. What information is given with the name of a mountain peak?

▼ Mauna Kea, an extinct volcano, is the highest peak in the state of Hawaii. Find Mauna Kea on the map.

Special Purpose Maps

As you explore the world, you will encounter many different kinds of special purpose maps. For example, a road map is a special purpose map. The title of each special purpose map tells the purpose and content of the map. Usually a special purpose map highlights only one kind of information. Examples of special purpose maps include land use, population distribution, recreation, transportation, natural resources, or weather.

The key on a special purpose map is very important. Even though a special purpose map shows only one kind of information, it may present many different pieces of data. This data can be shown in symbols, colors, or arrows. In this way, the key acts like a dictionary for the map.

Reading a special purpose map is a skill in itself. Look at the map below. First, try to get an overall sense of what it shows. Then, study the map to identify its main ideas. For example, one main idea of this map is that much of the petroleum production in the region takes place around the Persian Gulf.

1. What part of a special purpose map tells what information is contained on the map?

2. What part of a special purpose map acts like a dictionary for the map?

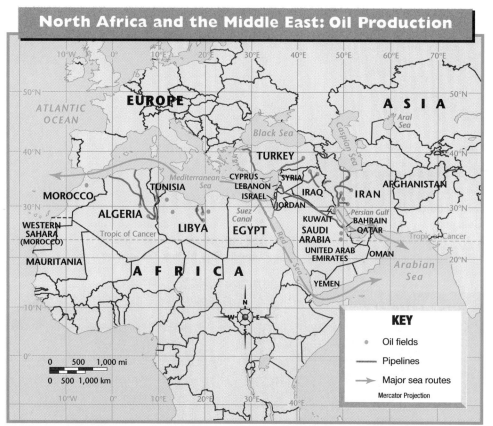

North Africa and the Middle East: Oil Production

◀ The title on a special purpose map indicates what information can be found on the map. The symbols used on the map are explained in the map's key.

KEY
- Oil fields
- Pipelines
- Major sea routes

Mercator Projection

Landforms, Climate Regions, and Natural Vegetation Regions

Maps that show landforms, climate, and vegetation regions are special purpose maps. Unlike the boundary lines on a political map, the boundary lines on these maps do not separate the land into exact divisions. A tropical wet climate gradually changes to a tropical wet and dry climate. A tundra gradually changes to an ice cap. Even though the boundaries between regions may not be exact, the information on these maps can help you understand the region and the lives of people in it.

Landforms

Understanding how people use the land requires an understanding of the shape of the land itself. The four most important landforms are mountains, hills, plateaus, and plains. Human activity in every region in the world is influenced by these landforms.

- **Mountains** are high and steep. Most are wide at the bottom and rise to a narrow peak or ridge. Most geographers classify a mountain as land that rises at least 2,000 feet (610 m) above sea level. A series of mountains is called a mountain range.

- **Hills** rise above surrounding land and have rounded tops. Hills are lower and usually less steep than mountains. The elevation of surrounding land determines whether a landform is called a mountain or a hill.
- A **plateau** is a large, mostly flat area of land that rises above the surrounding land. At least one side of a plateau has a steep slope.
- **Plains** are large areas of flat or gently rolling land. Plains have few changes in elevation. Many plains areas are located along coasts. Others are located in the interior regions of some continents.

▶ A satellite view of the Earth showing North and South America. What landforms are visible in the photograph?

Climate Regions

Another important influence in the ways people live their lives is the climate of their region. Climate is the weather of a given location over a long period of time. Use the descriptions in the table below to help you visualize the climate regions shown on maps.

Climate	Temperatures	Precipitation
Tropical		
Tropical wet	Hot all year round	Heavy all year round
Tropical wet and dry	Hot all year round	Heavy when sun is overhead, dry other times
Dry		
Semiarid	Hot summers, mild to cold winters	Light
Arid	Hot days, cold nights	Very light
Mild		
Mediterranean	Hot summers, cool winters	Dry summers, wet winters
Humid subtropical	Hot summers, cool winters	Year round, heavier in summer than in winter
Marine west coast	Warm summers, cool winters	Year round, heavier in winter than in summer
Continental		
Humid continental	Hot summers, cold winters	Year round, heavier in summer than in winter
Subarctic	Cool summers, cold winters	Light
Polar		
Tundra	Cool summers, very cold winters	Light
Ice Cap	Cold all year round	Light
Highlands	Varies, depending on altitude and direction of prevailing winds	Varies, depending on altitude and direction of prevailing winds

Natural Vegetation Regions

Natural vegetation is the plant life that grows wild without the help of humans. A world vegetation map tells what the vegetation in a place would be if people had not cut down forests or cleared grasslands. The table below provides descriptions of natural vegetation regions shown on maps. Comparing climate and vegetation regions can help you see the close relationship between climate and vegetation.

Vegetation	Description
Tropical rain forest	Tall, close-growing trees forming a canopy over smaller trees, dense growth in general
Deciduous forest	Trees and plants that regularly lose their leaves after each growing season
Mixed forest	Both leaf-losing and cone-bearing trees, no type of tree dominant
Coniferous forest	Cone-bearing trees, evergreen trees and plants
Mediterranean vegetation	Evergreen shrubs and small plants
Tropical savanna	Tall grasses with occasional trees and shrubs
Temperate grassland	Tall grasses with occasional stands of trees
Desert scrub	Low shrubs and bushes, hardy plants
Desert	Little or no vegetation
Tundra	Low shrubs, mosses, lichens; no trees
Ice Cap	Little or no vegetation
Highlands	Varies, depending on altitude and direction of prevailing winds

 How are mountains and hills similar? How are they different?

2 What is the difference between a plateau and a plain?

Atlas

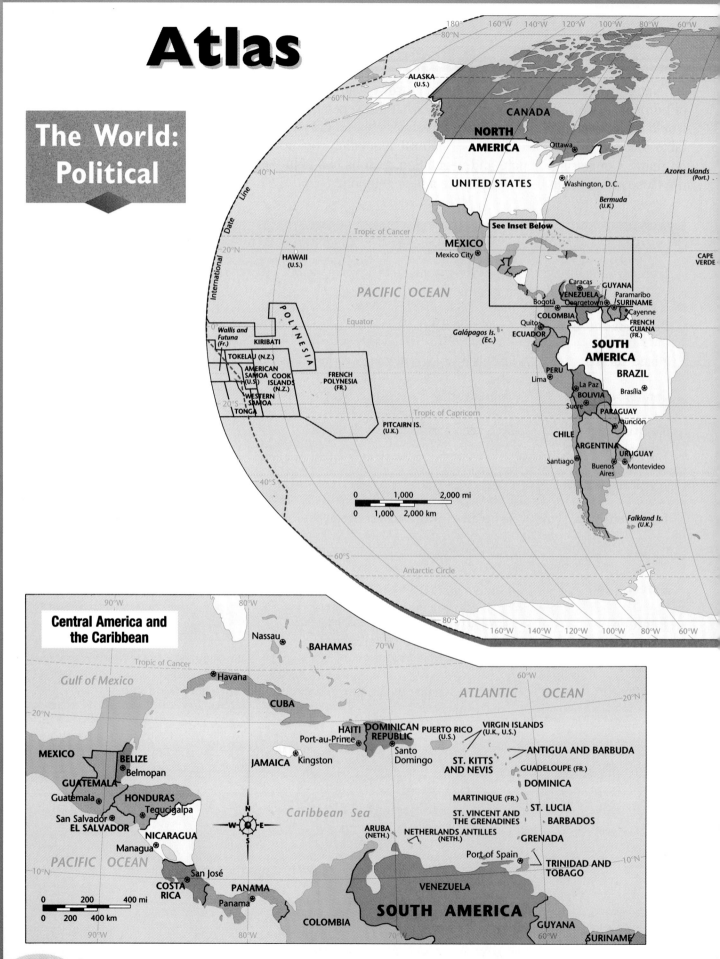

Central America and
the Caribbean

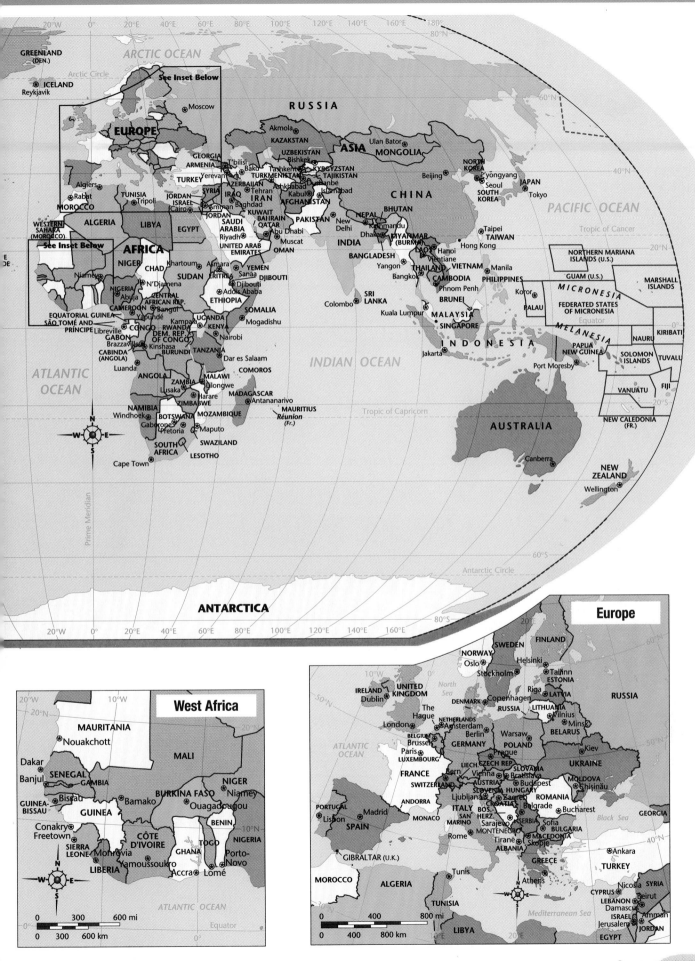

ARCTIC OCEAN

GREENLAND
(DEN.)

ICELAND
Reykjavik

EUROPE
See Inset Below

Moscow

RUSSIA

ASIA

KAZAKHSTAN

Akmola

UZBEKISTAN
T'bilisi
GEORGIA
ARMENIA
Baku
TURKEY
Yerevan
AZERBAIJAN
Tashkent
TURKMENISTAN
Bishkek
KYRGYZSTAN
TAJIKISTAN
Dushanbe
Ashkhabad

MONGOLIA
Ulan Bator

Beijing

NORTH
KOREA
P'yongyang
Seoul
SOUTH
KOREA

JAPAN

Tokyo

PACIFIC OCEAN

Algiers

TUNISIA
Tripoli

SYRIA
IRAQ
Baghdad
Tehran
IRAN
Kabul
AFGHANISTAN
Islamabad

CHINA

Taipei
TAIWAN

Hong Kong

Tropic of Cancer

Rabat
MOROCCO
JORDAN
ISRAEL
Cairo
Amman

PAKISTAN
NEPAL
Kathmandu
BHUTAN

WESTERN
SAHARA
(MOROCCO)

ALGERIA

LIBYA

EGYPT

SAUDI
ARABIA

KUWAIT
BAHRAIN
QATAR
Abu Dhabi
Riyadh
UNITED ARAB
EMIRATES
Muscat
OMAN

New
Delhi

Dhaka
INDIA

MYANMAR
(BURMA)

LAOS
Vientiane

Hanoi

VIETNAM
Manila

NORTHERN MARIANA
ISLANDS (U.S.)

GUAM (U.S.)

20°N

See Inset Below

AFRICA

NIGER
CHAD

Khartoum
N'Djamena

SUDAN

Asmara
ERITREA

Sanaa
YEMEN
DJIBOUTI
Djibouti

BANGLADESH

Yangon

THAILAND
Bangkok

CAMBODIA
Phnom Penh

PHILIPPINES

MARSHALL
ISLANDS

MICRONESIA

FEDERATED STATES
OF MICRONESIA

Niamey
NIGERIA
Abuja
CENTRAL
AFRICAN REP.
Bangui
CAMEROON

Addis Ababa
ETHIOPIA

SOMALIA

SRI
LANKA
Colombo

BRUNEI
Koror

PALAU

KIRIBATI

NAURU

EQUATORIAL GUINEA
SÃO TOMÉ AND
PRÍNCIPE
Libreville
GABON
CONGO
Brazzaville
Yaoundé
DEM. REP.
OF CONGO
Kinshasa

UGANDA
Kampala
RWANDA
KENYA
BURUNDI
Nairobi
TANZANIA

Kuala Lumpur
MALAYSIA
SINGAPORE

Jakarta

INDONESIA

MELANESIA

PAPUA
NEW GUINEA

SOLOMON
ISLANDS

TUVALU

Dar es Salaam

INDIAN OCEAN

Port Moresby

ATLANTIC
OCEAN

CABINDA
(ANGOLA)
Luanda

ANGOLA

Lusaka

ZAMBIA

COMOROS

MALAWI
Lilongwe

MADAGASCAR
Antananarivo

MAURITIUS
Réunion
(Fr.)

VANUATU

FIJI

Tropic of Capricorn

NEW CALEDONIA
(FR.)

Harare
NAMIBIA
Windhoek
BOTSWANA
Gaborone
Pretoria
Maputo
SOUTH
AFRICA
SWAZILAND
LESOTHO
Cape Town

ZIMBABWE
MOZAMBIQUE

AUSTRALIA

Canberra

NEW
ZEALAND

Wellington

ANTARCTICA

N
W   E
S

West Africa

MAURITANIA
Nouakchott

MALI

Dakar
SENEGAL
Banjul
GAMBIA
GUINEA-
BISSAU
Bissau
GUINEA
Conakry
Freetown
SIERRA
LEONE
Monrovia
LIBERIA

NIGER
Niamey

BURKINA FASO
Bamako
Ouagadougou

BENIN

CÔTE
D'IVOIRE
GHANA
Yamoussoukro
Accra

NIGERIA
TOGO
Porto-
Novo
Lomé

ATLANTIC OCEAN

N
W   E
S

| 0 | 300 | 600 mi |
| 0 | 300 | 600 km |

Europe

NORWAY
Oslo

SWEDEN

FINLAND

Helsinki

Stockholm

Tallinn
ESTONIA

RUSSIA

IRELAND
Dublin
UNITED
KINGDOM
North
Sea
DENMARK
Copenhagen

Riga
LATVIA

LITHUANIA
Vilnius
Minsk

London
The
Hague
NETHERLANDS
Amsterdam
BELGIUM
Brussels
Berlin

Warsaw
POLAND

BELARUS

Kiev

ATLANTIC
OCEAN

Paris
LUXEMBOURG
GERMANY
Prague
CZECH REP.
LIECH.
Vienna
SLOVAKIA
Bratislava
UKRAINE

MOLDOVA
Chişinău

FRANCE
SWITZERLAND
Bern
AUSTRIA
SLOVENIA
Budapest
HUNGARY
ROMANIA
Ljubljana
CROATIA
Zagreb
Belgrade
Bucharest

ANDORRA

ITALY
SAN
MARINO
BOS.
HERZ.
Sarajevo
SERBIA
Sofia
BULGARIA

GEORGIA

Black Sea

PORTUGAL
Lisbon

Madrid

MONACO

MONTENEGRO
MACEDONIA
Tirané
Skopje
ALBANIA

SPAIN

Rome

GIBRALTAR (U.K.)

GREECE

TURKEY

Ankara

Tunis

Athens

MOROCCO

ALGERIA

TUNISIA

LIBYA

Mediterranean Sea

CYPRUS
Nicosia
LEBANON
Beirut
Damascus
ISRAEL
Jerusalem
Amman
JORDAN

SYRIA

N
W   E
S

| 0 | 400 | 800 mi |
| 0 | 400 | 800 km |

The World: Physical

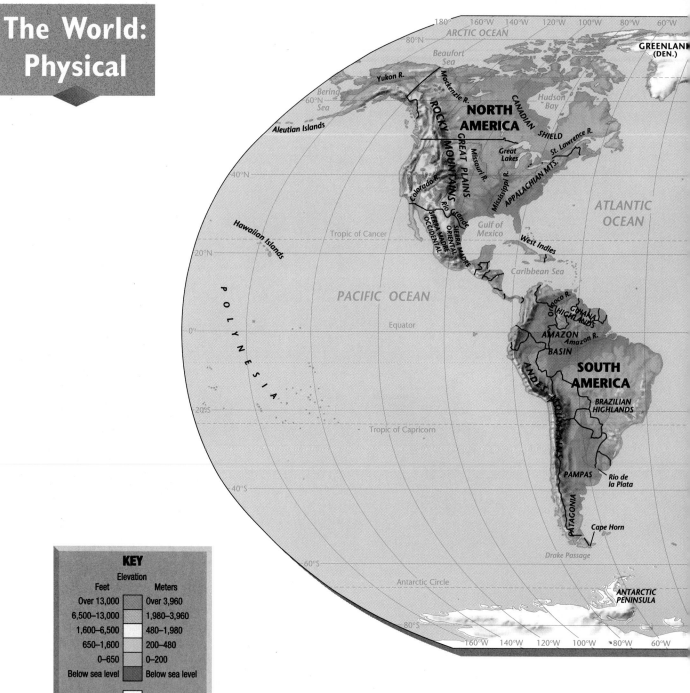

NORTH AMERICA

GREENLAND (DEN.)

ARCTIC OCEAN

Beaufort Sea

Yukon R.

Mackenzie R.

Bering Sea

Aleutian Islands

ROCKY MOUNTAINS

GREAT PLAINS

CANADIAN SHIELD

Hudson Bay

Great Lakes

St. Lawrence R.

Missouri R.

Mississippi R.

APPALACHIAN MTS.

Colorado R.

Rio Grande

SIERRA MADRE ORIENTAL

SIERRA MADRE OCCIDENTAL

Gulf of Mexico

West Indies

Caribbean Sea

ATLANTIC OCEAN

Hawaiian Islands

Tropic of Cancer

PACIFIC OCEAN

Equator

P O L Y N E S I A

Orinoco R.

GUIANA HIGHLANDS

AMAZON BASIN

Amazon R.

SOUTH AMERICA

BRAZILIAN HIGHLANDS

ANDES MTS.

PAMPAS

Rio de la Plata

PATAGONIA

Cape Horn

Tropic of Capricorn

Drake Passage

Antarctic Circle

ANTARCTIC PENINSULA

KEY

Elevation

Feet	Meters
Over 13,000	Over 3,960
6,500–13,000	1,980–3,960
1,600–6,500	480–1,980
650–1,600	200–480
0–650	0–200
Below sea level	Below sea level

Ice cap

Ice shelf

Robinson Projection

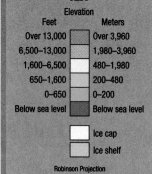

South Pole

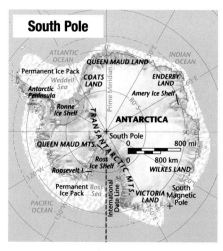

ATLANTIC OCEAN

INDIAN OCEAN

QUEEN MAUD LAND

Permanent Ice Pack

Weddell Sea

COATS LAND

ENDERBY LAND

Antarctic Peninsula

Amery Ice Shelf

Ronne Ice Shelf

ANTARCTICA

South Pole

QUEEN MAUD MTS.

TRANSANTARCTIC MTS.

Ross Ice Shelf

WILKES LAND

Roosevelt I.

Permanent Ice Pack

Ross Sea

VICTORIA LAND

South Magnetic Pole

PACIFIC OCEAN

Prime Meridian

International Date Line

0   800 mi

0   800 km

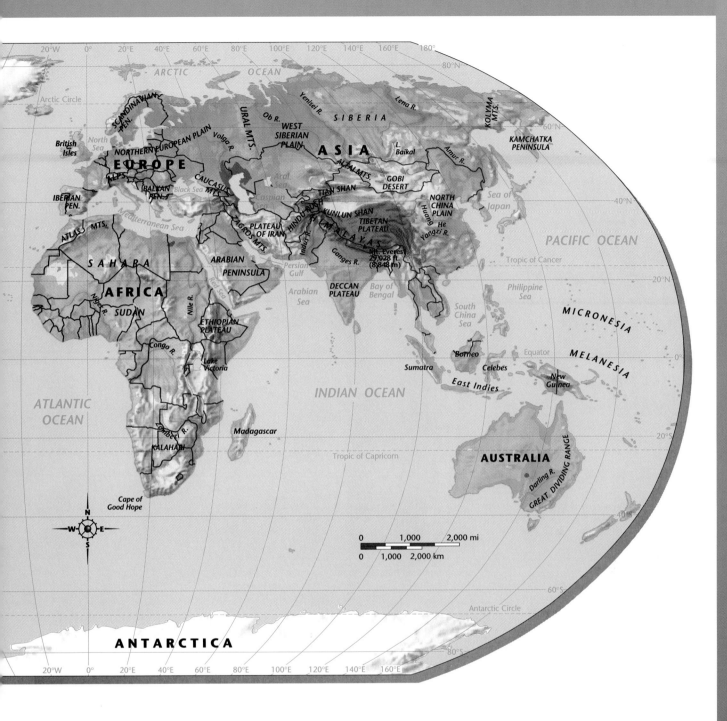

ARCTIC OCEAN

20°W 0° 20°E 40°E 60°E 80°E 100°E 120°E 140°E 160°E 180°

Arctic Circle

80°N

60°N

SCANDINAVIAN PEN.

British Isles

North Sea

NORTHERN EUROPEAN PLAIN

EUROPE

ALPS

IBERIAN PEN.

BALKAN PEN.

ATLAS MTS.

Mediterranean Sea

Black Sea

CAUCASUS MTS.

Caspian Sea

Aral Sea

URAL MTS.

Volga R.

Ob R.

Yenisei R.

WEST SIBERIAN PLAIN

SIBERIA

Lena R.

ASIA

ALTAI MTS.

TIAN SHAN

GOBI DESERT

Amur R.

KOLYMA MTS.

KAMCHATKA PENINSULA

L. Baikal

Sea of Japan

40°N

PLATEAU OF IRAN

ZAGROS MTS.

HINDU KUSH

KUNLUN SHAN

TIBETAN PLATEAU

HIMALAYAS

NORTH CHINA PLAIN

Huang He

Yangzi R.

PACIFIC OCEAN

Tropic of Cancer

ARABIAN PENINSULA

Persian Gulf

Indus R.

Mt. Everest 29,028 ft. (8,848 m)

Ganges R.

Red Sea

SAHARA

AFRICA

SUDAN

Niger R.

Nile R.

ETHIOPIAN PLATEAU

Arabian Sea

DECCAN PLATEAU

Bay of Bengal

Philippine Sea

MICRONESIA

20°N

Congo R.

Lake Victoria

South China Sea

Sumatra

Borneo

Celebes

East Indies

New Guinea

MELANESIA

Equator

0°

ATLANTIC OCEAN

INDIAN OCEAN

Zambezi R.

KALAHARI

Madagascar

Tropic of Capricorn

AUSTRALIA

Darling R.

GREAT DIVIDING RANGE

20°S

Cape of Good Hope

N
W   E
S

0   1,000   2,000 mi

0   1,000   2,000 km

40°S

60°S

Antarctic Circle

ANTARCTICA

80°S

20°W 0° 20°E 40°E 60°E 80°E 100°E 120°E 140°E 160°E

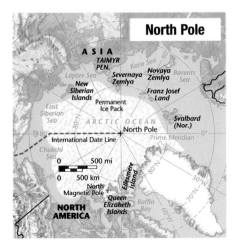

North Pole

ASIA

TAIMYR PEN.

Laptev Sea

New Siberian Islands

Severnaya Zemlya

Novaya Zemlya

Kara Sea

Barents Sea

Franz Josef Land

Permanent Ice Pack

Svalbard (Nor.)

East Siberian Sea

ARCTIC OCEAN

North Pole

Prime Meridian

0°

International Date Line

Chukchi Sea

0   500 mi

0   500 km

North Magnetic Pole

Queen Elizabeth Islands

Ellesmere Island

Baffin Bay

NORTH AMERICA

United States: Political

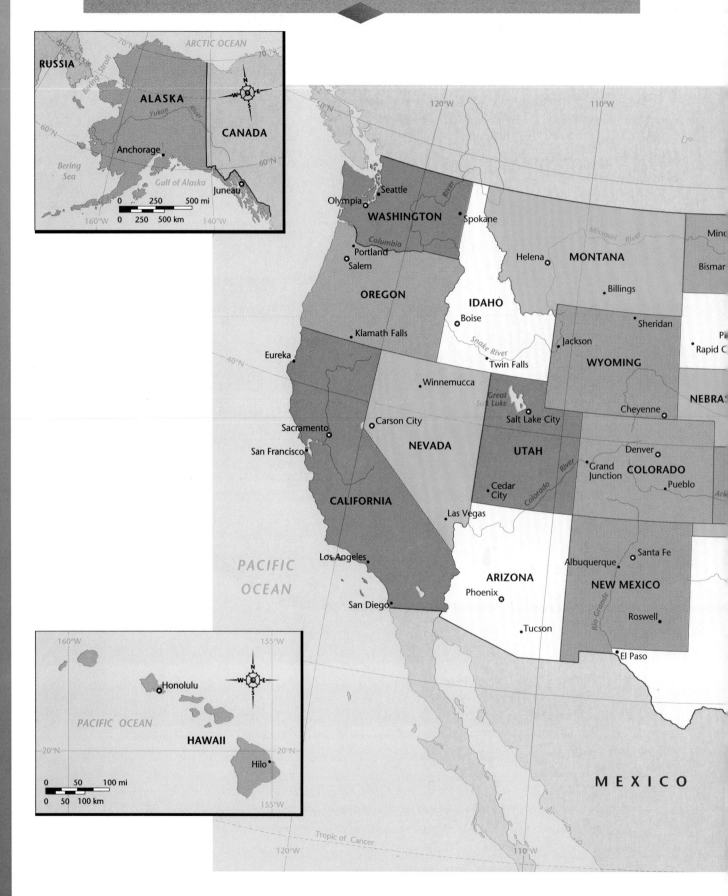

ALASKA

ARCTIC OCEAN

RUSSIA

70°N

70°N

Arctic Circle

Bering Strait

Yukon River

60°N

CANADA

60°N

Bering Sea

Anchorage

Gulf of Alaska

Juneau

0   250   500 mi

0   250   500 km

160°W   140°W

HAWAII

160°W   155°W

Honolulu

PACIFIC OCEAN

20°N   20°N

Hilo

0   50   100 mi

0   50   100 km

155°W

PACIFIC OCEAN

50°N

120°W   110°W

Mino

Seattle

WASHINGTON

Olympia

Spokane

Columbia

River

Helena

MONTANA

Bismar

Portland

Salem

Billings

OREGON

IDAHO

Boise

Sheridan

Rapid C

Klamath Falls

Snake River

Jackson

Eureka

40°N

Twin Falls

WYOMING

Winnemucca

Great
Salt Lake

Cheyenne

NEBRA

Sacramento

Carson City

Salt Lake City

San Francisco

NEVADA

UTAH

Denver

Colorado River

Grand
Junction

COLORADO

Pueblo

Cedar
City

Ark

CALIFORNIA

Las Vegas

PACIFIC

Los Angeles

Santa Fe

OCEAN

Albuquerque

ARIZONA

NEW MEXICO

San Diego

Phoenix

Rio Grande

Roswell

Tucson

El Paso

M E X I C O

120°W

110°W

Tropic of Cancer

C A N A D A

0 150 300 mi
0 150 300 km

NORTH DAKOTA
MINNESOTA
Duluth
Sault Ste. Marie
MICHIGAN
Lake Superior

SOUTH DAKOTA
Minneapolis
St. Paul
WISCONSIN
Milwaukee
Madison
Lansing
Detroit
Lake Michigan
Lake Huron

Presque Isle
MAINE
Augusta
Portland
Montpelier
VERMONT
NEW HAMPSHIRE
Concord
Boston
NEW YORK
Albany
Buffalo
Lake Ontario
MASSACHUSETTS
Providence
Hartford
New Haven
RHODE ISLAND
CONNECTICUT

Missouri
IOWA
Des Moines
Cedar Rapids
Chicago
ILLINOIS
Springfield
INDIANA
Indianapolis
OHIO
Columbus
Cincinnati
Cleveland
PENNSYLVANIA
Harrisburg
Pittsburgh
Lake Erie

New York City
Trenton
NEW JERSEY
Philadelphia
Dover
DELAWARE
Baltimore
Annapolis
Washington, D.C.
MARYLAND

Omaha
Lincoln
Topeka
Kansas City
KANSAS
Wichita
River
Jefferson City
MISSOURI
St. Louis
Louisville
Frankfort
KENTUCKY
Ohio River
WEST VIRGINIA
Charleston
Richmond
VIRGINIA
Norfolk

OKLAHOMA
Tulsa
Oklahoma City
ARKANSAS
Little Rock
Pine Bluff
Red River
Memphis
Nashville
TENNESSEE
Tennessee River
NORTH CAROLINA
Raleigh
Charlotte

TEXAS
Dallas
Austin
San Antonio
Houston
Shreveport
Baton Rouge
LOUISIANA
New Orleans
MISSISSIPPI
Jackson
Hattiesburg
Mississippi River
Birmingham
ALABAMA
Montgomery
GEORGIA
Columbus
Atlanta
Savannah
SOUTH CAROLINA
Columbia
Charleston

Jacksonville
Tallahassee
FLORIDA
Tampa
Lake Okeechobee
Miami

Rio Grande
Gulf of Mexico

ATLANTIC OCEAN

90°W   80°W   70°W
40°N
30°N

KEY
— National boundary
— State boundary
⊕ National capital
⊙ State capital
• Other city
Transverse Mercator Projection

North and South America: Political

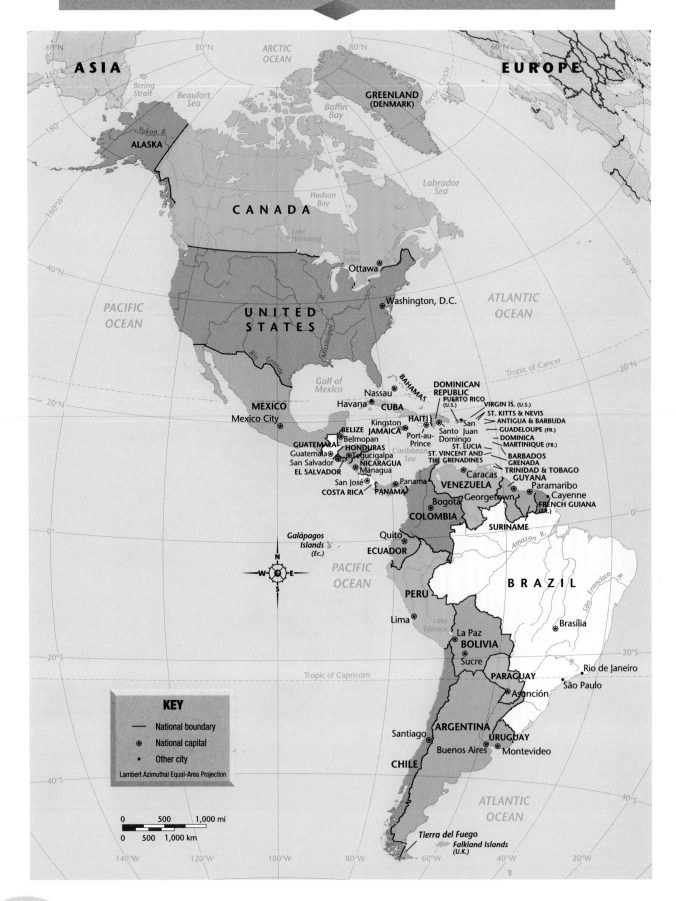

ASIA

ARCTIC OCEAN

EUROPE

60°N 80°N 80°N 60°N

160°E
180°
Bering Strait
Beaufort Sea
Baffin Bay

GREENLAND (DENMARK)

Arctic Circle

ALASKA
Yukon R.

Labrador Sea

CANADA

Hudson Bay

Lake Winnipeg

Great Lakes

40°N

Ottawa

20°W

UNITED STATES

Washington, D.C.

ATLANTIC OCEAN

PACIFIC OCEAN

160°W

Rio Grande

Mississippi R.

Tropic of Cancer

20°N

Gulf of Mexico

Nassau

BAHAMAS

DOMINICAN REPUBLIC
PUERTO RICO (U.S.)

VIRGIN IS. (U.S.)
ST. KITTS & NEVIS
ANTIGUA & BARBUDA
GUADELOUPE (FR.)
DOMINICA
MARTINIQUE (FR.)
BARBADOS
GRENADA
TRINIDAD & TOBAGO

MEXICO
Mexico City

Havana

CUBA

HAITI

San Juan

MEXICO

Santo Domingo

ST. LUCIA

Kingston

Port-au-Prince

20°N

BELIZE
Belmopan

JAMAICA

GUATEMALA
Guatemala
San Salvador
EL SALVADOR

HONDURAS
Tegucigalpa
NICARAGUA
Managua

Caribbean Sea

ST. VINCENT AND THE GRENADINES

San José
COSTA RICA

Panama

PANAMA

Caracas

VENEZUELA
Georgetown

GUYANA

Paramaribo
Cayenne
FRENCH GUIANA (FR.)

Bogotá

COLOMBIA

SURINAME

Galápagos Islands (Ec.)

Quito

ECUADOR

0°

Amazon R.

0°

PACIFIC OCEAN

BRAZIL

São Francisco R.

PERU

Lima

Lake Titicaca

Brasília

La Paz

BOLIVIA

Sucre

Rio de Janeiro

20°S

Tropic of Capricorn

PARAGUAY

São Paulo

Asunción

KEY

National boundary

National capital

Other city

Lambert Azimuthal Equal-Area Projection

ARGENTINA

URUGUAY

Santiago

Buenos Aires

Montevideo

CHILE

40°S

0   500   1,000 mi
0   500   1,000 km

ATLANTIC OCEAN

140°W   120°W   100°W   80°W

Tierra del Fuego

Falkland Islands (U.K.)

60°W   40°W   20°W

North and South America: Physical

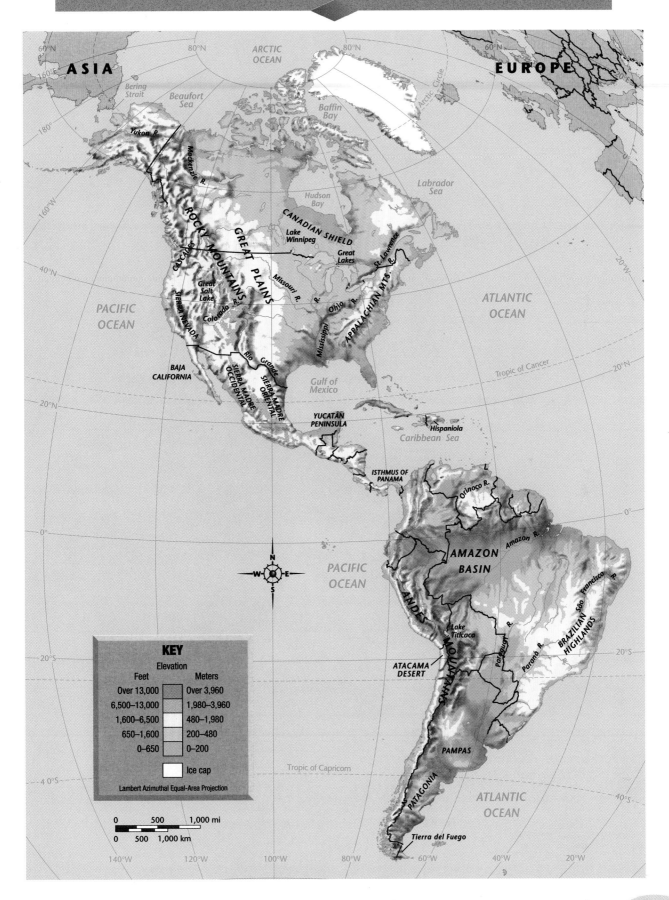

ASIA

EUROPE

ARCTIC OCEAN

60°N

80°N

80°N

60°N

160°E

180°

Bering Strait

Beaufort Sea

Baffin Bay

Arctic Circle

20°E

Yukon R.

Mackenzie R.

Hudson Bay

Labrador Sea

40°N

ROCKY MOUNTAINS

CASCADES

GREAT PLAINS

CANADIAN SHIELD

Lake Winnipeg

Great Lakes

St. Lawrence R.

160°W

40°N

20°W

Great Salt Lake

SIERRA NEVADA

Missouri R.

Colorado R.

Ohio R.

Mississippi R.

APPALACHIAN MTS.

ATLANTIC OCEAN

PACIFIC OCEAN

BAJA CALIFORNIA

SIERRA MADRE OCCIDENTAL

Rio Grande

SIERRA MADRE ORIENTAL

Gulf of Mexico

Tropic of Cancer

20°N

20°N

YUCATÁN PENINSULA

Hispaniola

Caribbean Sea

ISTHMUS OF PANAMA

Orinoco R.

L

0°

0°

Amazon R.

AMAZON BASIN

São Francisco R.

PACIFIC OCEAN

ANDES MOUNTAINS

Lake Titicaca

Juruá R.

Paraguay R.

BRAZILIAN HIGHLANDS

ATACAMA DESERT

20°S

20°S

Paraná R.

KEY

Elevation

Feet		Meters
Over 13,000		Over 3,960
6,500–13,000		1,980–3,960
1,600–6,500		480–1,980
650–1,600		200–480
0–650		0–200

Ice cap

Lambert Azimuthal Equal-Area Projection

PAMPAS

Tropic of Capricorn

PATAGONIA

ATLANTIC OCEAN

40°S

40°S

Tierra del Fuego

0   500   1,000 mi

0   500   1,000 km

140°W

120°W

100°W

80°W

60°W

40°W

20°W

Europe: Political

KEY

— National boundary
⊛ National capital
• Other city

Lambert Azimuthal Equal-Area Projection

ARCTIC OCEAN

ICELAND
Reykjavik

ATLANTIC OCEAN

Faeroe Is. (Den.)

Shetland Is. (U.K.)

NORWAY
Lillehammer
Oslo

SWEDEN
Stockholm
Göteborg

FINLAND
Turku
Helsinki
St. Petersburg

RUSSIA
Moscow

Tallinn
ESTONIA

Riga
LATVIA

LITHUANIA
Vilnius

BELARUS
Minsk

North Sea

Baltic Sea

DENMARK
Copenhagen

IRELAND
Dublin

UNITED KINGDOM
Manchester

London

Amsterdam
The Hague
NETHERLANDS

Brussels
BELGIUM

Berlin

RUSSIA

Gdańsk

POLAND
Warsaw
Łódź

Kiev

UKRAINE

GERMANY
Cologne
Bonn
Frankfurt

Katowice
Kraków

Prague
CZECH REPUBLIC
Brno

SLOVAKIA

MOLDOVA
Chişinău

LUXEMBOURG
Luxembourg

English Channel

Paris

Danube R.

Munich

LIECHTENSTEIN
Vienna

Bratislava
Budapest

Cluj

ROMANIA

FRANCE

Bay of Biscay

Bern
SWITZERLAND

AUSTRIA

HUNGARY

Bucharest

Black Sea

Ljubljana
SLOVENIA

Milan

Zagreb

CROATIA

BOSNIA & HERZEGOVINA
Sarajevo

Belgrade
SERBIA

BULGARIA
Sophia

SAN MARINO

Marseille

MONACO

ITALY

Adriatic Sea

Podgorica
MONTENEGRO

Skopje
MACEDONIA

PORTUGAL

ANDORRA

Corsica

VATICAN CITY
Rome

ALBANIA
Tiranë

Lisbon

Madrid

Barcelona

Sardinia

Naples

Aegean Sea

GREECE

SPAIN

Balearic Is.

Tyrrhenian Sea

Ionian Sea

Athens

Mediterranean Sea

Sicily

Crete

Strait of Gibraltar

GIBRALTAR (U.K.)

MALTA

AFRICA

0   250   500 mi
0   250   500 km

Europe: Physical

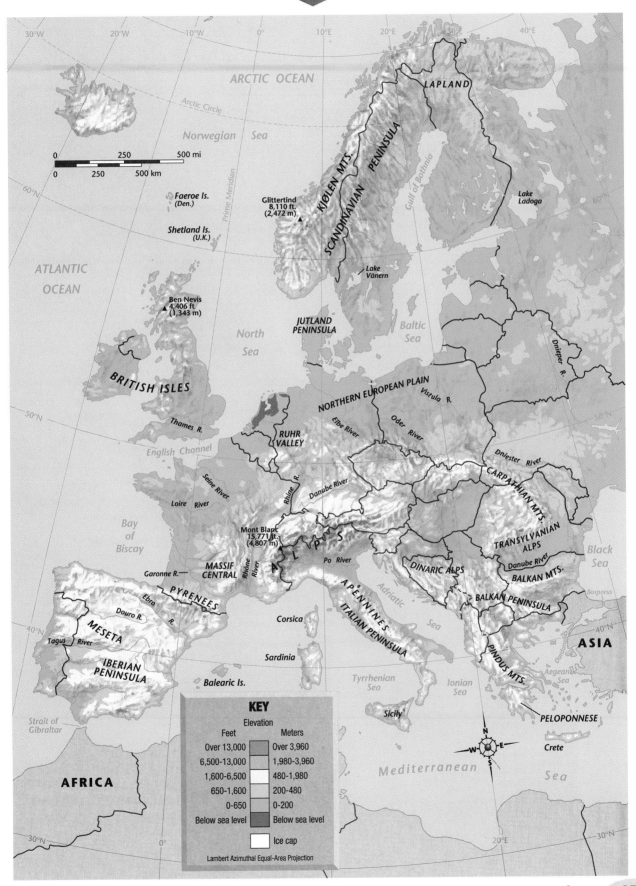

ARCTIC OCEAN

LAPLAND

Arctic Circle

Norwegian Sea

0   250   500 mi
0   250   500 km

Faeroe Is.
(Den.)

Glittertind
8,110 ft.
(2,472 m)

KJØLEN MTS.

SCANDINAVIAN PENINSULA

Gulf of Bothnia

Lake
Ladoga

Shetland Is.
(U.K.)

Lake
Vänern

ATLANTIC
OCEAN

Ben Nevis
4,406 ft.
(1,343 m)

North
Sea

JUTLAND
PENINSULA

Baltic
Sea

Dnieper R.

BRITISH ISLES

NORTHERN EUROPEAN PLAIN

Visrula R.

Thames R.

RUHR
VALLEY

Elbe River

Oder River

English Channel

Seine River

Rhine R.

Danube River

Dniester River

CARPATHIAN MTS.

Loire River

Bay
of
Biscay

Mont Blanc
15,771 ft.
(4,807 m)

ALPS

Po River

TRANSYLVANIAN
ALPS

Danube River

Black
Sea

MASSIF
CENTRAL

Garonne R.

Rhône River

DINARIC ALPS

BALKAN MTS.

Bosporus

PYRENEES

Ebro
R.

APENNINES

Adriatic

BALKAN PENINSULA

Douro R.

Corsica

ITALIAN PENINSULA

Sea

ASIA

MESETA

Tagus River

Sardinia

PINDUS MTS.

Aegean
Sea

IBERIAN
PENINSULA

Balearic Is.

Tyrrhenian
Sea

Ionian
Sea

PELOPONNESE

Strait of
Gibraltar

Crete

AFRICA

Mediterranean

Sea

KEY

Elevation

Feet		Meters
Over 13,000		Over 3,960
6,500–13,000		1,980–3,960
1,600–6,500		480–1,980
650–1,600		200–480
0–650		0–200
Below sea level		Below sea level
		Ice cap

Lambert Azimuthal Equal-Area Projection

30°W   20°W   10°W   0°   10°E   20°E   30°E   40°E

60°N

50°N

40°N

30°N

Africa: Political

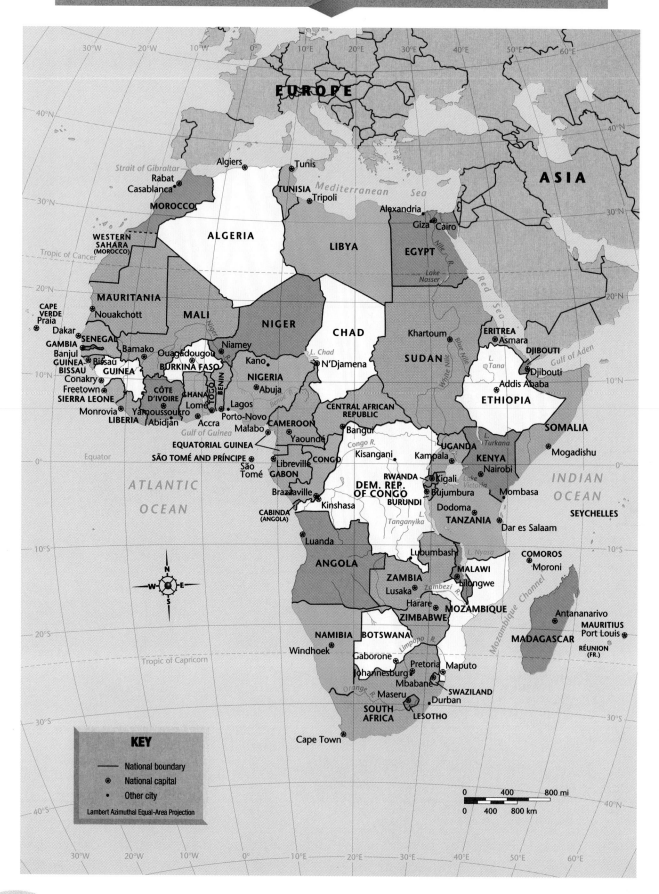

KEY
— National boundary
⊛ National capital
• Other city

Lambert Azimuthal Equal-Area Projection

0   400   800 mi
0   400   800 km

Africa: Physical

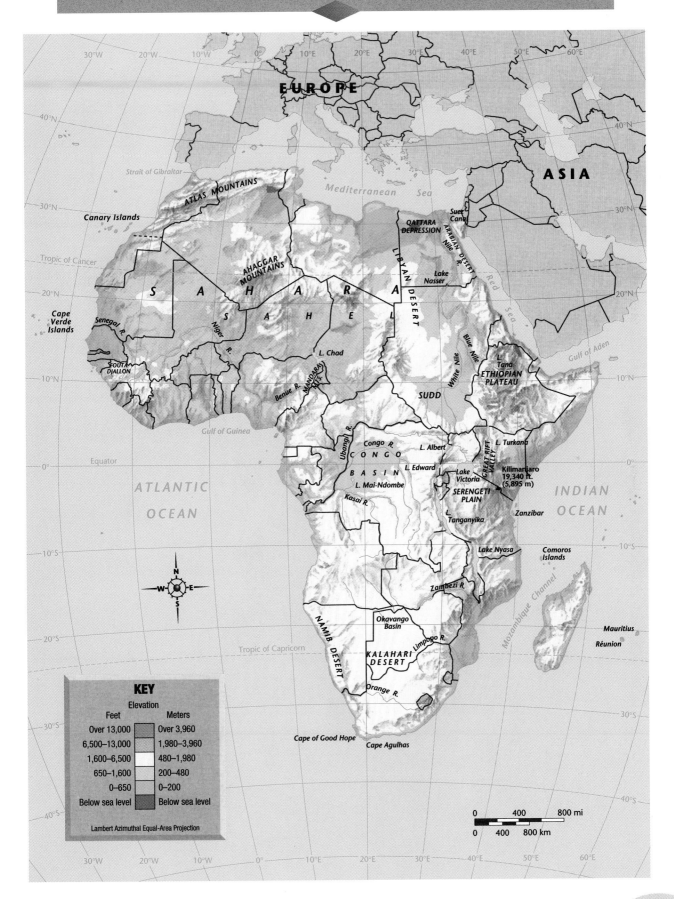

EUROPE

ASIA

Strait of Gibraltar

Mediterranean Sea

ATLAS MOUNTAINS

Canary Islands

Tropic of Cancer

QATTARA
DEPRESSION

Suez Canal

ARABIAN DESERT

Nile R.

AHAGGAR
MOUNTAINS

LIBYAN DESERT

Lake
Nasser

Red Sea

Cape
Verde
Islands

Senegal R.

S A H A R A

Niger R.

S A H E L

L. Chad

White Nile

Blue Nile

L.
Tana

Gulf of Aden

ETHIOPIAN
PLATEAU

FOUTA
DJALLON

MANDARA MTS.

Benue R.

SUDD

Gulf of Guinea

Ubangi R.

Congo R.

CONGO

L. Albert

L. Turkana

GREAT RIFT VALLEY

Equator

ATLANTIC

OCEAN

BASIN

L. Edward

Kilimanjaro
19,340 ft.
(5,895 m)

INDIAN

OCEAN

L. Mai-Ndombe

Lake
Victoria

Kasai R.

SERENGETI
PLAIN

Zanzibar

L.
Tanganyika

Lake Nyasa

Comoros
Islands

Zambezi R.

Mozambique Channel

Mauritius

Réunion

NAMIB DESERT

Okavango
Basin

Limpopo R.

Tropic of Capricorn

KALAHARI
DESERT

Orange R.

KEY

Elevation

Feet	Meters
Over 13,000	Over 3,960
6,500–13,000	1,980–3,960
1,600–6,500	480–1,980
650–1,600	200–480
0–650	0–200
Below sea level	Below sea level

Lambert Azimuthal Equal-Area Projection

Cape of Good Hope

Cape Agulhas

0   400   800 mi

0   400   800 km

Asia: Political

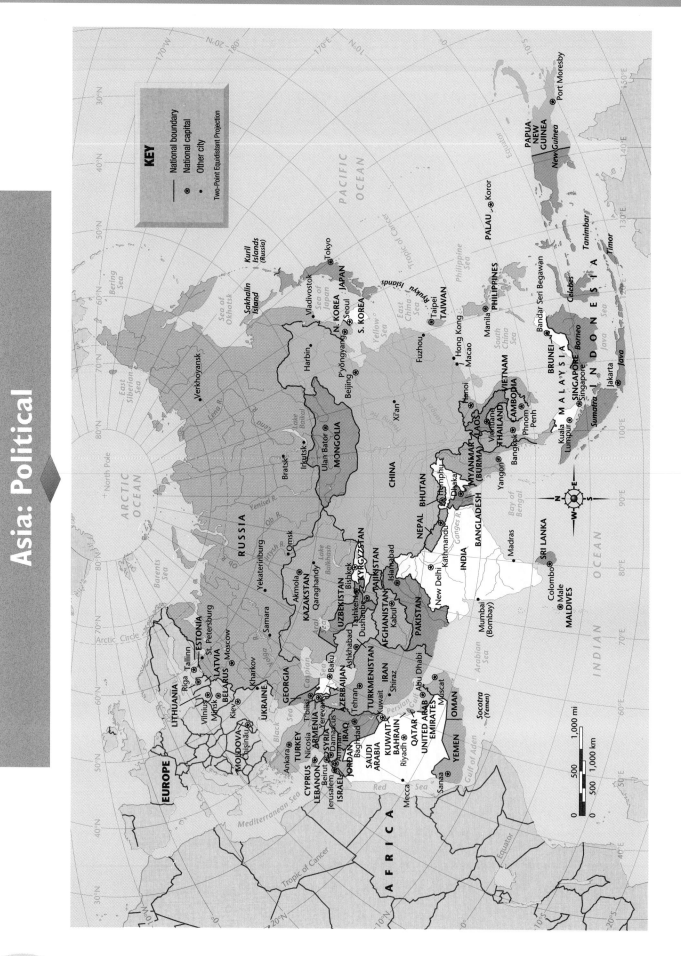

KEY
- National boundary
- National capital ⊛
- Other city •
Two-Point Equidistant Projection

PACIFIC OCEAN

ARCTIC OCEAN

North Pole

Bering Sea

Sea of Okhotsk

Kuril Islands (Russia)

Verkhoyansk

East Siberian Sea

Sakhalin Island

Vladivostok

Sea of Japan

Tokyo ⊛

N. KOREA
Pyŏngyang ⊛
Seoul ⊛
S. KOREA
JAPAN

East China Sea

Ryūkyū Islands

Taipei ⊛
TAIWAN

Philippine Sea

PALAU — Koror

PAPUA NEW GUINEA
New Guinea
Port Moresby

Equator

Barents Sea

RUSSIA

Lena R.

Lake Baikal

Harbin

Beijing ⊛

Fuzhou

Hong Kong
Macao

Manila ⊛
PHILIPPINES

South China Sea

Bandar Seri Begawan ⊛
BRUNEI
Celebes

Tanimbar

INDONESIA
Timor

Arctic Circle

Yenisey R.

Bratsk

Irkutsk

Ulan Bator ⊛
MONGOLIA

Xi'an

CHINA

Hanoi ⊛
VIETNAM
LAOS
Vientiane ⊛
THAILAND
Bangkok ⊛
CAMBODIA
Phnom Penh ⊛

MALAYSIA
Kuala Lumpur ⊛
SINGAPORE ⊛
Singapore
Sumatra
Borneo
Java
Jakarta ⊛
INDONESIA

Ob R.
Irtysh R.

Yekaterinburg

Omsk

Akmola

Lake Balkhash

KAZAKSTAN
Qaraghandy

Bishkek ⊛
KYRGYZSTAN
Tashkent ⊛
UZBEKISTAN
Dushanbe ⊛
TAJIKISTAN
Islamabad ⊛

NEPAL
Kathmandu ⊛
BHUTAN
Thimphu ⊛
Dhaka ⊛
BANGLADESH

MYANMAR (BURMA)
Yangon ⊛

Bay of Bengal

Samara

Volga R.

Aral Sea

Ashkhabad ⊛

AFGHANISTAN
Kabul ⊛
PAKISTAN

New Delhi ⊛

Ganges R.

INDIA

Madras

SRI LANKA
Colombo ⊛

INDIAN OCEAN

ESTONIA
Tallinn ⊛
Riga ⊛
St. Petersburg
LATVIA
Moscow ⊛
LITHUANIA
Vilnius ⊛
Minsk ⊛
BELARUS
Kiev ⊛
UKRAINE
Kharkov

MOLDOVA
Chişinău ⊛

EUROPE

Black Sea

Caspian Sea

Baku ⊛
AZERBAIJAN
Yerevan ⊛
ARMENIA
T'bilisi ⊛
GEORGIA

TURKMENISTAN

Tehran ⊛
IRAN
Shiraz

Mumbai (Bombay)

Arabian Sea

Male ⊛
MALDIVES

Muscat ⊛
OMAN

Socotra (Yemen)

Ankara ⊛
TURKEY
Nicosia ⊛
CYPRUS
LEBANON
Beirut ⊛
Damascus ⊛
SYRIA
Jerusalem ⊛
ISRAEL
Amman ⊛
JORDAN
Baghdad ⊛
IRAQ

KUWAIT
Kuwait ⊛
BAHRAIN
QATAR
UNITED ARAB EMIRATES
Abu Dhabi ⊛

YEMEN

SAUDI ARABIA
Riyadh ⊛

Mecca
Red Sea

Sanaa ⊛

Persian Gulf

Gulf of Aden

Mediterranean Sea

AFRICA

Tropic of Cancer

Equator

1,000 mi
0   500   1,000 km
0   500

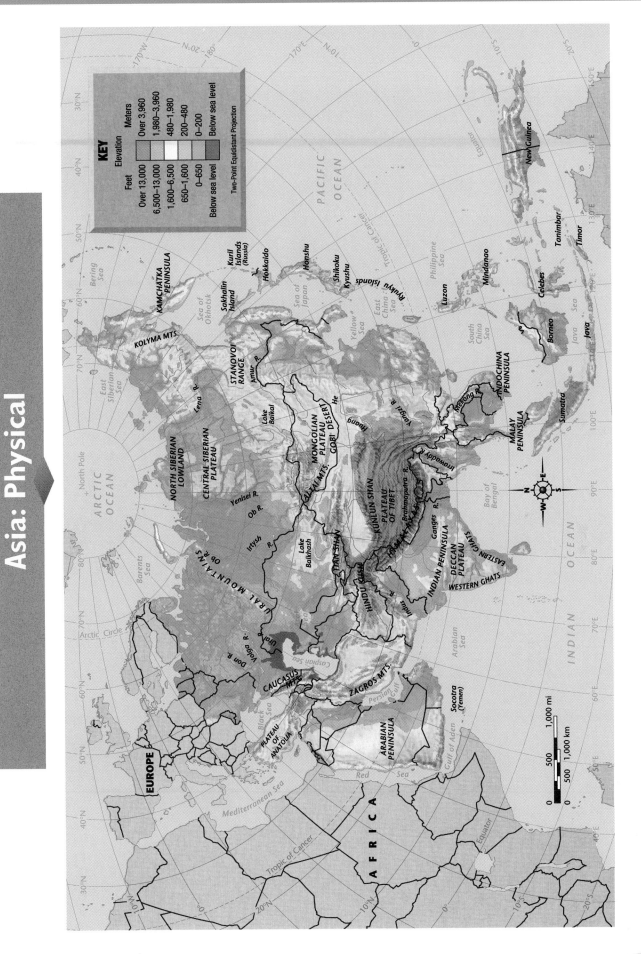

Asia: Physical

KEY
Elevation

Feet	Meters	
Over 13,000	Over 3,960	
6,500–13,000	1,980–3,960	
1,600–6,500	480–1,980	
650–1,600	200–480	
0–650	0–200	
Below sea level	Below sea level	

Two-Point Equidistant Projection

PACIFIC OCEAN

New Guinea

Tanimbar

Timor

Philippine Sea

Mindanao

Celebes

Luzon

Borneo

Java Sea

Java

Ryukyu Islands

East China Sea

Sumatra

South China Sea

INDOCHINA PENINSULA

MALAY PENINSULA

Bay of Bengal

INDIAN OCEAN

Arabian Sea

Socotra (Yemen)

Gulf of Aden

Red Sea

AFRICA

Mediterranean Sea

PLATEAU OF ANATOLIA

ARABIAN PENINSULA

Persian Gulf

ZAGROS MTS.

CAUCASUS MTS.

Black Sea

Caspian Sea

Don R.

Volga R.

Ural R.

EUROPE

URAL MOUNTAINS

Ob R.

Irtysh R.

Yenisei R.

Ob R.

Lake Balkhash

TIAN SHAN

HINDU KUSH

Indus R.

Ganges R.

Brahmaputra R.

HIMALAYAS

KUNLUN SHAN

PLATEAU OF TIBET

WESTERN GHATS

EASTERN GHATS

DECCAN PLATEAU

INDIAN PENINSULA

Irrawaddy R.

Mekong R.

Yangtze R.

Huang He

GOBI DESERT

MONGOLIAN PLATEAU

ALTAI MTS.

Lake Baikal

CENTRAL SIBERIAN PLATEAU

NORTH SIBERIAN LOWLAND

Lena R.

Amur R.

STANOVOI RANGE

KOLYMA MTS.

KAMCHATKA PENINSULA

Sea of Okhotsk

Bering Sea

East Siberian Sea

Barents Sea

ARCTIC OCEAN

North Pole

Arctic Circle

Sakhalin Island

Kuril Islands (Russia)

Hokkaido

Honshu

Sea of Japan

Shikoku

Kyushu

Yellow Sea

Equator

Tropic of Cancer

Tropic of Cancer

0   500   1,000 mi

0   500   1,000 km

Australia, New Zealand, and the Pacific Islands: Physical–Political

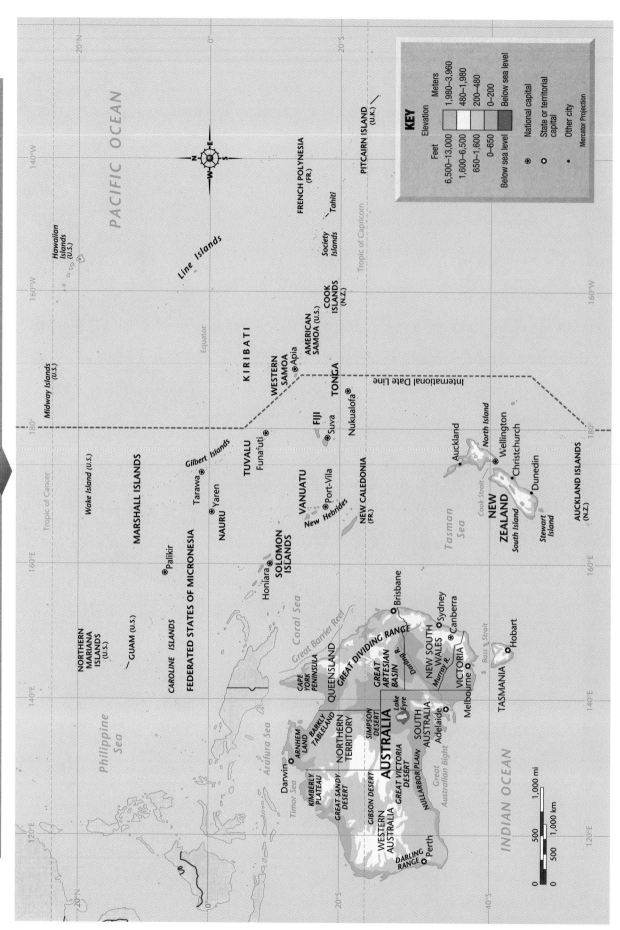

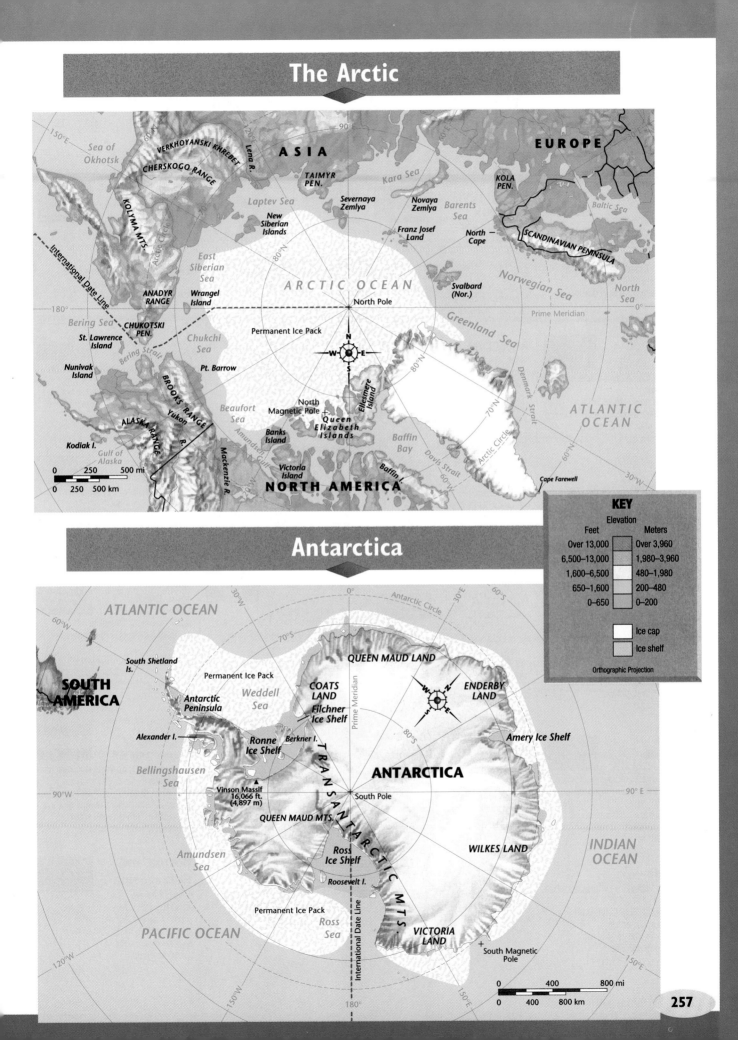

The Arctic

150°E · Sea of Okhotsk · VERKHOYANSKI KHREBET · Lena R. · CHERSKOGO RANGE · ASIA · 90°E · 60°N · TAIMYR PEN. · Kara Sea · EUROPE · KOLA PEN. · Baltic Sea

KOLYMA MTS. · Laptev Sea · New Siberian Islands · Severnaya Zemlya · Novaya Zemlya · Barents Sea · SCANDINAVIAN PENINSULA

East Siberian Sea · 80°N · Franz Josef Land · North Cape · Norwegian Sea · North Sea

ANADYR RANGE · Wrangel Island · ARCTIC OCEAN · North Pole · Svalbard (Nor.) · Prime Meridian · 0°

International Date Line · 180° · Bering Sea · CHUKOTSKI PEN. · Chukchi Sea · Permanent Ice Pack · Greenland Sea · 80°N · Denmark Strait · ATLANTIC OCEAN

St. Lawrence Island · Bering Strait · 70°N

Nunivak Island · Pt. Barrow · Beaufort Sea · North Magnetic Pole · Ellesmere Island · 60°N

BROOKS RANGE · Yukon R. · ALASKA RANGE · Banks Island · Queen Elizabeth Islands · Baffin Bay · Arctic Circle

Kodiak I. · Gulf of Alaska · Mackenzie R. · Victoria Island · Baffin I. · Davis Strait · 60°W · 30°W · Cape Farewell

0 250 500 mi
0 250 500 km

NORTH AMERICA

Antarctica

KEY

Elevation

Feet		Meters
Over 13,000		Over 3,960
6,500–13,000		1,980–3,960
1,600–6,500		480–1,980
650–1,600		200–480
0–650		0–200

Ice cap

Ice shelf

Orthographic Projection

ATLANTIC OCEAN · 30°W · 0° · Antarctic Circle · 30°E · 60°E

60°W · 70°S · QUEEN MAUD LAND · ENDERBY LAND

South Shetland Is. · Permanent Ice Pack · COATS LAND · Weddell Sea · Antarctic Peninsula · Filchner Ice Shelf · Prime Meridian · Amery Ice Shelf

Alexander I. · Berkner I. · Ronne Ice Shelf · 80°S · TRANSANTARCTIC MTS. · ANTARCTICA · 90°E

Bellingshausen Sea · 90°W · Vinson Massif 16,066 ft. (4,897 m) · South Pole · QUEEN MAUD MTS. · WILKES LAND · INDIAN OCEAN

Amundsen Sea · Ross Ice Shelf · Roosevelt I. · VICTORIA LAND

Permanent Ice Pack · Ross Sea · International Date Line · South Magnetic Pole

PACIFIC OCEAN · 120°W · 150°W · 180° · 150°E

0 400 800 mi
0 400 800 km

257

World View

Afghanistan

CAPITAL: Kabul
POPULATION: 24,792,375
MAJOR LANGUAGES: Pashtu, Afghan Persian, Turkic, and 30 various languages
AREA: 250,010 sq mi; 647,500 sq km
LEADING EXPORTS: fruits and nuts, handwoven carpets, and wool
CONTINENT: Asia

Albania
CAPITAL: Tiranë
POPULATION: 3,330,754
MAJOR LANGUAGES: Albanian, Tosk dialect, and Greek
AREA: 11,101 sq mi; 28,750 sq km
LEADING EXPORTS: asphalt, metals and metallic ores, and electricity
CONTINENT: Europe

Algeria
CAPITAL: Algiers
POPULATION: 30,480,793
MAJOR LANGUAGES: Arabic (official), French, and Berber dialects
AREA: 919,626 sq mi; 2,381,740 sq km
LEADING EXPORTS: petroleum and natural gas
CONTINENT: Africa

Andorra
CAPITAL: Andorra La Vella
POPULATION: 64,716
MAJOR LANGUAGES: Catalan (official), French, and Castilian
AREA: 174 sq mi; 450 sq km
LEADING EXPORTS: electricity, tobacco products, and furniture
CONTINENT: Europe

Angola
CAPITAL: Luanda
POPULATION: 10,864,512
MAJOR LANGUAGES: Portuguese (official), Bantu, and various languages
AREA: 481,370 sq mi; 1,246,700 sq km
LEADING EXPORTS: oil, diamonds, and refined petroleum products
CONTINENT: Africa

Anguilla

CAPITAL: The Valley
POPULATION: 11,147
MAJOR LANGUAGE: English (official)
AREA: 35 sq mi; 91 sq km
LEADING EXPORTS: lobster and salt
LOCATION: Caribbean Sea

Antigua and Barbuda

CAPITAL: Saint John's
POPULATION: 64,006
MAJOR LANGUAGES: English (official) and various dialects
AREA: 170 sq mi; 440 sq km
LEADING EXPORTS: petroleum products and manufactures
LOCATION: Caribbean Sea

Argentina

CAPITAL: Buenos Aires
POPULATION: 36,265,463
MAJOR LANGUAGES: Spanish (official), English, Italian, German, and French
AREA: 1,068,339 sq mi; 2,766,890 sq km
LEADING EXPORTS: meat, wheat, corn, oilseed, and manufactures
CONTINENT: South America

Armenia

CAPITAL: Yerevan
POPULATION: 3,421,775
MAJOR LANGUAGES: Armenian and Russian
AREA: 11,506 sq mi; 29,800 sq km
LEADING EXPORTS: gold and jewelry, and aluminum
CONTINENT: Asia

Australia

CAPITAL: Canberra
POPULATION: 18,613,087
MAJOR LANGUAGES: English and various languages
AREA: 2,968,010 sq mi; 7,686,850 sq km
LEADING EXPORTS: coal, gold, meat, wool, and alumina
CONTINENT: Australia

Austria

CAPITAL: Vienna
POPULATION: 8,133,611
MAJOR LANGUAGE: German
AREA: 32,376 sq mi; 83,850 sq km
LEADING EXPORTS: machinery and equipment, and iron and steel
CONTINENT: Europe

Azerbaijan

CAPITAL: Baku
POPULATION: 7,855,576
MAJOR LANGUAGES: Azeri, Russian, Armenian, and various languages
AREA: 33,438 sq mi; 86,600 sq km
LEADING EXPORTS: oil and gas, chemicals, and oil field equipment
CONTINENT: Asia

Bahamas

CAPITAL: Nassau
POPULATION: 279,833
MAJOR LANGUAGES: English and Creole
AREA: 5,382 sq mi; 13,940 sq km
LEADING EXPORTS: pharmaceuticals, cement, rum, and crawfish
LOCATION: Caribbean Sea

Bahrain

CAPITAL: Manama
POPULATION: 616,342
MAJOR LANGUAGES: Arabic, English, Farsi, and Urdu
AREA: 239 sq mi; 620 sq km
LEADING EXPORTS: petroleum and petroleum products
CONTINENT: Asia

Bangladesh

CAPITAL: Dhaka
POPULATION: 127,567,002
MAJOR LANGUAGES: Bangla and English
AREA: 55,600 sq mi; 144,000 sq km
LEADING EXPORTS: garments, jute and jute goods, and leather
CONTINENT: Asia

Barbados

CAPITAL: Bridgetown
POPULATION: 259,025
MAJOR LANGUAGE: English
AREA: 166 sq mi; 430 sq km
LEADING EXPORTS: sugar and molasses, and rum
LOCATION: Caribbean Sea

Belarus

CAPITAL: Minsk
POPULATION: 10,409,050
MAJOR LANGUAGES: Byelorussian and Russian
AREA: 79,926 sq mi; 207,600 sq km
LEADING EXPORTS: machinery and transportation equipment
CONTINENT: Europe

Belgium

CAPITAL: Brussels
POPULATION: 10,174,922
MAJOR LANGUAGES: Dutch, French, and German
AREA: 11,780 sq mi; 30,510 sq km
LEADING EXPORTS: iron and steel, and transportation equipment
CONTINENT: Europe

Belize

CAPITAL: Belmopan
POPULATION: 230,160
MAJOR LANGUAGES: English (official), Spanish, Maya, and Garifuna
AREA: 8,865 sq mi; 22,960 sq km
LEADING EXPORTS: sugar, citrus fruits, bananas, and clothing
CONTINENT: North America

Benin

CAPITAL: Porto-Novo
POPULATION: 6,100,799
MAJOR LANGUAGES: Fon, Yoruba, and at least 6 various languages
AREA: 43,484 sq mi; 112,620 sq km
LEADING EXPORTS: cotton, crude oil, palm products, and cocoa
LOCATION: Atlantic Ocean

Bermuda

CAPITAL: Hamilton
POPULATION: 62,009
MAJOR LANGUAGE: English
AREA: 19.3 sq mi; 50 sq km
LEADING EXPORTS: semitropical produce and light manufactures
LOCATION: Atlantic Ocean

Bhutan

CAPITAL: Thimphu
POPULATION: 1,908,307
MAJOR LANGUAGES: Dzongkha (official), Tibetan dialects, and Nepalese dialects
AREA: 18,147 sq mi; 47,000 sq km
LEADING EXPORTS: cardamon, gypsum, timber, and handicrafts
CONTINENT: Asia

Bolivia

CAPITAL: La Paz
POPULATION: 7,826,352
MAJOR LANGUAGES: Spanish, Quechua, and Aymara
AREA: 424,179 sq mi; 1,098,580 sq km
LEADING EXPORTS: metals, natural gas, soybeans, jewelry, and wood
CONTINENT: South America

Bosnia and Herzegovina
CAPITAL: Sarajevo
POPULATION: 3,365,727
MAJOR LANGUAGE: Serbo-Croatian
AREA: 19,782 sq mi; 51,233 sq km
LEADING EXPORTS: none
CONTINENT: Europe

Botswana

CAPITAL: Gaborone
POPULATION: 1,448,454
MAJOR LANGUAGES: English and Setswana
AREA: 231,812 sq mi; 600,370 sq km
LEADING EXPORTS: diamonds, copper and nickel, and meat
CONTINENT: Africa

Brazil

CAPITAL: Brasília
POPULATION: 169,806,557
MAJOR LANGUAGES: Portuguese, Spanish, English, and French
AREA: 3,286,600 sq mi; 8,511,965 sq km
LEADING EXPORTS: iron ore, soybean, bran, and orange juice
CONTINENT: South America

British Virgin Islands

CAPITAL: Road Town
POPULATION: 13,368
MAJOR LANGUAGE: English
AREA: 58 sq mi; 150 sq km
LEADING EXPORTS: rum, fresh fish, gravel, sand, and fruits
LOCATION: Caribbean Sea

Brunei

CAPITAL: Bandar Seri Begawan
POPULATION: 315,292
MAJOR LANGUAGES: Malay, English, and Chinese
AREA: 2,228 sq mi; 5,770 sq km
LEADING EXPORTS: crude oil and liquefied natural gas
LOCATION: South China Sea

Bulgaria

CAPITAL: Sofia
POPULATION: 8,240,426
MAJOR LANGUAGE: Bulgarian
AREA: 42,824 sq mi; 110,910 sq km
LEADING EXPORTS: machinery and agricultural products
CONTINENT: Europe

Burkina Faso

CAPITAL: Ouagadougou
POPULATION: 11,266,393
MAJOR LANGUAGES: French (official) and Sudanic languages
AREA: 105,873 sq mi; 274,200 sq km
LEADING EXPORTS: cotton, gold, and animal products
CONTINENT: Africa

Burundi

CAPITAL: Bujumbura
POPULATION: 5,537,387
MAJOR LANGUAGES: Kirundi, French, and Swahili
AREA: 10,746 sq mi; 27,830 sq km
LEADING EXPORTS: coffee, tea, cotton, and hides and skins
CONTINENT: Africa

Cambodia

CAPITAL: Phnom Penh
POPULATION: 11,339,562
MAJOR LANGUAGES: Khmer and French
AREA: 69,902 sq mi; 181,040 sq km
LEADING EXPORTS: timber, rubber, soybeans, and sesame
CONTINENT: Asia

Cameroon

CAPITAL: Yaounde
POPULATION: 15,029,433
MAJOR LANGUAGES: 24 various languages, English, and French
AREA: 183,574 sq mi; 475,440 sq km
LEADING EXPORTS: petroleum products and lumber
CONTINENT: Africa

Canada

CAPITAL: Ottawa
POPULATION: 30,675,398
MAJOR LANGUAGES: English and French
AREA: 3,851,940 sq mi; 9,976,140 sq km
LEADING EXPORTS: newsprint, wood pulp, timber, and crude petroleum
CONTINENT: North America

Cape Verde

CAPITAL: Praia
POPULATION: 399,857
MAJOR LANGUAGES: Portuguese and Crioulo
AREA: 1,556 sq mi; 4,030 sq km
LEADING EXPORTS: fish, bananas, and hides and skins
CONTINENT: Africa

Cayman Islands

CAPITAL: George Town
POPULATION: 37,716
MAJOR LANGUAGE: English
AREA: 100 sq mi; 260 sq km
LEADING EXPORTS: turtle products and manufactured goods
LOCATION: Caribbean Sea

Central African Republic

CAPITAL: Bangui
POPULATION: 3,375,771
MAJOR LANGUAGES: French, Sangho, Arabic, Hunsa, and Swahili
AREA: 240,542 sq mi; 622,980 sq km
LEADING EXPORTS: diamonds, timber, cotton, coffee, and tobacco
CONTINENT: Africa

Chad

CAPITAL: N'Djamena
POPULATION: 7,359,512
MAJOR LANGUAGES: French, Arabic, Sara, Songo, and over 100 various languages and dialects
AREA: 495,772 sq mi; 1,284,000 sq km
LEADING EXPORTS: cotton, cattle, textiles, and fish
CONTINENT: Africa

Chile

CAPITAL: Santiago
POPULATION: 14,787,781
MAJOR LANGUAGE: Spanish
AREA: 292,269 sq mi; 756,950 sq km
LEADING EXPORTS: copper and other metals and minerals
CONTINENT: South America

China

CAPITAL: Beijing
POPULATION: 1,236,914,658
MAJOR LANGUAGES: Mandarin, Putonghua, Yue, Wu, Minbei, Minnan, Xiang, and Gan and Hakka dialects
AREA: 3,705,533 sq mi; 9,596,960 sq km
LEADING EXPORTS: textiles, garments, footwear, and toys
CONTINENT: Asia

Colombia

CAPITAL: Bogota
POPULATION: 38,580,949
MAJOR LANGUAGE: Spanish
AREA: 439,751 sq mi; 1,138,910 sq km
LEADING EXPORTS: petroleum, coffee, coal, and bananas
CONTINENT: South America

Comoros

CAPITAL: Moroni
POPULATION: 545,528
MAJOR LANGUAGES: Arabic, French, and Comoran
AREA: 838 sq mi; 2,170 sq km
LEADING EXPORTS: vanilla, ylang-ylang, cloves, and perfume oil
LOCATION: Indian Ocean

Congo (Democratic Republic of)

CAPITAL: Kinshasa
POPULATION: 49,000,511
MAJOR LANGUAGES: French, Lingala, Swahili, Kingwana, Kikongo, and Tshiluba
AREA: 905,599 sq mi; 2,345,410 sq km
LEADING EXPORTS: copper, coffee, diamonds, cobalt, and crude oil
CONTINENT: Africa

Congo (Republic of the)

CAPITAL: Brazzaville
POPULATION: 2,658,123
MAJOR LANGUAGES: French, Lingala, Kikongo, and other languages
AREA: 132,051 sq mi; 342,000 sq km
LEADING EXPORTS: crude oil, lumber, plywood, sugar, and cocoa
CONTINENT: Africa

Cook Islands

CAPITAL: Avarua
POPULATION: 19,989
MAJOR LANGUAGES: English and Maori
AREA: 95 sq mi; 240 sq km
LEADING EXPORTS: copra, fresh and canned fruit, and clothing
LOCATION: Pacific Ocean

Costa Rica

CAPITAL: San José
POPULATION: 3,604,642
MAJOR LANGUAGES: Spanish and English
AREA: 19,730 sq mi; 51,100 sq km
LEADING EXPORTS: coffee, bananas, textiles, and sugar
CONTINENT: North America

Côte d'Ivoire

CAPITAL: Yamoussoukro
POPULATION: 15,446,231
MAJOR LANGUAGES: French, Dioula, and 59 other dialects
AREA: 124,507 sq mi; 322,460 sq km
LEADING EXPORTS: cocoa, coffee, tropical woods, and petroleum
CONTINENT: Africa

Croatia

CAPITAL: Zagreb
POPULATION: 4,671,584
MAJOR LANGUAGE: Serbo-Croatian
AREA: 21,830 sq mi; 56,538 sq km
LEADING EXPORTS: machinery and transportation equipment
CONTINENT: Europe

Cuba

CAPITAL: Havana
POPULATION: 11,050,729
MAJOR LANGUAGE: Spanish
AREA: 42,805 sq mi; 110,860 sq km
LEADING EXPORTS: sugar, nickel, shellfish, and tobacco
LOCATION: Caribbean Sea

Cyprus

CAPITAL: Nicosia
POPULATION: 748,982
MAJOR LANGUAGES: Greek, Turkish, and English
AREA: 3,572 sq mi; 9,250 sq km
LEADING EXPORTS: citrus, potatoes, grapes, wines, and cement
LOCATION: Mediterranean Sea

Czech Republic

CAPITAL: Prague
POPULATION: 10,286,470
MAJOR LANGUAGES: Czech and Slovak
AREA: 30,388 sq mi; 78,703 sq km
LEADING EXPORTS: manufactured goods
CONTINENT: Europe

Denmark

CAPITAL: Copenhagen
POPULATION: 5,333,617
MAJOR LANGUAGES: Danish, Faroese, Greenlandic, and German
AREA: 16,630 sq mi; 43,070 sq km
LEADING EXPORTS: meat and meat products, and dairy products
CONTINENT: Europe

Djibouti

CAPITAL: Djibouti
POPULATION: 440,727
MAJOR LANGUAGES: French, Arabic, Somali, and Afar
AREA: 8,495 sq mi; 22,000 sq km
LEADING EXPORTS: hides and skins, and coffee (in transit)
CONTINENT: Africa

Dominica

CAPITAL: Roseau
POPULATION: 65,777
MAJOR LANGUAGES: English and French patois
AREA: 290 sq mi; 750 sq km
LEADING EXPORTS: bananas, soap, bay oil, and vegetables
LOCATION: Caribbean Sea

Dominican Republic

CAPITAL: Santo Domingo
POPULATION: 7,998,776
MAJOR LANGUAGE: Spanish
AREA: 18,815 sq mi; 48,730 sq km
LEADING EXPORTS: ferronickel, sugar, gold, coffee, and cocoa
LOCATION: Caribbean Sea

Ecuador

CAPITAL: Quito
POPULATION: 12,336,572
MAJOR LANGUAGES: Spanish, Quechua, and various languages
AREA: 109,487 sq mi; 283,560 sq km
LEADING EXPORTS: petroleum, bananas, shrimp, and cocoa
CONTINENT: South America

Egypt

CAPITAL: Cairo
POPULATION: 66,050,004
MAJOR LANGUAGES: Arabic, English, and French
AREA: 386,675 sq mi; 1,001,450 sq km
LEADING EXPORTS: crude oil and petroleum products
CONTINENT: Africa

El Salvador

CAPITAL: San Salvador
POPULATION: 5,752,067
MAJOR LANGUAGES: Spanish and Nahua
AREA: 8,124 sq mi; 21,040 sq km
LEADING EXPORTS: coffee, sugar cane, and shrimp
CONTINENT: North America

Equatorial Guinea

CAPITAL: Malabo
POPULATION: 454,001
MAJOR LANGUAGES: Spanish, Pidgin English, Fang, Bubi, and Ibo
AREA: 10,831 sq mi; 28,050 sq km
LEADING EXPORTS: coffee, timber, and cocoa beans
CONTINENT: Africa

Eritrea

CAPITAL: Asmara
POPULATION: 3,842,436
MAJOR LANGUAGES: Tigre, Kunama, Cushitic dialects, Nora Bana, and Arabic
AREA: 46,844 sq mi; 121,320 sq km
LEADING EXPORTS: salt, hides, cement, and gum arabic
CONTINENT: Africa

Estonia

CAPITAL: Tallinn
POPULATION: 1,421,335
MAJOR LANGUAGES: Estonian, Latvian, Lithuanian, and Russian
AREA: 17,414 sq mi; 45,100 sq km
LEADING EXPORTS: textiles, food products, vehicles, and metals
CONTINENT: Europe

Ethiopia

CAPITAL: Addis Ababa
POPULATION: 58,390,351
MAJOR LANGUAGES: Amharic, Tigrinya, Orominga, Guaraginga, Somali, Arabic, English, and various languages
AREA: 435,201 sq mi; 1,127,127 sq km
LEADING EXPORTS: coffee, leather products, and gold
CONTINENT: Africa

Fiji

CAPITAL: Suva
POPULATION: 802,611
MAJOR LANGUAGES: English, Fijian, and Hindustani
AREA: 7,054 sq mi; 18,270 sq km
LEADING EXPORTS: sugar, clothing, gold, processed fish, and lumber
LOCATION: Pacific Ocean

Finland

CAPITAL: Helsinki
POPULATION: 5,149,242
MAJOR LANGUAGES: Finnish, Swedish, Lapp, and Russian
AREA: 130,132 sq mi; 337,030 sq km
LEADING EXPORTS: paper and pulp, machinery, and chemicals
CONTINENT: Europe

France

CAPITAL: Paris
POPULATION: 58,804,944
MAJOR LANGUAGES: French and regional dialects and languages
AREA: 211,217 sq mi; 547,030 sq km
LEADING EXPORTS: machinery and transportation equipment
CONTINENT: Europe

Gabon

CAPITAL: Libreville
POPULATION: 1,207,844
MAJOR LANGUAGES: French, Fang, Myene, Bateke, Bapounou/Eschira, and Bandjabi
AREA: 103,351 sq mi; 267,670 sq km
LEADING EXPORTS: crude oil, timber, manganese, and uranium
CONTINENT: Africa

The Gambia

CAPITAL: Banjul
POPULATION: 1,291,858
MAJOR LANGUAGES: English, Mandinka, Wolof, Fula, and various languages
AREA: 4,363 sq mi; 11,300 sq km
LEADING EXPORTS: peanuts and peanut products, and fish
CONTINENT: Africa

Georgia

CAPITAL: T'bilisi
POPULATION: 5,108,527
MAJOR LANGUAGES: Armenian, Azeri, Georgian, Russian, and various languages
AREA: 26,912 sq mi; 69,700 sq km
LEADING EXPORTS: citrus fruits, tea, and wine
CONTINENT: Asia

Germany

CAPITAL: Berlin
POPULATION: 82,079,454
MAJOR LANGUAGE: German
AREA: 137,808 sq mi; 356,910 sq km
LEADING EXPORTS: machines and machine tools, and chemicals
CONTINENT: Europe

Ghana

CAPITAL: Accra
POPULATION: 18,497,206
MAJOR LANGUAGES: English, Akan, Moshi-Dagomba, Ewe, Ga, and various languages
AREA: 92,104 sq mi; 238,540 sq km
LEADING EXPORTS: cocoa, gold, timber, tuna, and bauxite
CONTINENT: Africa

Greece

CAPITAL: Athens
POPULATION: 10,662,138
MAJOR LANGUAGES: Greek, English, and French
AREA: 50,944 sq mi; 131,940 sq km
LEADING EXPORTS: manufactured goods, foodstuffs, and fuels
CONTINENT: Europe

Grenada

CAPITAL: Saint George's
POPULATION: 96,217
MAJOR LANGUAGES: English and French patois
AREA: 131 sq mi; 340 sq km
LEADING EXPORTS: bananas, cocoa, nutmeg, and fruits and vegetables
LOCATION: Caribbean Sea

Guatemala

CAPITAL: Guatemala
POPULATION: 12,007,580
MAJOR LANGUAGES: Spanish, Quiche, Cakchiquel, Kekchi, and various languages and dialects
AREA: 42,044 sq mi; 108,890 sq km
LEADING EXPORTS: coffee, sugar, bananas, cardamom, and beef
CONTINENT: North America

Guinea

CAPITAL: Conakry
POPULATION: 7,477,110
MAJOR LANGUAGES: French and various languages
AREA: 94,930 sq mi; 245,860 sq km
LEADING EXPORTS: bauxite, alumina, diamonds, gold, and coffee
CONTINENT: Africa

Guinea-Bissau

CAPITAL: Bissau
POPULATION: 1,206,311
MAJOR LANGUAGES: Portuguese, Criolo, and various languages
AREA: 13,946 sq mi; 36,210 sq km
LEADING EXPORTS: cashews, fish, peanuts, and palm kernels
CONTINENT: Africa

Guyana

CAPITAL: Georgetown
POPULATION: 707,954
MAJOR LANGUAGES: English and various
  dialects
AREA: 83,003 sq mi; 214,970 sq km
LEADING EXPORTS: sugar, bauxite/alumina,
  rice, and shrimp
CONTINENT: South America

Haiti

CAPITAL: Port-au-Prince
POPULATION: 6,780,501
MAJOR LANGUAGES: French and Creole
AREA: 8,784 sq mi; 22,750 sq km
LEADING EXPORTS: light manufactures and
  coffee
LOCATION: Caribbean Sea

Holy See (Vatican City)

CAPITAL: Vatican City
POPULATION: 840
MAJOR LANGUAGES: Italian, Latin, and
  various languages
AREA: 0.17 sq mi; 0.44 sq km
LEADING EXPORTS: none
CONTINENT: Europe

Honduras

CAPITAL: Tegucigalpa
POPULATION: 5,861,955
MAJOR LANGUAGES: Spanish and various
  dialects
AREA: 43,280 sq mi; 112,090 sq km
LEADING EXPORTS: bananas, coffee, shrimp,
  lobsters, and minerals
CONTINENT: North America

Hungary

CAPITAL: Budapest
POPULATION: 10,208,127
MAJOR LANGUAGES: Hungarian and various
  languages
AREA: 35,920 sq mi; 93,030 sq km
LEADING EXPORTS: raw materials and semi-
  finished goods
CONTINENT: Europe

Iceland

CAPITAL: Reykjavik
POPULATION: 271,033
MAJOR LANGUAGE: Icelandic
AREA: 39,770 sq mi; 103,000 sq km
LEADING EXPORTS: fish and fish products,
  and animal products
LOCATION: Atlantic Ocean

India

CAPITAL: New Delhi
POPULATION: 984,003,683
MAJOR LANGUAGES: English, Hindi, Bengali,
  Telugu, Marathi, Tamil, Urdu,
  Gujarati, Malayam, Kannada, Oriya,
  Punjabi, Assamese, Kashmiri, Sindhi,
  Sanskrit, and Hindustani (all official)
AREA: 1,269,389 sq mi; 3,287,590 sq km
LEADING EXPORTS: clothing, and gems and
  jewelry
CONTINENT: Asia

Indonesia

CAPITAL: Jakarta
POPULATION: 212,941,810
MAJOR LANGUAGES: Bahasa Indonesia,
  English, Dutch, Javanese, and
  various dialects
AREA: 741,052 sq mi; 1,919,251 sq km
LEADING EXPORTS: manufactures, fuels, and
  foodstuffs
CONTINENT: Asia

Iran

CAPITAL: Tehran
POPULATION: 68,959,931
MAJOR LANGUAGES: Farsi (official) and
  Turkic languages
AREA: 634,562 sq mi; 1,643,452 sq km
LEADING EXPORTS: petroleum, carpets, fruit,
  nuts, and hides
CONTINENT: Asia

Iraq

CAPITAL: Baghdad
POPULATION: 21,722,287
MAJOR LANGUAGES: Arabic, Kurdish,
  Assyrian, and Armenian
AREA: 168,760 sq mi; 437,072 sq km
LEADING EXPORTS: crude oil and refined
  products, and fertilizers
CONTINENT: Asia

Ireland

CAPITAL: Dublin
POPULATION: 3,619,480
MAJOR LANGUAGES: Irish Gaelic and English
AREA: 27,136 sq mi; 70,280 sq km
LEADING EXPORTS: chemicals and data
  processing equipment
CONTINENT: Europe

Israel

CAPITAL: Jerusalem
POPULATION: 5,643,966
MAJOR LANGUAGES: Hebrew, Arabic, and
  English
AREA: 8,019 sq mi; 20,849 sq km
LEADING EXPORTS: machinery and
  equipment, and cut diamonds
CONTINENT: Asia

Italy

CAPITAL: Rome
POPULATION: 56,782,748
MAJOR LANGUAGES: Italian, German,
  French, and Slovene
AREA: 116,310 sq mi; 301,230 sq km
LEADING EXPORTS: metals, and textiles and
  clothing
CONTINENT: Europe

Jamaica

CAPITAL: Kingston
POPULATION: 2,634,678
MAJOR LANGUAGES: English and Creole
AREA: 4,243 sq mi; 10,990 sq km
LEADING EXPORTS: alumina, bauxite, sugar,
  bananas, and rum
LOCATION: Caribbean Sea

Japan

CAPITAL: Tokyo
POPULATION: 125,931,533
MAJOR LANGUAGE: Japanese
AREA: 145,888 sq mi; 377,835 sq km
LEADING EXPORTS: machinery, motor
  vehicles, and electronics
CONTINENT: Asia

Jordan

CAPITAL: Amman
POPULATION: 4,434,978
MAJOR LANGUAGES: Arabic and English
AREA: 34,447 sq mi; 89,213 sq km
LEADING EXPORTS: phosphates, fertilizers,
  and potash
CONTINENT: Asia

Kazakstan

CAPITAL: Akmola
POPULATION: 16,846,808
MAJOR LANGUAGES: Kazakh and Russian
AREA: 1,049,191 sq mi; 2,717,300 sq km
LEADING EXPORTS: oil, and ferrous and
  nonferrous metals
CONTINENT: Asia

Kenya

CAPITAL: Nairobi
POPULATION: 28,337,071
MAJOR LANGUAGES: English,
  Swahili, and various languages
AREA: 224,970 sq mi; 582,650 sq km
LEADING EXPORTS: tea, coffee, and
  petroleum products
CONTINENT: Africa

Kiribati

CAPITAL: Tarawa
POPULATION: 83,976
MAJOR LANGUAGES: English and Gilbertese
AREA: 277 sq mi; 717 sq km
LEADING EXPORTS: copra, seaweed, and fish
LOCATION: Pacific Ocean

Korea, North

CAPITAL: P'yongyang
POPULATION: 21,234,387
MAJOR LANGUAGE: Korean
AREA: 46,542 sq mi; 120,540 sq km
LEADING EXPORTS: minerals and
  metallurgical products
CONTINENT: Asia

Korea, South

CAPITAL: Seoul
POPULATION: 46,416,796
MAJOR LANGUAGES: Korean and English
AREA: 38,025 sq mi; 98,480 sq km
LEADING EXPORTS: electronic and electrical
  equipment
CONTINENT: Asia

Kuwait

CAPITAL: Kuwait
POPULATION: 1,913,285
MAJOR LANGUAGES: Arabic and English
AREA: 6,881 sq mi; 17,820 sq km
LEADING EXPORT: oil
CONTINENT: Asia

Kyrgyzstan

CAPITAL: Bishkek
POPULATION: 4,522,281
MAJOR LANGUAGES: Kyrgyz and Russian
AREA: 76,644 sq mi; 198,500 sq km
LEADING EXPORTS: wool, chemicals, cotton,
  metals, and shoes
CONTINENT: Asia

Laos

CAPITAL: Vientiane
POPULATION: 5,260,842
MAJOR LANGUAGES: Lao,
  French, English, and various
  languages
AREA: 91,432 sq mi; 236,800 sq km
LEADING EXPORTS: electricity, wood
  products, coffee, and tin
CONTINENT: Asia

Latvia

CAPITAL: Riga
POPULATION: 2,385,396
MAJOR LANGUAGES: Lettish, Lithuanian,
  Russian, and various languages
AREA: 24,750 sq mi; 64,100 sq km
LEADING EXPORTS: oil products, timber, and
  ferrous metals
CONTINENT: Europe

Lebanon

CAPITAL: Beirut
POPULATION: 3,505,794
MAJOR LANGUAGES: Arabic, French,
  Armenian, and English
AREA: 4,016 sq mi; 10,400 sq km
LEADING EXPORTS: agricultural products,
  chemicals, and textiles
CONTINENT: Asia

Lesotho

CAPITAL: Maseru
POPULATION: 2,089,829
MAJOR LANGUAGES: Sesotho, English, Zulu, and Xhosa
AREA: 11,719 sq mi; 30,350 sq km
LEADING EXPORTS: wool, mohair, wheat, cattle, and peas
CONTINENT: Africa

Liberia

CAPITAL: Monrovia
POPULATION: 2,771,901
MAJOR LANGUAGES: English and Niger-Congo
AREA: 43,002 sq mi; 111,370 sq km
LEADING EXPORTS: iron ore, rubber, timber, and coffee
CONTINENT: Africa

Libya

CAPITAL: Tripoli
POPULATION: 5,690,727
MAJOR LANGUAGES: Arabic, Italian, and English
AREA: 679,385 sq mi; 1,759,540 sq km
LEADING EXPORTS: crude oil and refined petroleum products
CONTINENT: Africa

Liechtenstein

CAPITAL: Vaduz
POPULATION: 31,717
MAJOR LANGUAGES: German and Alemannic
AREA: 62 sq mi; 160 sq km
LEADING EXPORTS: small specialty machinery and dental products
CONTINENT: Europe

Lithuania

CAPITAL: Vilnius
POPULATION: 3,600,158
MAJOR LANGUAGES: Lithuanian, Polish, and Russian
AREA: 25,175 sq mi; 65,200 sq km
LEADING EXPORTS: electronics, petroleum products, and food
CONTINENT: Europe

Luxembourg

CAPITAL: Luxembourg
POPULATION: 425,017
MAJOR LANGUAGES: Luxembourgisch, German, French, and English
AREA: 998 sq mi; 2,586 sq km
LEADING EXPORTS: finished steel products and chemicals
CONTINENT: Europe

Macedonia

CAPITAL: Skopje
POPULATION: 2,009,387
MAJOR LANGUAGES: Macedonian, Albanian, Turkish, Serb, Gypsy, and various languages
AREA: 9,781 sq mi; 25,333 sq km
LEADING EXPORTS: manufactured goods and machinery
CONTINENT: Europe

Madagascar

CAPITAL: Antananarivo
POPULATION: 14,462,509
MAJOR LANGUAGES: French and Malagasy
AREA: 226,665 sq mi; 587,040 sq km
LEADING EXPORTS: coffee, vanilla, cloves, shellfish, and sugar
CONTINENT: Africa

Malawi

CAPITAL: Lilongwe
POPULATION: 9,840,474
MAJOR LANGUAGES: English, Chichewa, and various languages
AREA: 45,747 sq mi; 118,480 sq km
LEADING EXPORTS: tobacco, tea, sugar, coffee, and peanuts
CONTINENT: Africa

Malaysia

CAPITAL: Kuala Lumpur
POPULATION: 20,932,901
MAJOR LANGUAGES: Malay, English, Mandarin, Tamil, Chinese dialects, and various languages and dialects
AREA: 127,322 sq mi; 329,750 sq km
LEADING EXPORTS: electronic equipment
CONTINENT: Asia

Maldives

CAPITAL: Male
POPULATION: 290,211
MAJOR LANGUAGES: Divehi dialect and English
AREA: 116 sq mi; 300 sq km
LEADING EXPORTS: fish and clothing
CONTINENT: Asia

Mali

CAPITAL: Bamako
POPULATION: 10,108,569
MAJOR LANGUAGES: French, Bambara, and various languages
AREA: 478,783 sq mi; 1,240,000 sq km
LEADING EXPORTS: cotton, livestock, and gold
CONTINENT: Africa

Malta

CAPITAL: Valletta
POPULATION: 379,563
MAJOR LANGUAGES: Maltese and English
AREA: 124 sq mi; 320 sq km
LEADING EXPORTS: machinery and transportation equipment
LOCATION: Mediterranean Sea

Marshall Islands

CAPITAL: Majuro
POPULATION: 63,031
MAJOR LANGUAGES: English, Marshallese dialects, and Japanese
AREA: 70 sq mi; 181.3 sq km
LEADING EXPORTS: coconut oil, fish, live animals, and trichus shells
LOCATION: Pacific Ocean

Mauritania

CAPITAL: Nouakchott
POPULATION: 2,511,473
MAJOR LANGUAGES: Hasaniya Arabic, Wolof, Pular, and Soninke
AREA: 397,969 sq mi; 1,030,700 sq km
LEADING EXPORTS: iron ore, and fish and fish products
CONTINENT: Africa

Mauritius

CAPITAL: Port Louis
POPULATION: 1,168,256
MAJOR LANGUAGES: English (official), Creole, French, Hindi, Urdu, Hakka, and Bojpoori
AREA: 718 sq mi; 1,860 sq km
LEADING EXPORTS: textiles, sugar, and light manufactures
LOCATION: Indian Ocean

Mayotte

CAPITAL: Mamoutzou
POPULATION: 141,944
MAJOR LANGUAGES: Mahorian and French
AREA: 145 sq mi; 375 sq km
LEADING EXPORTS: ylang-ylang and vanilla
CONTINENT: Africa

Mexico

CAPITAL: Mexico City
POPULATION: 98,552,776
MAJOR LANGUAGES: Spanish and Mayan dialects
AREA: 761,632 sq mi; 1,972,550 sq km
LEADING EXPORTS: crude oil, oil products, coffee, and silver
CONTINENT: North America

Micronesia

CAPITAL: Federated states of Kolonia (on the Island of Pohnpei)
*a new capital is being built about 10 km southwest in the Palikir Valley
POPULATION: 129,658
MAJOR LANGUAGES: English, Turkese, Pohnpeian, Yapese, and Kosrean
AREA: 271 sq mi; 702 sq km
LEADING EXPORTS: fish, copra, bananas, and black pepper
LOCATION: Pacific Ocean

Moldova

CAPITAL: Chisinau
POPULATION: 4,457,729
MAJOR LANGUAGES: Moldovan (official), Russian, and Gagauz dialect
AREA: 13,012 sq mi; 33,700 sq km
LEADING EXPORTS: foodstuffs, wine, and tobacco
CONTINENT: Europe

Monaco

CAPITAL: Monaco
POPULATION: 32,035
MAJOR LANGUAGES: French (official), English, Italian, and Monegasque
AREA: .73 sq mi; 1.9 sq km
LEADING EXPORTS: exports through France
CONTINENT: Europe

Mongolia

CAPITAL: Ulaanbaatar
POPULATION: 2,578,530
MAJOR LANGUAGES: Khalkha Mongol, Turkic, Russian, and Chinese
AREA: 604,270 sq mi; 1,565,000 sq km
LEADING EXPORTS: copper, livestock, animal products, and cashmere
CONTINENT: Asia

Morocco

CAPITAL: Rabat
POPULATION: 29,114,497
MAJOR LANGUAGES: Arabic (official), Berber dialects, and French
AREA: 172,420 sq mi; 446,550 sq km
LEADING EXPORTS: food and beverages
CONTINENT: Africa

Mozambique

CAPITAL: Maputo
POPULATION: 18,641,469
MAJOR LANGUAGES: Portuguese and various dialects
AREA: 309,506 sq mi; 801,590 sq km
LEADING EXPORTS: shrimp, cashews, cotton, sugar, copra, and citrus
CONTINENT: Africa

Myanmar (Burma)

CAPITAL: Rangoon
POPULATION: 47,305,319
MAJOR LANGUAGE: Burmese
AREA: 261,979 sq mi; 678,500 sq km
LEADING EXPORTS: pulses and beans, teak, rice, and hardwood
CONTINENT: Asia

Namibia

CAPITAL: Windhoek
POPULATION: 1,622,328
MAJOR LANGUAGES: English (official),
 Afrikaans, German, Oshivambo,
 Herero, Nama, and various languages
AREA: 318,707 sq mi; 825,418 sq km
LEADING EXPORTS: diamonds, copper, gold,
 zinc, and lead
CONTINENT: Africa

Nauru

CAPITAL: Government
 offices in Yaren
 District
POPULATION: 10,501
MAJOR LANGUAGES: Nauruan and English
AREA: 8 sq mi; 21 sq km
LEADING EXPORTS: phosphates
LOCATION: Pacific Ocean

Nepal

CAPITAL: Kathmandu
POPULATION: 23,698,421
MAJOR LANGUAGES: Nepali (official) and 20
 various languages divided into
 numerous dialects
AREA: 54,365 sq mi; 140,800 sq km
LEADING EXPORTS: carpets, clothing, and
 leather goods
CONTINENT: Asia

Netherlands

CAPITAL: Amsterdam
POPULATION: 15,731,112
MAJOR LANGUAGE: Dutch
AREA: 14,414 sq mi; 37,330 sq km
LEADING EXPORTS: metal products and
 chemicals
CONTINENT: Europe

New Caledonia

CAPITAL: Noumea
POPULATION: 194,197
MAJOR LANGUAGES: French and 28
 Melanesian-Polynesian dialects
AREA: 7,359 sq mi; 19,060 sq km
LEADING EXPORTS: nickel metal and
 nickel ore
LOCATION: Pacific Ocean

New Zealand

CAPITAL: Wellington
POPULATION: 3,625,388
MAJOR LANGUAGES: English and Maori
AREA: 103,741 sq mi; 268,680 sq km
LEADING EXPORTS: wool, lamb, mutton,
 beef, fish, and cheese
LOCATION: Pacific Ocean

Nicaragua

CAPITAL: Managua
POPULATION: 4,583,379
MAJOR LANGUAGES: Spanish (official),
 English, and various languages
AREA: 50,000 sq mi; 129,494 sq km
LEADING EXPORTS: meat, coffee, cotton,
 sugar, seafood, and gold
CONTINENT: North America

Niger

CAPITAL: Niamey
POPULATION: 9,671,848
MAJOR LANGUAGES: French (official),
 Hausa, and Djerma
AREA: 489,208 sq mi; 1,267,000 sq km
LEADING EXPORTS: uranium ore and
 livestock products
CONTINENT: Africa

Nigeria

CAPITAL: Abuja
POPULATION: 110,532,242
MAJOR LANGUAGES: English (official),
 Hausa, Yoruba, Ibo, and Fulani
AREA: 356,682 sq mi; 923,770 sq km
LEADING EXPORTS: oil, cocoa, and rubber
CONTINENT: Africa

Niue

CAPITAL: (Free association
 with New Zealand)
POPULATION: 1,800
MAJOR LANGUAGES: Polynesian and English
AREA: 100 sq mi; 260 sq km
LEADING EXPORTS: canned coconut cream,
 copra, and honey
LOCATION: Pacific Ocean

Norway

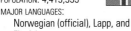

CAPITAL: Oslo
POPULATION: 4,419,955
MAJOR LANGUAGES:
 Norwegian (official), Lapp, and
 Finnish
AREA: 125,186 sq mi; 324,220 sq km
LEADING EXPORTS: petroleum and
 petroleum products
CONTINENT: Europe

Oman

CAPITAL: Muscat
POPULATION: 2,363,591
MAJOR LANGUAGES: Arabic (official),
 English, Baluchi, Urdu, and Indian
 dialects
AREA: 82,034 sq mi; 212,460 sq km
LEADING EXPORTS: petroleum, re-exports,
 and fish
CONTINENT: Asia

Pakistan

CAPITAL: Islamabad
POPULATION: 135,135,195
MAJOR LANGUAGES: Urdu (official), English
 (official), Punjabi, Sindhi, Pashtu,
 Urdu, Balochi, and other languages
AREA: 310,414 sq mi; 803,940 sq km
LEADING EXPORTS: cotton, textiles, clothing,
 rice, and leather
CONTINENT: Asia

Palau

CAPITAL: Koror
POPULATION: 18,110
MAJOR LANGUAGES: English (official),
 Sonsorolese, Angaur, Japanese, Tobi,
 and Palauan
AREA: 177 sq mi; 458 sq km
LEADING EXPORTS: trochus, tuna, copra, and
 handicrafts
LOCATION: Pacific Ocean

Panama

CAPITAL: Panama
POPULATION: 2,735,943
MAJOR LANGUAGES: Spanish (official) and
 English
AREA: 30,194 sq mi; 78,200 sq km
LEADING EXPORTS: bananas, shrimp, sugar,
 clothing, and coffee
CONTINENT: North America

Papua New Guinea

CAPITAL: Port Moresby
POPULATION: 4,599,785
MAJOR LANGUAGES: English, pidgin English,
 and Motu
AREA: 178,266 sq mi; 461,690 sq km
LEADING EXPORTS: gold, copper ore, oil,
 logs, and palm oil
LOCATION: Pacific Ocean

Paraguay

CAPITAL: Asuncion
POPULATION: 5,291,020
MAJOR LANGUAGES: Spanish (official) and
 Guarani
AREA: 157,052 sq mi; 406,750 sq km
LEADING EXPORTS: cotton, soybeans, timber,
 and vegetable oils
CONTINENT: South America

Peru

CAPITAL: Lima
POPULATION: 26,111,110
MAJOR LANGUAGES: Spanish (official),
 Quechua (official), and Aymara
AREA: 496,243 sq mi; 1,285,220 sq km
LEADING EXPORTS: copper, zinc, and
 fish meal
CONTINENT: South America

Philippines

CAPITAL: Manila
POPULATION: 77,725,862
MAJOR LANGUAGES: Filipino and English
 (official)
AREA: 115,834 sq mi; 300,000 sq km
LEADING EXPORTS: electronics, textiles, and
 coconut products
CONTINENT: Asia

Poland

CAPITAL: Warsaw
POPULATION: 38,606,922
MAJOR LANGUAGE: Polish
AREA: 120,731 sq mi; 312,680 sq km
LEADING EXPORTS: intermediate goods
CONTINENT: Europe

Portugal

CAPITAL: Lisbon
POPULATION: 9,927,556
MAJOR LANGUAGE: Portuguese
AREA: 35,553 sq mi; 92,080 sq km
LEADING EXPORTS: clothing and footwear,
 and machinery
CONTINENT: Europe

Qatar

CAPITAL: Doha
POPULATION: 697,126
MAJOR LANGUAGES: Arabic (official) and
 English
AREA: 4,247 sq mi; 11,000 sq km
LEADING EXPORTS: petroleum products,
 steel, and fertilizers
CONTINENT: Asia

Romania

CAPITAL: Bucharest
POPULATION: 22,395,848
MAJOR LANGUAGES: Romanian, Hungarian,
 and German
AREA: 91,702 sq mi; 237,500 sq km
LEADING EXPORTS: metals and metal
 products, and mineral products
CONTINENT: Europe

Russia

CAPITAL: Moscow
POPULATION: 146,861,022
MAJOR LANGUAGES: Russian and various
 languages
AREA: 6,952,996 sq mi; 17,075,200 sq km
LEADING EXPORTS: petroleum and
 petroleum products
CONTINENT: Europe and Asia

Rwanda

CAPITAL: Kigali
POPULATION: 7,956,172
MAJOR LANGUAGES: Kinyarwanda (official),
 French (official), and Kiswahili
AREA: 10,170 sq mi; 26,340 sq km
LEADING EXPORTS: coffee, tea, cassiterite,
 and wolframite
CONTINENT: Africa

Saint Kitts and Nevis

CAPITAL: Basseterre
POPULATION: 42,291
MAJOR LANGUAGE: English
AREA: 104 sq mi; 269 sq km
LEADING EXPORTS: machinery, food, and electronics
LOCATION: Caribbean Sea

Saint Lucia

CAPITAL: Castries
POPULATION: 152,335
MAJOR LANGUAGES: English and French patois
AREA: 239 sq mi; 620 sq km
LEADING EXPORTS: bananas, clothing, cocoa, and vegetables
LOCATION: Caribbean Sea

Saint Vincent and the Grenadines

CAPITAL: Kingstown
POPULATION: 119,818
MAJOR LANGUAGES: English and French patois
AREA: 131 sq mi; 340 sq km
LEADING EXPORTS: bananas, and eddoes and dasheen (taro)
LOCATION: Caribbean Sea

Samoa

CAPITAL: Apia
POPULATION: 224,713
MAJOR LANGUAGES: Samoan and English
AREA: 1,104 sq mi; 2,860 sq km
LEADING EXPORTS: coconut oil and cream, taro, copra, and cocoa
LOCATION: Pacific Ocean

San Marino

CAPITAL: San Marino
POPULATION: 24,894
MAJOR LANGUAGE: Italian
AREA: 23 sq mi; 60 sq km
LEADING EXPORTS: building stone, lime, wood, and chestnuts
CONTINENT: Europe

São Tomé and Príncipe

CAPITAL: São Tomé
POPULATION: 150,123
MAJOR LANGUAGE: Portuguese (official)
AREA: 371 sq mi; 960 sq km
LEADING EXPORTS: cocoa, copra, coffee, and palm oil
CONTINENT: Africa

Saudi Arabia

CAPITAL: Riyadh
POPULATION: 20,785,955
MAJOR LANGUAGE: Arabic
AREA: 757,011 sq mi; 1,960,582 sq km
LEADING EXPORTS: petroleum and petroleum products
CONTINENT: Asia

Senegal

CAPITAL: Dakar
POPULATION: 9,723,149
MAJOR LANGUAGES: French (official), Wolof, Pulaar, Diola, and Mandingo
AREA: 75,752 sq mi; 196,190 sq km
LEADING EXPORTS: fish, ground nuts, and petroleum products
CONTINENT: Africa

Serbia and Montenegro

CAPITAL: Belgrade
POPULATION: 11,206,039
MAJOR LANGUAGES: Serbo-Croatian and Albanian
AREA: 39,436 sq mi; 102,350 sq km
LEADING EXPORTS: none
CONTINENT: Europe

Seychelles

CAPITAL: Victoria
POPULATION: 78,641
MAJOR LANGUAGES: English (official), French (official), and Creole
AREA: 176 sq mi; 455 sq km
LEADING EXPORTS: fish, cinnamon bark, and copra
CONTINENT: Africa

Sierra Leone

CAPITAL: Freetown
POPULATION: 5,080,004
MAJOR LANGUAGES: English (official), Mende, Temne, and Krio
AREA: 27,700 sq mi; 71,740 sq km
LEADING EXPORTS: rutile, bauxite, diamonds, coffee, and cocoa
CONTINENT: Africa

Singapore

CAPITAL: Singapore
POPULATION: 3,490,356
MAJOR LANGUAGES: Chinese, Malay, Tamil, and English
AREA: 244 sq mi; 633 sq km
LEADING EXPORTS: computer equipment
CONTINENT: Asia

Slovakia

CAPITAL: Bratislava
POPULATION: 5,392,982
MAJOR LANGUAGES: Slovak and Hungarian
AREA: 18,860 sq mi; 48,845 sq km
LEADING EXPORTS: machinery and transportation equipment
CONTINENT: Europe

Slovenia

CAPITAL: Ljubljana
POPULATION: 1,971,739
MAJOR LANGUAGES: Slovenian, Serbo-Croatian, and various languages
AREA: 7,837 sq mi; 20,296 sq km
LEADING EXPORTS: machinery and transportation equipment
CONTINENT: Europe

Solomon Islands

CAPITAL: Honiara
POPULATION: 441,039
MAJOR LANGUAGES: Melanesian pidgin and English
AREA: 10,985 sq mi; 28,450 sq km
LEADING EXPORTS: fish, timber, palm oil, cocoa, and copra
LOCATION: Pacific Ocean

Somalia

CAPITAL: Mogadishu
POPULATION: 6,841,695
MAJOR LANGUAGES: Somali (official), Arabic, Italian, and English
AREA: 246,210 sq mi; 637,660 sq km
LEADING EXPORTS: bananas, live animals, fish, and hides
CONTINENT: Africa

South Africa

CAPITAL: Pretoria (administrative), Cape Town (legislative), Bloemfontein (judicial)
POPULATION: 42,834,520
MAJOR LANGUAGES: Afrikaans, English, Ndebele, Pedi, Sotho, Swazi, Tsonga, Tswana, Venda, Xhosa, and Zulu (all official)
AREA: 471,027 sq mi; 1,219,912 sq km
LEADING EXPORTS: gold, other minerals and metals, and food
CONTINENT: Africa

Spain

CAPITAL: Madrid
POPULATION: 39,133,996
MAJOR LANGUAGES: Spanish, Catalan, Galician, and Basque
AREA: 194,892 sq mi; 504,750 sq km
LEADING EXPORTS: cars and trucks, and semifinished goods
CONTINENT: Europe

Sri Lanka

CAPITAL: Colombo
POPULATION: 18,933,558
MAJOR LANGUAGES: Sinhala (official) and Tamil
AREA: 25,333 sq mi; 65,610 sq km
LEADING EXPORTS: garments and textiles, teas, and diamonds
CONTINENT: Asia

Sudan

CAPITAL: Khartoum
POPULATION: 33,550,552
MAJOR LANGUAGES: Arabic (official), Nubian, Ta Bedawie, Nilotic, Nilo-Hamitic, and Sudanic dialects
AREA: 967,532 sq mi; 2,505,810 sq km
LEADING EXPORTS: gum arabic, livestock/meat, and cotton
CONTINENT: Africa

Suriname

CAPITAL: Paramaribo
POPULATION: 427,980
MAJOR LANGUAGES: Dutch (official), English, Sranang, Tongo, Hindustani, and Japanese
AREA: 63,041 sq mi; 163,270 sq km
LEADING EXPORTS: alumina, aluminum, and shrimp and fish
CONTINENT: South America

Swaziland

CAPITAL: Mbabane
POPULATION: 966,462
MAJOR LANGUAGES: English (official) and SiSwati (official)
AREA: 6,641 sq mi; 17,360 sq km
LEADING EXPORTS: sugar, edible concentrates, and wood pulp
CONTINENT: Africa

Sweden

CAPITAL: Stockholm
POPULATION: 8,886,738
MAJOR LANGUAGES: Swedish, Lapp, and Finnish
AREA: 173,738 sq mi; 449,964 sq km
LEADING EXPORTS: machinery, motor vehicles, and paper products
CONTINENT: Europe

Switzerland

CAPITAL: Bern
POPULATION: 7,260,357
MAJOR LANGUAGES: German, French, Italian, Romansch, and various languages
AREA: 15,943 sq mi; 41,290 sq km
LEADING EXPORTS: machinery and equipment
CONTINENT: Europe

Syria

CAPITAL: Damascus
POPULATION: 16,673,282
MAJOR LANGUAGES: Arabic (official), Kurdish, Armenian, Aramaic, Circassian, and French
AREA: 71,501 sq mi; 185,180 sq km
LEADING EXPORTS: petroleum, textiles, cotton, and fruits
CONTINENT: Asia

Taiwan

CAPITAL: Taipei
POPULATION: 21,908,135
MAJOR LANGUAGES: Mandarin Chinese (official), Taiwanese, and Hakka dialects
AREA: 13,892 sq mi; 35,980 sq km
LEADING EXPORTS: electrical machinery and electronics
CONTINENT: Asia

Tajikistan

CAPITAL: Dushanbe
POPULATION: 6,020,095
MAJOR LANGUAGES: Tajik (official) and Russian
AREA: 55,253 sq mi; 143,100 sq km
LEADING EXPORTS: cotton, aluminum, fruits, and vegetable oil
CONTINENT: Asia

Tanzania

CAPITAL: Dar Es Salaam
POPULATION: 30,608,769
MAJOR LANGUAGES: Swahili, English, and various languages
AREA: 364,914 sq mi; 945,090 sq km
LEADING EXPORTS: coffee, cotton, tobacco, tea, and cashew nuts
CONTINENT: Africa

Thailand

CAPITAL: Bangkok
POPULATION: 60,037,366
MAJOR LANGUAGES: Thai and English
AREA: 198,463 sq mi; 511,770 sq km
LEADING EXPORTS: machinery and manufactures
CONTINENT: Asia

Togo

CAPITAL: Lome
POPULATION: 4,905,827
MAJOR LANGUAGES: French, Ewe and Mina, Dagomba, and Kabye
AREA: 21,927 sq mi; 56,790 sq km
LEADING EXPORTS: phosphates, cotton, cocoa, and coffee
CONTINENT: Africa

Tonga

CAPITAL: Nukualofa
POPULATION: 108,207
MAJOR LANGUAGES: Tongan and English
AREA: 289 sq mi; 748 sq km
LEADING EXPORTS: squash, vanilla, fish, root crops, and coconut oil
LOCATION: Pacific Ocean

Trinidad and Tobago

CAPITAL: Port-of-Spain
POPULATION: 1,116,595
MAJOR LANGUAGES: English, Hindu, French, and Spanish
AREA: 1,981 sq mi; 5,130 sq km
LEADING EXPORTS: petroleum and petroleum products
LOCATION: Caribbean Sea

Tunisia

CAPITAL: Tunis
POPULATION: 9,380,404
MAJOR LANGUAGES: Arabic and French
AREA: 63,172 sq mi; 163,610 sq km
LEADING EXPORTS: hydrocarbons and agricultural products
CONTINENT: Africa

Turkey

CAPITAL: Ankara
POPULATION: 65,566,511
MAJOR LANGUAGES: Turkish, Kurdish, and Arabic
AREA: 301,394 sq mi; 780,580 sq km
LEADING EXPORTS: manufactured products, and foodstuffs
CONTINENT: Europe and Asia

Turkmenistan

CAPITAL: Ashgabat
POPULATION: 4,297,629
MAJOR LANGUAGES: Turkmen, Russian, Uzbek, and various languages
AREA: 188,463 sq mi; 488,100 sq km
LEADING EXPORTS: natural gas, cotton, and petroleum products
CONTINENT: Asia

Tuvalu

CAPITAL: Fongafale, on Funafuti atoll
POPULATION: 10,444
MAJOR LANGUAGES: Tuvaluan and English
AREA: 10 sq mi; 26 sq km
LEADING EXPORT: copra
LOCATION: Pacific Ocean

Uganda

CAPITAL: Kampala
POPULATION: 22,167,195
MAJOR LANGUAGES: English, Luganda, Swahili, Bantu languages, and Nilotic languages
AREA: 91,139 sq mi; 236,040 sq km
LEADING EXPORTS: coffee, cotton, and tea
CONTINENT: Africa

Ukraine

CAPITAL: Kiev
POPULATION: 50,125,108
MAJOR LANGUAGES: Ukranian, Russian, Romanian, Polish, and Hungarian
AREA: 233,098 sq mi; 603,700 sq km
LEADING EXPORTS: coal, electric power, and metals
CONTINENT: Europe

United Arab Emirates

CAPITAL: Abu Dhabi
POPULATION: 2,303,088
MAJOR LANGUAGES: Arabic, Persian, English, Hindi, and Urdu
AREA: 29,183 sq mi; 75,581 sq km
LEADING EXPORTS: crude oil, natural gas, re-exports, and dried fish
CONTINENT: Asia

United Kingdom

CAPITAL: London
POPULATION: 58,970,119
MAJOR LANGUAGES: English, Welsh, and Scottish Gaelic
AREA: 94,529 sq mi; 244,820 sq km
LEADING EXPORTS: manufactured goods, machinery, and fuels
CONTINENT: Europe

United States

CAPITAL: Washington, D.C.
POPULATION: 270,311,758
MAJOR LANGUAGES: English and Spanish
AREA: 3,618,908 sq mi; 9,372,610 sq km
LEADING EXPORTS: capital goods and automobiles
CONTINENT: North America

Uruguay

CAPITAL: Montevideo
POPULATION: 3,284,841
MAJOR LANGUAGES: Spanish and Brazilero
AREA: 68,041 sq mi; 176,220 sq km
LEADING EXPORTS: wool and textile manufactures
CONTINENT: South America

Uzbekistan

CAPITAL: Tashkent
POPULATION: 23,784,321
MAJOR LANGUAGES: Uzbek, Russian, Tajik, various languages
AREA: 172,748 sq mi; 447,400 sq km
LEADING EXPORTS: cotton, gold, natural gas, and minerals
CONTINENT: Asia

Vanuatu

CAPITAL: Port-Vila
POPULATION: 185,204
MAJOR LANGUAGES: English, French, pidgin, and Bislama
AREA: 5,699 sq mi; 14,760 sq km
LEADING EXPORTS: copra, beef, cocoa, timber, and coffee
LOCATION: Pacific Ocean

Venezuela

CAPITAL: Caracas
POPULATION: 22,803,409
MAJOR LANGUAGES: Spanish and various languages
AREA: 352,156 sq mi; 912,050 sq km
LEADING EXPORTS: petroleum, bauxite and aluminum, and steel
CONTINENT: South America

Vietnam

CAPITAL: Hanoi
POPULATION: 76,236,259
MAJOR LANGUAGES: Vietnamese, French, Chinese, English, Khmer, and various languages
AREA: 127,248 sq mi; 329,560 sq km
LEADING EXPORTS: petroleum, rice, and agricultural products
CONTINENT: Asia

Yemen

CAPITAL: Sanaa
POPULATION: 16,387,963
MAJOR LANGUAGE: Arabic
AREA: 203,857 sq mi; 527,970 sq km
LEADING EXPORTS: crude oil, cotton, coffee, hides, and vegetables
CONTINENT: Asia

Zambia

CAPITAL: Lusaka
POPULATION: 9,460,736
MAJOR LANGUAGES: English (official) and about 70 various languages
AREA: 290,594 sq mi; 752,610 sq km
LEADING EXPORTS: copper, zinc, cobalt, lead, and tobacco
CONTINENT: Africa

Zimbabwe

CAPITAL: Harare
POPULATION: 11,044,147
MAJOR LANGUAGES: English, Shona, and Sindebele
area: 150,809 sq mi; 390,580 sq km
LEADING EXPORTS: agricultural products and manufactures
CONTINENT: Africa

Glossary of Geographic Terms

basin
a depression in the surface of the land; some basins are filled with water

bay
a part of a sea or lake that extends into the land

butte
a small raised area of land with steep sides

▲ butte

canyon
a deep, narrow valley with steep sides; often has a stream flowing through it

cataract
a large waterfall; any strong flood or rush of water

◀ cataract

delta
a triangular-shaped plain at the mouth of a river, formed when sediment is deposited by flowing water

flood plain
a broad plain on either side of a river, formed when sediment settles on the riverbanks

glacier
a huge, slow-moving mass of snow and ice

hill
an area that rises above surrounding land and has a rounded top; lower and usually less steep than a mountain

island
an area of land completely surrounded by water

isthmus
a narrow strip of land that connects two larger areas of land

mesa
a high, flat-topped landform with cliff-like sides; larger than a butte

mountain
an area that rises steeply at least 2,000 feet (610 m) above surrounding land; usually wide at the bottom and rising to a narrow peak or ridge

▶ glacier

◄ delta

mountain pass
a gap between mountains

peninsula
an area of land almost completely surrounded by water and connected to the mainland by an isthmus

plain
a large area of flat or gently rolling land

plateau
a large, flat area that rises above the surrounding land; at least one side has a steep slope

river mouth
the point where a river enters a lake or sea

strait
a narrow stretch of water that connects two larger bodies of water

tributary
a river or stream that flows into a larger river

volcano
an opening in the Earth's surface through which molten rock, ashes, and gasses from the Earth's interior escape

▶ volcano

Gazetteer

A

Acropolis (38°N, 23°E) a hill in Athens, Greece, on which many temples and archaeological sites are located, p. 157

Africa world's second-largest continent, surrounded by the Mediterranean Sea, the Atlantic Ocean, and the Red Sea, p. 21

Alexandria (31°N, 30°E) ancient Hellenistic city in Egypt, p. 178

Amazon River the second-longest river in the world, flows from northern Peru across northern Brazil into the Atlantic Ocean, p. 17

Americas the land areas of the Western Hemisphere, including North America, South America, Mexico, and Central America, p. 21

Andes Mountains a mountain system extending along the western coast of South America, p. 16

Arabian Peninsula (22°N, 46°E) a peninsula of Southwest Asia, on which are located the present-day nations of Saudi Arabia, Yemen, Oman, the United Arab Emirates, Qatar, Bahrain, and Kuwait, p. 89

Arctic Circle (66°N) line of latitude around Earth near the North Pole, p. 16

Asia the world's largest continent, surrounded by the Arctic Ocean, the Pacific Ocean, the Indian Ocean, and Europe, p. 16

Asia Minor a peninsula in western Asia, between the Black Sea and the Mediterranean Sea; the site of present-day eastern Turkey, p. 36

Assyria a historical kingdom of northern Mesopotamia around present-day Iraq and Turkey, p. 35

Athens (38°N, 23°E) the capital city of Greece, pp. 157, 260

B

Babylonia (32°N, 45°E) an ancient region around southeastern Mesopotamia and between the Tigris and Euphrates rivers; now present-day Iraq, p. 36

Bay of Bengal (17°N, 87°E) part of the Indian Ocean, between eastern India and Southeast Asia, p. 96

Brazil (9°S, 53°W) the largest country in South America, pp. 54, 259

Byzantium city of ancient Greece; the site of present-day Istanbul, Turkey, p. 216

C

Cairo (30°N, 31°E) the capital and largest city of Egypt, located on the Nile River, p. 68

Canaan a region occupied by the ancient Israelites, also known as Palestine, located between the Jordan River, Mediterranean Sea and the Dead Sea, on a site that includes present-day Israel and part of Jordan, p. 48

Carthage (37°N, 10°E) an ancient city on the northern coast of Africa; now a suburb of the city of Tunis, p. 195

Ceylon (8°N, 82°E) an island country off the southeast coast of India, now known as Sri Lanka, p. 115

Chang Jiang (30°N, 117°E) the longest river in China and Asia and the third-longest river in the world, p. 124

Colosseum (42°N, 12°E) a large amphitheatre built in Rome around A.D. 70; site of contests and combats between people and animals, p. 200

Constantinople (41°N, 29°E) the ancient capital of Byzantium; now Istanbul, Turkey, p. 216

D

Damascus (33°N, 36°E) the capital and largest city of Syria, p. 211

Dead Sea (31°N, 35°E) a salt lake between Israel and Jordan; the Dead Sea is the lowest point on Earth, p. 53

E

East Africa an eastern region of the continent of Africa that is made up of the countries of Burundi, Kenya, Rwanda, Tanzania, Uganda, and Somalia, p. 14

Egypt (27°N, 27°E) a country in North Africa, pp. 13, 260

Euphrates River (36°N, 40°E) a river flowing south from Turkey through Syria and Iraq, p. 21

F

Fertile Crescent a region in Southwest Asia; site of the world's first civilizations, p. 30

G

Ganges River (24°N, 89°E) a river in northern India and Bangladesh, flowing from the Himalaya Mountains to the Bay of Bengal, p. 96

Gaul a region inhabited by the ancient Gauls; now present-day France and parts of Belgium, Germany, and Italy, p. 196

Giza (30°N, 31°E) an ancient city capital of Upper Egypt; site of the Great Pyramids, p. 77

Gobi Desert (43°N, 103°E) a desert in Mongolia and northern China, p. 141

Great Wall of China (38°N, 109°E) a wall that extends about 1,400 miles across northern China; built in the third century B.C., p. 136

Greece (39°N, 21°E) a country in Mediterranean Europe; site of a great ancient civilization, pp. 153, 260

H

Himalaya Mountains (29°N, 85°E) a mountain system of south central Asia, extending along the border between India and Tibet and through Pakistan, Nepal, and Bhutan, p. 95

Hindu Kush a mountain range in central Asia, p. 95

Huang He (35°N, 113°E) the second-longest river in China, p. 125

I

India (23°N, 77°E) a large country occupying most of the Indian subcontinent in South Asia, pp. 54, 261

Indian Ocean (10°S, 40°E) the world's third-largest ocean lying between Africa, Asia, and Australia, p. 96

Indus River Valley (26°N, 67°E) a valley and early civilization along the Indus River, one of the longest rivers in the world, p. 96

Iraq (32°N, 42°E) a country in Southwest Asia, pp. 21, 261

Israel (32°N, 34°E) a country in Southwest Asia, pp. 50, 261

Italy (44°N, 11°E) a boot-shaped country in southern Europe, including the islands of Sicily and Sardinia, pp. 192, 261

J

Japan (36°N, 133°E) an island country in the Pacific Ocean off the east coast of Asia, pp. 110, 261

Jerusalem (31°N, 35°E) the capital city of modern Israel; a holy city for Jews, Christians, and Muslims, p. 49

Judah the name of the southern half of the Kingdom of the Israelites (the northern half retained the name Israel); Jerusalem was its capital; also spelled *Judea,* p. 50

K

Kalahari Desert (23°S, 22°E) a desert region in southern Africa, p. 17

Kemet term used by ancient Egyptians to describe their land; means "the black land" and refers to the dark soil left by the Nile River, p. 63

Kerma a market town in present-day Sudan; an ancient Nubian city, p. 86

Khartoum (15°N, 32°E) the capital and largest city of Sudan, on the Nile River, p. 62

Koreas (40°N, 127°E) the nations of North and South Korea, which occupy the Korean peninsula in east Asia, surrounded by the Yellow Sea and the Sea of Japan, pp. 110, 261

L

Lake Nasser (24°N, 33°E) a lake located in southeast Egypt and northern Sudan, formed by the construction of the Aswan Dam on the Nile River, p. 64

Los Angeles (34°N, 118°W) a seaport city in California in the southwestern United States, p. 20

Lower Egypt an area in ancient Egypt, in the northern Nile River region, p. 62

Lower Nubia an ancient region in northern Africa extending from the Nile Valley in Egypt to present-day Sudan, specifically, between the first and second Nile cataracts, p. 62

M

Macedonia (41°N, 22°E) an ancient kingdom on the Balkan Peninsula in southeastern Europe, the site of the present-day nation of Macedonia, northern Greece, and southwest Bulgaria, p. 175

Marathon a city in the Attic Peninsula where the Greeks defeated the Persians in 490 B.C., p. 172

Maurya Empire Indian empire founded by Chandragupta; began with his kingdom in north-eastern India and spread to most of northern and central India, p. 111

Mediterranean Sea the large sea that separates Europe and Africa, p. 30

Meroë a city of ancient Nubia in present-day Sudan, p. 86

Mesopotamia (34°N, 44°E) an ancient region between the Tigris and Euphrates rivers in Southwest Asia, p. 29

Mohenjo-Daro (27°N, 68°E) an ancient city on the banks of the Indus River in southern Pakistan, p. 96

Mount Everest (28°N, 87°E) highest point on Earth, located in the Great Himalaya Range, p. 95

N

Napata one of the three most powerful Nubian kingdoms; located between the third and fourth cataracts of the Nile River in Upper Nubia, p. 86

New Babylonian empire a revival of the old Babylonian empire stretching from the Persian Gulf to the Mediterranean Sea, p. 39

New Guinea (5°S, 140°E) an island in the Pacific Ocean north of Australia; Indonesia occupies the western half of the island and Papua New Guinea the eastern half, p. 17

Nile River the longest river in the world, flows through northeastern Africa into the Mediterranean Sea, p. 13

North China Plain a large plain in East Asia, built up by soil deposits of the Huang He, p. 124

Nubia a desert region and ancient kingdom in the Nile River Valley, on the site of present-day southern Egypt and northern Sudan, p. 62

P

Pakistan (28°N, 67°E) country in South Asia, between India and Afghanistan, officially the Islamic Republic of Pakistan, pp. 21, 263

Parthenon the chief temple of the Greek goddess Athena on the hill of the Acropolis in Athens, Greece, p. 161

Persia a vast ancient empire of Southwest Asia; the historical name for the region in and around present-day Iran, p. 172

Persian Gulf (27°N, 50°E) an arm of the Arabian Sea, located between the Arabian Peninsula and southwest Iran, p. 38

Peru (10°S, 75°W) a country in northwestern South America, pp. 16, 263

Phoenicia an ancient region in present-day Lebanon, p. 46

R

Rome (42°N, 12°E) the capital city of Italy; capital of the ancient Roman Empire, p. 191

S

Sahara largest tropical desert in the world, covers almost all of North Africa, p. 64

Silk Road an ancient trade route between China and Europe, p. 140

Sinai Peninsula (29°N, 33°E) a peninsula on the northern end of the Red Sea that links southwest Asia with northeast Africa, p. 48

Spain (40°N, 4°W) a country in southwest Europe, occupying most of the Iberian Peninsula, pp. 54, 264

Sparta an ancient city-state in Greece, p. 170

Sumer the site of the earliest known civilization; located in Mesopotamia, in present-day southern Iraq; later became Babylonia, p. 29

Syria (35°N, 37°E) a country in Southwest Asia, pp. 71, 264

T

Tiber River a major river in Italy; Rome is built on its banks, p. 191

Tibet (32°N, 83°E) a historical region of central Asia north of the Himalayas; currently under Chinese control, p. 110

Tigris River a river in Iraq and Turkey, p. 30

Troy (40°N, 26°E) an ancient city in northwestern Anatolia, the Asiatic part of Turkey; the site of the mythical Trojan War, p. 154

Tyre (33°N, 35°E) a rich tradeport and the major city of Phoenicia, located on the eastern Mediterranean Sea in present-day southern Lebanon, p. 45

U

Upper Egypt an area in ancient Egypt in the Nile Valley, south of the river's delta and the 30th northern parallel, p. 62

Upper Nubia an ancient region in northeastern Africa that extended from the Nile Valley in Egypt to present-day Sudan, specifically, between the second and sixth cataracts, p. 62

Ur a city of ancient Sumer in southern Mesopotamia, located in present-day southeast Iraq, p. 33

V

Vietnam (18°N, 107°E) a country located in Southeast Asia, pp. 110, 265

Biographical Dictionary

A

Abraham first leader of the Israelites; according to the Bible, he led his family to Canaan, where he became the founder of a new nation, p. 48

Akhenaton (ah kuh NAH tuhn) (died c. 1354 B.C.) king of ancient Egypt (c. 1372–1354 B.C.), introduced monotheism; under Akhenaton Egypt lost much of its provincial territories, p. 75

Alexander the Great king of Macedonia (356–323 B.C.); conquered Persia and Egypt and invaded India; spread Hellenism, p. 176

Archimedes (ar kuh MEE deez) (born 290 B.C.) Greek inventor and mathematician; invented the formulas for the surface area and volume of a sphere, p. 179

Aristarchus (AIR uh STAHR kus) (lived c. 310–230 B.C.) Greek astronomer who was the first to hold the theory that Earth moves around the sun, p. 179

Aristotle (AIR uh staht ul) (384–322 B.C.) Greek philosopher who was a student of Plato and became a famous teacher; wrote about and taught logic, politics, science, and poetry; his works became the basis for medieval church scholarship, p. 175

Asoka (uh SOH kuh) (died c. 238 B.C.) Chandragupta's grandson and last major emperor of India's Maurya empire; credited with having built the greatest empire in India's history; helped spread Buddhism, p. 113

Augustus (63 B.C.–A.D. 14) first Roman emperor; ruled after Julius Caesar's death in 44 B.C. until his own death, p. 196

C

Caligula (kuh LIG yuh luh) (A.D. 12–41) Roman emperor (A.D. 37–41) believed to be insane for much of his rule; was responsible for many disturbances during his reign, p. 198

Champollion, Jean François (zhahn frahn SWAH shahm poh LYOHN) (A.D. 1790–1832) French scholar; first to decode Egyptian hieroglyphics, p. 83

Chandragupta (chuhn druh GUP tuh) (died 297 B.C.) founded India's Maurya empire in 321 B.C.; unified most of India under one ruler, p. 111

Cicero (SIS uh roh) (106–43 B.C.) the greatest and best-known Roman orator and the author of many famous speeches; also famous as a philosopher and politician, p. 202

Commodus (161–192 B.C.) Roman emperor who succeeded his father Marcus Aurelius; he was a poor ruler and was assassinated; his reign marks the beginning of the decline of the Roman Empire, p. 214

Confucius (kuhn FYOO shuhs) (551–479 B.C.) Chinese philosopher and teacher; his beliefs, known as Confucianism, greatly influenced Chinese life, p. 128

Constantine (KAHN stuhn teen) (c. A.D. 278–337) emperor of Rome from A.D. 312 to 337; encouraged the spread of Christianity, p. 213

J

Jesus (c. 4 B.C.–A.D. 30) founder of Christianity; believed by Christians to be the Messiah; executed by the Roman government; followers said he spoke to them after the death and rose bodily to heaven, p. 208

Julius Caesar (c. 100–44 B.C.) Roman political and military leader; became dictator for life in 44 B.C.; greatly improved the Roman government; was murdered by Roman senators because of his great power, p. 195

Justinian (juh STIHN ee uhn) (A.D. 483–565) Byzantine emperor, responsible for codifying Roman law; his work would influence all later legal history, p. 202

L

Liu Bang (LEE oo bahng) founder of the Han dynasty of China in 202 B.C.; born a peasant; stabilized the government and promoted education, p. 138

M

Marcus Aurelius (aw REE lee uhs) (A.D. 121–180) Roman emperor, generally tolerant and promoter of humanitarian causes, p. 199

Martial (MAR shuhl) Roman poet (c. A.D. 38–103); wrote poems about the early Roman Empire, p. 203

Menes (MEE neez) (lived c. 2925 B.C.) founder of the first Egyptian dynasty; unified Upper and Lower Egypt; founded the capital of Memphis, p. 68

Moses (c. 1200s B.C.) Israelite leader; led the Israelites from Egypt to Canaan; according to the Bible, he received the Ten Commandments from God, p. 48

N

Nebuchadnezzar II (nehb uh kuhd NEHZ uhr) (c. 630–561 B.C.) king of the New Babylonian empire from about 605 to 561 B.C., p. 39

Nero (c. A.D. 37–68) Roman emperor from A.D. 54 to 68; known for his mistreatment of the Christians, p. 198

O

Octavian (63 B.C.–A.D. 14) Rome's first emperor; wise and strong leader whose rule led to peace and wealth; also known as Augustus, p. 196

P

Paul (died c. A.D. 64) disciple of Jesus, spent his later life spreading Jesus' teachings; his writings helped turn Christianity into an organized religion, p. 210

Pericles (PEHR ih kleez) (c. 495–429 B.C.) Athenian leader; played a major role in the development of democracy and the Athenian empire, p. 159

Philip (382–336 B.C.) king of Macedonia; seized power in 359 B.C.; conquered the Greek city-states; father of Alexander the Great, p. 175

Ptolemy V (TALL uh mee) (died 180 B.C.) king of ancient Egypt (205–180 B.C.), married to Cleopatra; his ascension to the throne is recorded on the Rosetta Stone, p. 83

R

Ramses II (died 1224 B.C.) king of ancient Egypt (1292–1225 B.C.); his reign is marked by great splendor and the building of monuments, p. 75

Romulus and Remus twin brothers; according to legend, founded Rome in 753 B.C., p. 191

Romulus Augustulus (died c. A.D. 476) the last Roman emperor (A.D. 475–476), p. 217

S

Sargon II (died 705 B.C.) king of Assyria (722–705 B.C.), conquered Babylonia and founded the last great Assyrian dynasty, p. 35

Saul first king of the Israelites, p. 49

Seneca (c. 4 B.C.–A.D. 65) writer, philosopher, and statesman of ancient Rome, p. 206

Shi Huangdi (shee hoo ahng DEE) (c. 259–210 B.C.) emperor of the Qin dynasty (c. 221–210 B.C.); was the first to unify the Chinese empire, p. 134

Sima Qian (soo MAH chen) (c. 495–429 B.C.) Chinese scholar, astronomer, and historian; wrote the most important history of ancient China, *Historical Records,* p. 144

Socrates (SOK ruh teez) (c. 135–87 B.C.) Athenian philosopher of late 400s B.C.; taught through questioning; helped form many values of Western culture; was put to death for challenging Athenian values, p. 162

Solomon (died c. 932 B.C.) king of the Israelites (c. 972–c. 932 B.C.) after his father David; built cities, temples, and established foreign trade and alliances, p. 49

Solon (c. 630–560 B.C.) Athenian statesman; made Athens more democratic, p. 158

T

Taharka prince of Nubia; became king of Nubia and Egypt in 690 B.C., p. 85

Thales (c. 636–546 B.C.) Greek philosopher, the first recorded Western philosopher; first to look for ways to explain the physical world other than mythological explanations, p. 162

Thutmose III (thoot MOH suh) (died 1426 B.C.) stepson of Hatshepsut; considered the greatest pharaoh of the New Kingdom of Egypt; reigned from 1479 to 1426 B.C.; expanded the empire to include Syria and Nubia; p. 70

Tutankhamen (toot ahng KAH muhn) king of ancient Egypt (ruled c. 1333–1323 B.C.); the excavation of his tomb in 1922 provided new knowledge about Egyptian art and history, p. 75

W

Wudi (woo dee) (c. 156–86 B.C.) Chinese emperor from 140 to 86 B.C.; brought the Han dynasty to its peak; expanded the Chinese empire; made Confucianism the state religion, p. 139

Glossary

A

absolute power complete control over someone or something, p. 112

acropolis a high, rocky hill on or near which early people built cities, p. 156

afterlife the next life, in which the dead are believed to live again, p. 73

agora [AG uh ruh] a public market and meeting place in an ancient Greek city, p. 165

ahimsa [uh HIM sah] in Hinduism, the idea of being nonviolent, p. 105

alphabet a set of symbols that represent the sounds of a language, p. 47

ancestor a person from whom one is descended, especially if of a generation earlier than a grandparent, p. 14

aqueduct a structure that carries water over long distances, p. 202

archaeologist a scientist who examines bones, tools, structures, and other objects to learn about past peoples and cultures, p. 11

archer a person who uses a bow and arrow, p. 38

architecture the art and work of designing and constructing buildings or other large structures; the style and design of a building, p. 22

aristocrat a member of a rich and powerful family, p. 157

artisan a worker who is especially skilled in making something, such as baskets, leather goods, tools, jewelry, pottery, or clothes, p. 20

assassinate to murder for political reasons, p. 176

astronomer a scientist who studies the stars and other objects in the sky, p. 83

astronomy the branch of science that studies the planets, stars, moon, and other objects in the universe, p. 81

B

barbarian a person who belongs to a group that another group considers to be savage or uncivilized, p. 175

barge a large, flat-bottomed boat that carries loads of goods or materials on rivers, canals, or other waterways, p. 77

battering ram a heavy wooden beam on wheels used to knock down walls or buildings, p. 38

bazaar a market selling different kinds of goods, p. 37

blockade the cutting off of an area by enemy forces that closes it to travel and trade, p. 174

boomerang a flat, curved object, traditionally made of wood, that can be thrown so that it returns to the thrower, p. 66

bronze a yellowish-brown alloy of copper, tin, and traces of other metals; used by people during the Bronze Age to make tools and weapons, p. 22

Buddhism [BOO diz ihm] religion based on the teachings of Buddha; characterized by the belief that enlightenment comes from within rather than from worshipping gods, p. 106

C

canal a waterway dug into the earth or modified by people to transport water or people, or provide drainage, p. 19

caravan a group of traders traveling together, p. 37

caste a social class of people, p. 100

catacombs underground cemetery of many tunnels and passageways, p. 211

chieftain leader or head of a group, such as a clan or a tribe, p. 157

Christianity the Christian religion, based on the life and teachings of Jesus and on the Christian holy book, the Bible, p. 55

circus an arena in ancient Rome; also the show held there, p. 205

citadel a fortress in a city, p. 97

city-state a city with its own traditions and its own government and laws; both a city and a separate independent state, p. 32

civil service the group of people whose job is to carry out the work of the government, p. 132

civilization a society with cities, a central government run by official leaders, and workers who specialize in certain jobs, leading to social classes. Writing, art, and architecture also characterize a civilization, p. 21

code an organized list of laws or rules, p. 40

conquerer person who uses force to gain control of other people, land, or possessions, p. 37

consul one of two officials who led the ancient Roman Republic, p. 194

convert to change one's beliefs; used in particular to describe a change from one religion to another, p. 113

copper reddish-brown metal; used by early civilizations, before the Bronze Age, to make tools and weapons, p. 22

covenant a binding agreement, p. 52

culture language, religious beliefs, values, customs, and other ways of life shared by a group of people, p. 22

cuneiform [kyoo NEE uh form] a form of writing that uses groups of wedges and lines; used to write several languages of the Fertile Crescent, p. 44

currency the kind of money used by a group or a nation, p. 138

D

dam a barrier across a waterway to control the level of water, p. 19

Dead Sea scrolls ancient parchment manuscripts containing the earliest version of the first few books of the Bible, p. 53

delta the place at the mouth of a river where it splits into several streams to form an area shaped like a triangle, p. 63

democracy a form of government in which citizens govern themselves, p. 157

descendant child, grandchild, great-grandchild (and so on) of an ancestor, p. 51

desert a hot, dry region with little vegetation, p. 64

dharma [DAHR muh] in Hinduism, the religious and moral duties of each person, p. 104

diaspora [dy AS puhr uh] the scattering of people who have a common background or beliefs, p. 54

dictator a person in the ancient Roman Republic appointed to rule for six months in times of emergency, with all the powers of a king, p. 194

dike a protective wall that controls or holds back water, p. 126

disciple a follower of a person or belief, p. 209

district an area set by law for a particular purpose; an area having particular characteristics, p. 137

domesticate to tame animals and raise them to be used by humans, p. 17

drama a literary work, such as a play, that tells a story and is written to be performed by actors, p. 163

dynasty a series of rulers from the same family, p. 68

emperor a ruler of widespread lands, p. 136

empire many territories and people who are controlled by one government, p. 36

epic a long poem that tells a story, p. 155

epistle [ee PIS uhl] a letter; in the Christian Bible, letters written by disciples like Paul to Christian groups, p. 211

exile to force someone to live in another country, p. 50

extended family closely related people of several generations, such as brothers and sisters, parents, uncles and aunts, grandparents, and great-grandparents, p. 127

F

famine a time when there is so little food that many people starve, p. 48

farmer person who makes a living by raising crops or animals, p. 23

fertile land or soil that contains substances plants need in order to grow well, p. 17

finances the amounts of money or money-related resources a person has; the management of money, p. 169

flood waters water from a flood; generally used to describe floods caused in the spring by excess water from rain and melting snow, p. 19

G

geography the study of Earth's surface and the processes that shape it, the connections between places, and the relationship between people and their environment, pp. 12–13

gladiator in ancient Rome, a person who fought to the death in an arena for the entertainment of the public; usually a slave, p. 205

god a being considered to be the creator or ruler of the universe or parts of the universe; the object of worship in some cultures and societies, p. 102

goddess a female being considered to be the creator or ruler of the universe or parts of the universe; the object of worship in some cultures and societies, p. 102

gold a soft, yellow, durable element; has great value as a substance used to make jewelry and other valuable goods; has historically been used as money, p. 22

Gospel in the Christian Bible, the books of Matthew, Mark, Luke, and John, which are the first four books of the New Testament, p. 209

H

Hammurabi's Code a set of laws created by Babylonian king Hammurabi, telling his people how to live and settle conflicts, p. 40

Hellenistic describing Greek culture after the death of Alexander the Great, including the three main kingdoms formed by the breakup of Alexander's empire, p. 177

helot [HEL ut] in ancient Sparta, the term for a slave, p. 171

herbalism the art of creating medicines from plants, p. 84

hieroglyphs [HY ur oh glifs] a kind of picture writing in which some pictures stand for ideas or things and others stand for sounds, p. 82

Hinduism a religion developed in India, introduced by the Aryans, and based on sacred books called the Vedas and Upanishads; Hindus accept many gods as different aspects of one supreme being, p. 101

history the written and other recorded events of people, p. 10

hunters and gatherers people who gather wild food and hunt animals to survive, p. 16

I

Iliad a Greek epic, credited to the poet Homer, telling about quarrels among Greek leaders in the last year of the Trojan War, p. 155

immortal someone or something that lives forever, p. 162

incense blocks or sticks of material, such as gum or wood, that are burned to make a perfumed scent, p. 33

inflation an economic situation in which there is more money of less value, p. 216

irrigation supplying land with water through a network of canals, p. 19

Islam the religion practiced by Muslims; based on the teachings of the prophet Muhammad and on the holy book of Islam, the Koran, p. 55

ivory hard, smooth yellowish-white material that forms in the tusks of elephants and some other animals; valued as a material used to make jewelry, piano keys, and ornaments, p. 67

J

jade hard, pale-green or white mineral; valued as a gemstone or as a material from which to make boxes, carved tablets, or other ornaments, p. 143

Judaism the religion of the Jewish people which developed from ancient Israelite beliefs; based on belief in one God and the teachings of the sacred texts, the Torah and the Bible, p. 52

L

landform an area of Earth's surface with a definite shape; mountains and hills are examples of landforms, p. 153

linen smooth, strong cloth made of the fibers of the flax plant, p. 142

loess [les] yellow-brown soil, p. 125

M

martyr a person who chooses to die for a cause he or she believes in, p. 212

meditate to think deeply about sacred things, p. 107

mercenary a foreign soldier who serves in an army only for pay, p. 215

merchant person who buys or sells goods for a profit; person who runs a store or business, p. 23

messiah a savior in Judaism and Christianity, p. 209

Middle Kingdom the middle time period of the groups of Egyptian dynasties, p. 68

migrate to relocate; to move from one place to settle in another area, p. 99

mina a unit of weight or money used in ancient Greece and Asia, p. 41

missionary a person who spreads his or her religious beliefs to others, p. 108

monotheism the belief in one god, p. 48

monsoon the winds that blow across East Asia at certain times of the year; in summer, they are very wet; in winter, they are generally dry unless they have crossed warm ocean currents, p. 96

moral acting in a way that is considered good and just by a society's standards, p. 104

mummy a dead body preserved in lifelike condition, p. 75

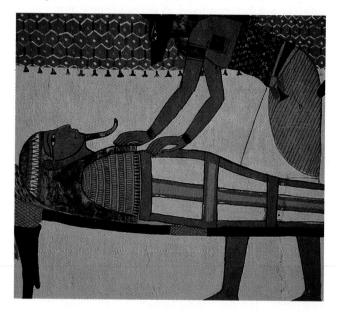

myth a traditional story; in some cultures, a legend that explains people's beliefs, p. 33

N

New Kingdom the latest time period of the groups of Egyptian dynasties, p. 68

New Stone Age the later part of the Stone Age during which people began to grow their own foods and lived in the same place year after year, p. 17

nirvana the lasting peace that Buddhists seek by giving up selfish desires, p. 108

noble in certain societies, a person of high rank, sometimes inherited through family connections, p. 41

nomad a person who has no single, settled home, p. 16

O

Odyssey a Greek epic, credited to the poet Homer, describing the adventures of the hero Odysseus after the Trojan War, p. 155

Old Kingdom the earliest time period of the groups of Egyptian dynasties, p. 68

Old Stone Age the early part of the Stone Age during which people learned to hunt in groups, discovered how to use fire, and became nomads, p. 15

oral traditions stories passed down through generations by word of mouth, p. 12

orchestra the round space at the bottom of a Greek theater where the action took place; the main floor of a theater; a group of musicians who play together on different instruments, p. 164

outdoor stalls small stands, usually located on busy streets, from which merchants sell food or goods, p. 32

P

papyrus [puh PY ruhs] an early form of paper made from a reedlike plant found in the marshy areas of the Nile delta, p. 82

parchment heavy piece of material used to write on, made from animal skin, p. 51

patrician member of a wealthy, upper-class family in the ancient Roman Republic, p. 194

peasant a member of a class that makes its living through small-scale farming and labor, p. 80

peninsula an area of land nearly surrounded by water, p. 153

pharaoh [FAIR oh] the title of the kings of ancient Egypt, p. 67

philosopher someone who uses reason to understand the world; in Greece, the earliest philosophers used reason to explain natural events, p. 162

philosophy system of beliefs and values, p. 131

plague a widespread disease, p. 174

playwright a person who writes plays and dramas; also called a dramatist, p. 164

plebeian an ordinary citizen in the ancient Roman Republic, p. 194

polytheism the belief in many gods, p. 33

prehistory before history; the events in the period of time before writing was invented, p. 10

priestess a woman who has the authority to carry out religious rites, p. 169

prophet a religious leader who told the Israelites what God wanted them to do, p. 54

province a unit of an empire; the provinces of the Roman Empire each had a governor supported by an army, p. 198

pyramid a huge building with four sloping outside walls shaped like triangles; in Egypt, pyramids were built as royal tombs, p. 77

Q

quarry a site where large holes are dug into the ground and stone collected by digging, cutting, or other means, p. 77

R

rapids a very fast-moving part of a river, p. 61

rebellion an organized resistance to the government or other authority, p. 137

reeds tall, hollow-stemmed grasses that grow in wet places, p. 31

regent someone who rules for a child until the child is old enough to rule, p. 70

reincarnation rebirth of a soul in the body of another living thing, p. 104

republic a type of government in which citizens who have the right to vote select their leaders; the leaders rule in the name of the people, p. 194

Roman Empire an empire lasting from 27 B.C. to A.D. 576, whose boundaries changed over time but at its greatest extent stretched from Britain to North Africa and the Persian Gulf, p. 72

Rosetta Stone an ancient tablet covered with Egyptian and Greek hieroglyphics; provided a key to deciphering hieroglyphics, p. 83

rubble pieces of rock or other materials left on the ground after a building or some other structure has been destroyed or has decayed over time, p. 38

S

sandstorm a strong wind that carries clouds of sand and dust as it blows, p. 140

scribe a professional writer, p. 29

senate the governing council of ancient Rome and the later Roman Empire, p. 196

shepherd a person who guards, herds, and takes care of sheep, p. 54

silk a valuable cloth originally made only in China from threads spun by caterpillars called silkworms, p. 142

silt rich, fertile soil deposited by the flooding of a river, p. 63

silver a soft, shiny, white metal; has great value as a substance used for jewelry and other ornaments; has historically been used as money, p. 41

slavery condition of being owned by, and forced to work for, someone else, p. 168

slinger a person who shoots rocks or stones by means of a slingshot, p. 38

social class a group, or class, that is made up of people with similar backgrounds, wealth, and ways of living, p. 23

society a group of people distinct from other groups, who share a common culture, p. 17

spiritual concerned with religious or sacred matters, p. 114

Stone Age a period of time during which people made tools and weapons mainly from stone; the earliest known period of human culture, p. 14

subcontinent a large landmass that juts out from a continent; India is considered a subcontinent, p. 95

surplus more of a thing or product than is needed, p. 20

synagogue in the Jewish religion, a building or meeting place for worship, p. 51

T

Ten Commandments according to the Bible, a code of laws given to the Israelites by God, p. 48

terra cotta a hard, ceramic-like clay used in pottery and building construction, p. 134

time line a simple diagram showing how dates and events relate to one another, p. 24

tomb a grave or place of burial, p. 73

topsoil the layer of soil on the top of the ground, p. 31

Torah the most sacred text of the early Israelites, that recorded laws and events of their history, p. 51

trade buying and selling goods; an exchange of one thing for another, p. 22

trader person who makes a living by trading goods, p. 22

tragedy a type of serious drama that ends in disaster for the main character, p. 163

tribute a payment made by a less powerful state or nation to a more powerful one, p. 160

Trojan War in Greek epic poems and myths, a 10-year war between Greece and the city of Troy in Asia Minor, p. 154

tyrant a ruler who takes power with the support of the middle and working classes; not necessarily cruel and violent, p. 157

U

Upanishads [oo PAN uh shadz] one of the Hindu religious texts; written in the style of questions by students and answers by teachers, p. 103

V

Vedas a series of religious texts, written in Sanskrit by the Aryan peoples, which became a basis for Hinduism, p. 100

veto the Latin word for "forbid"; the rejection of a bill by the President or of any planned action or rule by a person in power, p. 194

viaduct a series of arches built to provide a road or railroad over valleys or other roads or railroads, p. 216

W

warlord a leader of an armed group, p. 139

welfare health, happiness, and good fortune; financial or other aid provided to people, especially by the state, p. 114

woolens cloth or clothes made from wool, p. 142

Z

ziggurat [ZIHG uh raht] a temple of the ancient Sumerians and Babylonians, made of terraces connected by ramps and stairs, roughly in the shape of a pyramid, p. 32

Index

Acknowledgments

Cover Design
Bruce Bond, Suzanne Schineller, and Olena Serbyn

Cover Photo
Jon Chomitz

Maps
MapQuest.com, Inc.
Map information sources: Columbia Encyclopedia, Encyclopaedia Britannica, Microsoft® Encarta®, National Geographic Atlas of the World, Rand McNally Commercial Atlas, The Times Atlas of the World.

Staff Credits
The people who made up the *World Explorer* team—representing editorial, editorial services, design services, on-line services/multimedia development, product marketing, production services, project office, and publishing processes—are listed below. Bold type denotes core team members.

Barbara Bertell, **Paul Gagnon, Mary Hanisco, Dotti Marshall,** Susan Swan, and Carol Signorino.

Additional Credits
Art and Design: Emily Soltanoff. Editorial: Debra Reardon, Nancy Rogier. Market Research: Marilyn Leitao. Production Services: **Joyce Barisano.** Publishing Processes: **Wendy Bohannan.**

Text
16, map from *World Civilizations: The Global Experience,* Volume A by Peter N. Stearns, Michael Adas, and Stuart B. Schwartz. Copyright 1993 by HarperCollins College Publishers. Reprinted by permission of Addison Wesley Educational Publishers Inc. **33,** from Mary Anne Frese Witt et al, *The Humanities: Cultural Roots and Continuities, Volume 1, Three Cultural Roots,* Fourth Edition. Copyright 1993 by D.C. Heath and Company. **40,** from *Everyday Life in Babylonia and Assyria,* by H.W.F. Saggs. Copyright 1965 by H. W. F. Saggs. Used by permission of B.T. Batsford Ltd. **51,** from *The Torah: A Modern Commentary.* Copyright 1981 by The Union of American Hebrew Congregations. Reprinted by permission of The Union of American Hebrew Congregations. **101,** from the Rig-Veda, 1.154, verses 1–3 adapted from *Hinduism* by V.P. (Hermant) Kanitkar, Stanley Thornes (Publishers) Ltd, 1989. **120,** from *The Fables of India* by Joseph Gaer. Copyright 1955 by Joseph Gaer; © renewed 1983 by Fay Gaer. By permission of Little, Brown and Company. **131,** from *Book of Songs,* translated by Arthur Waley. Copyright 1937 by Arthur Waley. Used by permission of Grove/Atlantic, Inc. **159,** from *The Peloponnesian War,* by Thucydides. Copyright 1951 by Random House, Inc. **186,** from THE ADVENTURES OF ULYSSES by Bernard Evslin. Copyright 1969 by Scholastic Inc. Reprinted by permission of Scholastic Inc.

Photos
1 TL, © D.J. Dianellis/Photri, **1 TR,** © Charles Walker Collection/Stock Montage, **1 B,** © D.E. Cox/Tony Stone Images, **4 TL, TR,** © SuperStock International, **4 BL,** © Doug Armand/Tony Stone Images, **4 BR,** © Christopher Arensen/Tony Stone Images, **4 inset,** © Mark Thayer, Boston,

5, © The Granger Collection, **6–7,** © Erich Lessing/PhotoEdit, **8,** © Douglas Mazonowicz/Art Resource, **9,** © SyGMA, **10 L, R,** © Kenneth Garrett/National Geographic Society Image Collection, **11 TL, BL, R,** © Lee Boltin/Boltin Picture Library, **12,** © Jason Laure'/Laure' Communications, **13,** © Yann Layma/Tony Stone Images, **14,** © Lee Boltin/Boltin Picture Library, **17,** © Robert S. Peabody Museum of Archaeology, Phillips Academy, Andover, Massachusetts All Rights Reserved/Robert S. Pcabody Muscum of Archaeology, **18,** © Ed Simpson/Tony Stone Images, **19, 21,** © SuperStock International, **23 L, R,** © Erich Lessing/Art Resource, **24,** © Michael Newman/PhotoEdit, **29,** © Lee Boltin/Boltin Picture Library, **31,** © SuperStock International, **32,** © British Museum, **33,** © The Granger Collection, **34,** © Courtesy University of Chicago/Oriental Institute, **35,** © Erich Lessing/Art Resource, **37,** © The Granger Collection, **38,** © Erich Lessing/Art Resource, **39,** © British Museum, **40,** © Giraudon/Art Resource, **41 L,** © The Granger Collection, **41 R,** © Erich Lessing/Art Resource, **42,** © Giraudon/Art Resource, **43 L, R,** © The Granger Collection, **45,** © Art Resource, **47,** © The Granger Collection, **49,** © SuperStock International, **50,** © Corbis-Bettmann, **51,** © Jewish Museum/Art Resource, **53 T, B,** © The Granger Collection, **54,** © Erich Lessing/Art Resource, **56,** © Lucas Films/Kobal Collection, **61,** © Werner Forman/Art Resource, **62,** © The Bettmann Archive/Corbis-Bettmann, **63,** © Eliot Elisofon/National Geographic Society Image Collection, **64, 65,** © SuperStock International, **66,** © Lee Boltin/Boltin Picture Library, **67,** © SuperStock International, **68,** © Werner Forman Archive/Art Resource, **71,** © SuperStock International, **72 L,** © The Granger Collection, **72 R,** © SuperStock International, **73,** © Erich Lessing/Art Resource, **74,** © Scala/Art Resource, **75 L,** © The Granger Collection, **75 R,** Egyptian National Museum, Cairo/SuperStock International, **77,** © Hugh Sitton/Tony Stone Images, **78,** © Richard T. Nowitz/Photri, **79,** © Chip & Rosa María de la Cueva Peterson, **80,** © Erich Lessing/Art Resource, **81 T,** © Robert Frerck/Odyssey Productions, **81 B,** **82,** © The Granger Collection, **83 TR,** © Bridgeman/Art Resource, **83 BL,** © The Granger Collection, **84 L, R,** © Lee Boltin/Boltin Picture Library, **85,** © The Granger Collection, **87 T,** © Director's Contingent Fund (40.469) Courtesy of/Museum of Fine Arts Boston, **87 B,** © The Granger Collection, **88,** © Museum Expedition, Nubian Gallery (20.333) Courtesy of/Museum of Fine Arts Boston, **89,** © Museum Expedition, Nubian Gallery (20.1059) Courtesy of/Museum of Fine Arts Boston, **90–91,** © The Granger Collection, **95,** © Nicholas DeVore/Tony Stone Images, **97,** © Trip/Trip Photographic, **98 T, BL, BR,** © Jehangir Gazdar/Woodfin Camp & Associates, **99,** © Kevin Downey Photography, **101,** © Robert & Linda Mitchell Photography, **102,** Krishna, by Dhruv Khanna, age 12, India. Courtesy of the International Children's Art Museum, **103,** © GUPTA/Dinodia Picture Agency, **104,** © Robert & Linda Mitchell/Robert & Linda Mitchell Photography, **105,** © Anil A. Dave/Dinodia Picture Agency, **106,** © Lee Boltin/Boltin Picture Library, **107,** © Robert & Linda Mitchell Photography, **108,** © D.E. Cox/Tony Stone Images, **109,** © Robert & Linda Mitchell Photography, **111, 112,** © Corbis-Bettmann, **113,** © Dinodia/Dinodia Picture Agency, **114,** © Chris Haigh/Tony Stone Images, **115,** © Kevin Miller/Tony Stone Images, **116 T,** © David W. Hamilton, **116 B,** © Michael Newman/PhotoEdit, **123,** © Charles Walker Collection/Stock Montage, **124,** © Kevin Downey Photography, **125,** © Wolfgang Kaehler Photography, **126,** © H. Rogers/Trip Photographic, **127,** © The Granger Collection, **128,** © Photri, **129,** © The Granger Collection, **130,** © Giraudon/Bridgeman Art Library, **131,** © UPI/Corbis-Bettmann, **132,** © Thc Grcat Bronze Age of China/Metropolitan Museum, **134, 135, TL, B,** © O. Louis Mazzatenta/National Geographic Society Image Collection, **135 TR,** © K. Cardwell/Trip Photographic, **136,** © Keren Su/Tony Stone Images, **139,** © The Granger Collection, **140,** © Masaharu Uemura/Tony Stone Images, **142 L, R,** © The Granger Collection, **142 inset,** © Robert & Linda Mitchell/Robert & Linda Mitchell Photography, **143 L,** © J. Stanley/Trip Photographic, **143 R,** © Photri, **144 T, BL,** © The Granger Collection, **144 BR,** © Photri, **147,** © Michael Newman/PhotoEdit, **151,** © Ric Ergenbright/Ric Ergenbright Photography, **153,** © Werner Forman/Art Resource, **154,** © George Grigoriou/Tony Stone Images, **155,**